# The A-Z of Cool
# Computer Games

# The A-Z of Cool Computer Games

## Jack Railton

First published in Great Britain in 2005 by
Allison & Busby Limited
13 Charlotte Mews
London W1T 4EJ
www.allisonandbusby.com

A catalogue record for this book is available from
the British Library.

10 9 8 7 6 5 4 3 2 1

ISBN 0 7490 8206 2

Printed and bound in Wales by
Creative Print and Design, Ebbw Vale

Jack Railton is the pen-name of Jack Kibble-White who reviews and writes about popular culture for publications and websites such as *ScriptWriter Magazine*, bbc.co.uk, Off The Telly and TV Cream. He is the co-author of the book *TV Cream: The Ultimate Guide to '70s and '80s Pop Culture*, and has acted as programme consultant on a number of Channel Four entertainment documentaries. He has also contributed to BBC4's *Time Shift* series and makes the occasional appearance on radio and television, usually to talk about old telly.

This book is dedicated to Sweetpea

# Contents

# Acknowledgements

This book was inspired by happy computer game memories of beatings dished out and received courtesy of Stewart Campbell, Damon Chambers, Alistair Duguid, Andrew Henderson, Dee-Anne Herd, Keith Kinloch, Richard Macintyre, David Oliphant, Iain Russell, James Sands, Kenny Young and, of course, The Bob. In later years I also took several computer beatings from Jane Redfern and these should also be noted for the record.

In preparing this book I had to draw upon a number of resources. The following grizzled 'old skool' computer fans helped me on my way: Alex Smith, Ronnie Graham and Rob Stradling; and thanks also to Chris Diamond who kindly allowed me to nick a couple of his many good ideas.

Thanks are also due to Ian Jones, Steve Williams and Chris Hughes for stepping in and helping me out with other commitments that I had to meet whilst writing this book, as well as some five or so years of general encouragement; and to the Bullet List participants who gave me a few pointers on copyright stuff and the **ZX Spectrum**. Thanks also to Mark Beaver, Jason Darby, Chris Giggins, Gary Goldman, Richard Hewison, Nick Humphries, Tony Mott and Kevin Toms who all helped me organise images for the book.

Closer to home, I am indebted to my dad who gave me his old ZX Spectrum and ZX80 for inspiration, to my sister Gail who read some of the initial entries and made the right encouraging noises, and to my brother Graham who gave me the 'in' to Allison & Busby in the first place, and lots of advice and comments along the way. I would also like to thank Bob and Sheila Railton for allowing me to borrow their surname and their general support whilst writing this.

Finally though, the person I should thank most of all is my other half, Rose, who helped me work out a feasible way to get

this all done and was then unstinting in her support, encouragement and love, even when she had plenty of her own stuff to be
getting on with.

# Introduction

One of the strongest memories from my youth is of the day we played a game called *Pangolins* on our then brand new Sinclair **ZX Spectrum**. It probably occurred after a marathon **Hungry Horace** session (I would control the up and down keys and my sister the left and right). Anyway *Pangolins* was a simple computer program that attempted to guess the animal you were thinking of via a series of 'yes' and 'no' questions. If the computer failed to guess correctly it would ask you to reveal the mystery beast's identity and type in a question which, if asked next time, would allow the computer to discount or identify it. As such, the more you played it, the more 'intelligent' it got. Giddy with the thrill of it, me and my siblings played *Pangolins* for hours, such that by teatime we had in our possession a super intelligent computer program that possessed information on an entire menagerie of creatures both fantastical (we were obsessed with griffins back then) and real.

Then our dad came home from work. He had brought with him a colleague who he wanted to show off the ZX Spectrum to. Having discovered our session of *Pangolins*, our dad thought up an animal and began answering the various questions, all the while impressing upon his friend 'how clever these micro-computers were'. We stumbled upon this activity just at the point where the program had completed asking my dad if the animal in question had ever become mixed up with three pirates called Roderick the Red, Gregory the Green and Benjamin the Blue, and had moved on to quizzing him whether the animal in question was 'a stupid smelly shitbag who is a spaz and can't wipe her bum properly without mum's help'.

Had our dad answered 'yes' at that point, he would have been informed that the animal he was thinking of was most likely my sister. However, just to prolong the embarrassment he typed in 'no' and proceeded to type in 'no' to a whole range of, frankly, offensive questions relating to other members of my immediate family, plus friends, neighbours, distant relatives and, for some reason, the broadcaster Dickie Davies. The whole terrible ordeal only came to an end when I managed to 'accidentally' pull out the (admittedly never very secure) ZX Spectrum power lead.

I am not really sure if I learned any lessons from the experience but recalling it now, most of the elements of the story seem part of a bygone age. I mean, when was the last time that **dads** took an interest in their kids' computer? Also can you possibly imagine anyone today (let alone children) playing a game as simplistic as *Pangolins* for more than two minutes? In fact the only element of the story that feels in any way contemporary is the bit with the swearing. But all this happened within my lifetime, and most probably, yours too.

Computers are still here, but how we view them has changed fundamentally. Once they were a slice of the future sitting benignly in the front room, they were a taste of exotica, a portal to imaginary places. Now, they are an essential part of our everyday lives; for some even a primary means of communication. They are the tools upon which many of us carry out our day-to-day work, and are a great way to idle away a few hours achieving not very much in particular.

But what they aren't is new and exciting, or niche and exclusive in quite the same way as they once were. Indeed computers and video games now sit alongside a vast selection of leisure activities. Computer games are mainstream entertainment, the type of thing that men and women will talk about in the office before swapping notes on whether or not Kylie has had a temple lift. However, back in the day, it would only be a few of the bookish types at school who would dare to openly regale each other with tales of **Ant Attack** or *Valhalla* before going on to discuss their plans for their next *Call of Cthulhu*

**role-playing** campaign.

Okay, it is great that we all learned to stop worrying and love the **PC**, but now that computers are for everyone, and not just the hobbyists or the over-intelligent kids, something almost indefinable has been lost forever.

Which rather leads me to the point of this book.

# The Point of this Book

What you hold in your hands is a miscellany of the great and the good of the classic computer years. As you will see, entries cover a number of different decades, but in the main the book focuses on a nebulous golden era that if you pushed me I would say began in 1978 (with the dawn of *Space Invaders* and thus the rise of the video game industry) and ended at exactly the moment Sony launched the **PlayStation** (not that I have anything against the machine, it's just that it marks the point when computers went 'overground').

Within these pages you will find a pot pourri of memorable games from yesteryear, an assembly of computers and consoles and lots of stuff on some of the more bizarre and well-loved pieces of paraphernalia, attitudes and add-ons that helped define the glory years of the computing scene. In selecting the entries I have enlisted the help of a number of seasoned computer old timers, but, ultimately, this list is subjective. Please bear that in mind as you flick through and proclaim 'wot no *Paperboy*?' (although it does get a mention somewhere in the book).

Hopefully, what you will find in here are entries that will bring forth dormant memories of your own computing years and make you remember how great and fabulous it was to be growing up in the age of the silicon chip. One further note: there is a year attached to every entry (well, almost every entry). This usually denotes the year the object first came into being, but in some cases it's not quite that simple, in which case I have attempted to nail the year when the items in question first came to the attention of computer users.

# The Games

Whilst businessmen might debate which particular machine will offer them the best spreadsheet functionality or the most comprehensive accounting package, the computers that have won public support have been those that have featured the best games. Yet we seem to enjoy a curious love-hate relationship with these splendid creations. Over the years, a number of (usually failed) computers have been launched on the back of a publicity campaign proclaiming that the product in question can do much more than simply house a reasonable home conversion of *Paperboy*. The implication is that somehow clocking up hours in front of *Wizball* or *Schizoids* is a complete waste of time. Well, that may or may not be the case, but what those who seek to criticise games often fail to understand is that the pursuit of *Wizball* perfection is also a lot of fun.

However, it is worth noting that our definition of 'fun' in the context of computer games has radically altered over time. Spool back twenty-five years and game players had to content themselves with estimating their drive force on the fairway in the **ZX81** version of *Golf*. Such titles offered little interactivity, spectacle or even reward, but somehow they thrilled us. It was as if being able to run a game, any kind of game, on a home computer was satisfaction enough. In fact the notion of pushing our computer to its limits is one that is still important today, such that any new game that fails to fully exploit its hardware is often judged to be lacking, regardless of playability.

Development in the home computer games market during the early Eighties was content to take much of its lead from what was happening in the amusement arcades, and titles such as 1982's **Hungry Horace** and Quicksilva's 1983 release *Time Gate* were obviously inspired by the popular coin-ops of the day. In addition, almost as soon as home computers were able to support graphics, conversions of arcade hits such as *Scramble* began to appear. However, this situation wasn't wholly satisfactory. Arcade games are designed to appeal to the passing gamer with possibly only a few minutes to spare. Conversely, computer games suffer no such time impediment, so to create home computer games only in the mould of their arcade cousins was unnecessarily restrictive.

Luckily, the popularity of the text-based **adventure game** (which predated the home computer revolution by a good few years) proved that long-form games had a place too, and so the continuing obsession with creating arcade-style titles for the home market was accompanied by an equally concerted push to create titles that were ever more complex and vast in scale. An early highpoint of this trend came in 1984 with the release of the massive space game *Elite*.

From the mid-Eighties onwards, size became more and more important, with titles such as 1984's *Jet Set Willy* and *Sabre Wulf* offering massive playing areas to explore. Meanwhile, experiments in creating real-time **3-D** environments relied on the unique hardware attributes of home computers and in so doing offered a further differentiation from what was going on in the largely sprite-based coin-ops. By the time the 16-bit machines such as the **Atari ST** and **Amiga** arrived in the late Eighties, home computer games had stepped well and truly out of the shadow of the amusement arcade. Although arcade conversions still appeared, the home computer game scene had taken on a life of its own, spawning its own unique genres.

Undoubtedly, the most significant of these has been the **first-person shooter**, which relies on 3-D technology, as well as the player's commitment to stick with a game for a number of hours. Such was their appeal, more traditional genres like **platformers** and **shoot 'em ups** (both of which relied largely on a two dimensional playing environment) became increasingly marginalized. Even sports and **strategy games** felt the pinch, with the former moving from two dimensional to 3-D arenas, whilst the latter struggled to try and replicate the simplistic fun of *Tetris* within the extra dimension.

With the emergence of 3-D technology, the aspirations of games creators changed too. Where once games existed only to provide us with some kind of challenge to overcome, titles such as *Resident Evil* (released in 1996) tried to scare us, whilst **Nintendo's** 1998 *Zelda: Ocarina of Time* had a whole litany of characters that it wanted us to get to know and, ultimately, care for. The arrival of Electronic Arts' *The Sims* in 2000, challenged the whole notion of what constitutes a computer game. The title did not require us to achieve specific objectives, but instead asked us to participate in a kind of computerized soap opera, making a number of decisions along the way that would influence the growth of our on-screen avatar.

Although the simplistic fun of *Dizzy* can still hold our attention for a while, the modern day home computer gamer requires far more substance and sophistication from their computer games. By and large, we wish to operate within worlds that we can believe in, and interact with computer characters that possess at least some kind of inner life. Whether such games are any less of a waste of time then running round a maze devouring dots is a question best left to another time. Far better to expend the energy sitting back and thinking of triumphs past against end-of-level bosses and stubborn wizards.

# Adventure Games
## 1972

'You are in a small cave. It's grey and plain and there are exits to the north and west...' So would begin another exciting text-based traverse through a series of tediously similar looking locales that pretty much constituted your average adventure game back in the early Eighties. In recent years the fortunes of the adventure game appear to have dipped, as the chief characteristic of the genre – interacting with the computer via the medium of words – has fallen out of favour with a generation of players who deem typing in commands to be too much like hard work.

However, if the bell has tolled for the traditional text based adventure game, then we can at least reflect upon the fact that it had a good innings; and more importantly, has managed to annoy almost all of us at one time or another. Ironically a game that offers the player the entire English language as its control interface displays its shortcomings far more readily than, say, a **platformer** in which the player is confined to up, down, left, right and jump. Because we know the rules and restrictions of everyday grammar it seems unacceptable when commands such as 'kick Gandalf up the arse' are met with the response 'I do not know the word "kick"'. Yet during a session of the classic platform game **Manic Miner** it is unlikely you will attempt to give Eugene a swift smack in the chops because you know, and willingly accept, the parameters of the control system.

But such frustrations did not stop the proliferation of adventure games during their glory period (the Seventies and Eighties). Many claim the genre started back in 1972 with the 'interactive fiction' game *Adventure* (also known as *Colossal Caves*). Created by Will Crowther and later expanded upon by Don Woods, *Adventure* involved navigating your way around a series of caves, picking up objects along the way that might later prove helpful. As a formula it proved to have remarkable longevity, with most of the adventure games that followed adhering to these basic principles. Even the kids' television series of the Eighties and Nineties – *Knightmare* – was pretty much *Adventure*, except with fancy graphics and precocious youngsters.

Because they were so formulaic, the basic strategy for success in adventure games quickly became engrained on our psyche such that were we to get lost in a real-life cave we would know only too well to pick up the least helpful artefacts that we came across (for some reason things like grappling hooks, torches and weapons never turned out to be as useful as ancient scrolls, a bit of stale bread or a single white feather).

Undoubtedly, one of the key reasons for the genre's proliferation was that they were pig easy to write. Even a novice programmer could not fail to get to grips with the logic that underpinned such commands as 'IF player selects "west" Then Goto Line 1540'. From these basic cause-and-effect building blocks a myriad of different adventures and quests could be writ. Yet with countless worlds and fictional genres to choose from, most adventure games inhabited sub-Tolkein landscapes populated by dragons, orcs and halflings, and although over time this became accepted as a 'given' within the adventure genre, the proliferation of 'Middle Earth-lite' quests is largely down to the fact that Crowther, the man who kicked the whole thing off, was an ardent proponent of fantasy **role-playing** games.

Down the years, the adventure game's control interface has evolved. Recognising that **programming** a game to be able to understand a quintillion different text-based commands would still not legislate for when someone would attempt to 'tell his majesty to stick his daughter and his stinking kingdom up the back side of the next passing dragon', games such as ICOM Simulation's *Déjà vu: A nightmare comes true!!* (released in 1985) adopted a 'point-and-click' interface that side-stepped the whole tricky business of typing in words altogether. Although this was a welcome advancement it did mean the end for that occasional heady moment when your command 'I want to fart' actually got a legitimate response along the lines of 'you spread your legs and fart lustily' (as was allegedly the case in Rainbird's 1988 title *Legend of the Sword*). In fact, *Legend of the Sword* was even equipped to allow you to examine your penis – not that we ever did you understand.

As games have grown ever more graphically sophisticated, they have allowed players to interact with their environment in increasingly spontaneous ways, and as such the genre boundaries have eroded. Whilst titles such as *Grand Theft Auto: Vice City* contain storylines that unfold in a manner reminiscent of the traditional adventure game, the harsh, almost perverse trial and error torture of attempting to piece together the right noun-verb combination in order to get your character through a simple doorway has gone for good.

The black water evaporates, the fast river evaporates, the crack is dead.

## Ant Attack
## 1984

If the word 'isometric' doesn't conjure up images of double Technical Drawing then you've either never heard it before, or are already familiar with the impact of the mighty **ZX Spectrum** game *Ant Attack*.

Utter the phrase 'softsolid' now and it's likely that most people will conclude that you've just had a runny poo; however back in 1984 the UK Home computer industry went berserk as software publishing house Quicksilva unveiled their ant baiting masterpiece. Whilst the game's premise might have been relatively straightforward (the object of the exercise was to rescue various men or women enslaved somewhere in the post-apocalyptic maze-like city of Antescher, all the while fending off hordes of rampaging, giant ants), programmer Sandy White and his 'softsolid' algorithm produced a whole gaming world displayed in **3-D**.

The rapid development in computing technology means that we are quick to assimilate change, and so it is difficult now to appreciate just what a breakthrough this was. *Ant Attack* offered an isometric world populated by structures built from blocks of varying degrees of shade, which tiny little characters (apparently the humans in the game were only fourteen pixels high) could walk in front, behind or even on top of. White believes that he was the first person to write such a game (the 1982 arcade classic **Zaxxon** did offer an isometric 3-D view but White considers it to be a sideways scrolling **shoot-'em up** with fancy graphics).

As even the most ardent **Dragon's Lair** fan will grudgingly admit, nice graphics do not a good game make; and thankfully *Ant Attack* was almost as much fun to play as it was to look at. The introduction of a 3-D game world brought with it a freedom of player experimentation that had never been seen before. Whilst we knew the purpose of the exercise was to get on and save lives, it was possible to forget the day job for a while and simply wander around admiring Antescher's marvellous architecture (White was also a sculptor in his spare-time). There were also other bits of unscripted fun to be had, of which the most entertaining was trying to ride around on top of an ant.

However, whilst 3-D opened up areas of gaming that had previously been unexplored, it also brought with it some new problems. First of all, the isometric viewpoint became extremely problematic if your character disappeared behind a building. White's solution to this was to allow the player to effectively 'switch' cameras to obtain a reverse-angle view. However, as any good film student knows, crossing the 'line of action' can be disorientating for the viewer and too many times you found yourself no longer running away from a horrible salivating swarm of ants, but straight at them. Similarly, the extra dimension meant that controls for up, down, left and right were no longer enough, now we needed *in* and *out* as well. *Ant Attack's* control mechanism consisted of one set of keys to rotate you in increments of 90 degrees and another to move you in the direction you were facing. This was far from intuitive and could result in your hapless hero running around in circles.

But it was worth persevering if for nothing else than to see your character's skirt flap up and down (assuming you chose to play a girl) as you jumped from block to block – yes it was the little details that most entertained us.

## Bandersnatch
## 1984

'How will these four master computer game writers be feeling in a few weeks time? They have been brought together to pool their awesome talents to create the two most sensational, mind boggling games ever imagined...*Psyclapse* and *Bandersnatch*'.

So ran the hyperbolic press advertising campaign for what were clearly going to be the two greatest computer games of all time. Indeed the advertising blurb proclaimed *Psyclapse* and *Bandersnatch* to be 'the two most exhilarating experiences ever' and a later advert showed three graphic artists and two 'highly respected' musicians gathered round in front of a **programming** screen in the process of fine tuning these two 'megagames' that, unbelievably, were supposed to run on the humble **ZX Spectrum** and **Commodore 64**.

Software publisher Imagine had high hopes for both titles and so did the computer press. In July 1984 *Your Spectrum* spoke of 'an environmental experience, where the player will take part in **role-playing** games interacting with large, well-defined characters on-screen.' Imagine, sales reps were briefing retailers that the finished products would sell for £39.95 and would come with hardware add-ons to accommodate the sophisticated graphics and gameplay that the team of master developers were preparing.

There was also talk of a spin-off LP featuring a 'famous name' on voice-over. The computer press ran a series of adverts that featured one letter at a time of each game, and computer fans began to clamour for screenshots, concrete news of release dates and any other information they could get their hands on.

However, the project ran into serious difficulty when it became apparent it was going to take several months longer than the first mooted four-week development period. Then somewhat fatally, the money ran out. Or, as *Sinclair User* put in July 1985, 'Imagine went bust, and the *Bandersnatch* team was out of a job, along with dozens of others who gave their soul for the most spectacular, romantic and, ultimately, sordid software company this country is ever likely to see'. Requiring £2 million to support the project, Imagine's summer 1984 sales had been far lower than expected and the cost of developing the two megagames broke what was already a weakened bank. Indeed, things came to an ignominious end when Imagine employees returning from their lunch break were barred from company premises by a group of fearsome moustachioed bailiffs, and what's more all of this was lovingly caught on camera for the 1984 documentary series *Commercial Break*.

There was talk of remounting the game for the **Sinclair QL** but this came to nothing. Finally, some elements saw the light of day in *Brataccas* for the **Atari ST**. What we were left with was an acceptable **adventure game** set on a mining asteroid. Whilst reasonably interesting and featuring some clever artificial intelligence, it was certainly something of a comedown for those who had been hooked by Imagine's overheated campaign.

## Beat 'em Ups
### 1984

Once the king of all computer game genres, the beat 'em up is finally starting to look a little long in the tooth (not to mention

cauliflowered in the ear), and gamers seem at last to be weary-
ing of pulling off eight move combos. However in its day (the
late Eighties to early Nineties) the beat 'em up was all conquer-
ing, usurping the once ubiquitous **shoot 'em up** as the genre of
choice for over-excited boys.

For over twenty years, the beat 'em up was the fastest evolving game genre, with ever more elaborate ways of inflicting
pain being devised with each new title, and a myriad of sub-
genres birthing, evolving and (sometimes) becoming extinct.
However, all beat 'em ups comply to two basic tenets: namely the object of the exercise is to kick somebody's head in (be
they another player, or a character controlled by the computer); and secondly, that the efficacy of the administered beating
is largely dependent upon how many different **joystick** and
button combinations the player can muster during the course
of a bout. In truth, beat 'em ups were the great levellers of
computer games and the skilful game player could always
come undone if their human opponent was frantic enough at
button bashing.

The first ever fighting game is reputed to have been released in
1978 and was a two-player vector graphics sword-fighting game
called *Warrior*. However, the genre didn't really get going until six
years later when Data East released the arcade classic *Karate
Champ*. For its time this was a fearsomely complex game with
moves being deployed through the combined movement of two
separate joysticks. During the same year Bug-Byte released *Kung
Fu* for the **ZX Spectrum**. However it was Melbourne House's *Way
of the Exploding Fist* (released in 1985) that really got things
motoring. This game managed to find a decent compromise
between complexity and accessibility and soon Speccy owners
the land over were giving their bemused mothers a hugely satisfying and (in their minds) psychologically significant beating.

But it was within the confines of the amusement arcade that
beat 'em ups really flourished. Titles such as Taito's *Double*

*Dragon* (1987) and **Sega**'s *Altered Beast* (1988) introduced a quest element, but arcade beat 'em ups were at their best when you were pummelling all of your mates into a very public submission (and stuffing a few passing strangers too). The feeling of satisfaction was immense, and would often lead to the emission of outrageous *World Wresting Federation* style victory chants that deeply antagonized those subjected to your noxious outbursts.

The most important beat 'em up title of them all was Capcom's **Street Fighter II,** released in 1991. The reasons for the game's phenomenal success are not easy to pinpoint. Although technically accomplished, it was something about the variety of characters and the nature of their hidden moves that made *Street Fighter II* appeal to gamers the world over. Such was its success that it temporarily reversed the declining fortunes of the whole arcade industry.

After that point, beat 'em ups began to resemble variations on the *Street Fighter II* formula, with the *Street Fighter* franchise itself spawning multiple iterations (there were even **manga** versions). For those who didn't like the *Street Fighter* way, it must have got a little depressing. However, things brightened up a little bit in 1992 when Midway released a photo realistic beat 'em up with outrageously gory moves called **Mortal Kombat.** For a time these two titles tussled in the affections of arcade and home computer players (both *Mortal Kombat* and *Streetfighter II* appeared on multiple home formats), with *Mortal Kombat* never really managing to unseat the mighty Capcom classic.

This all changed in 1993, when Sega released *Virtua Fighter*, arguably the last beat 'em up to date to feature a substantially new element: namely characters rendered in **3-D**. Although this didn't really change much about the gaming mechanics (albeit you could now shuffle round an opponent) it somehow felt like a completely different playing experience.

From that day to this the 3-D beat 'em up has ruled, what has been of late, a dwindling roost, with beat 'em up fans of old having long since deserted the genre in favour of the delights of the **first-person shooter**.

## Bomberman
1985

Everyone knows that the most addictive games are those that are devilishly simple. Not that simplicity in itself makes for a good game (just ask **Atari** who had to literally bury thousands of *E.T.* cartridges for their 2600 system because the game was too simple to attract players). But a computer game based on the right simple premise can be a thing of beauty (one need look no further than *Tetris* for an example).

Hudson Soft's *Bomberman* is – in those terms – quite simply a bit of a looker. Having first appeared in 1985, it has gone on to sell in excess of ten million copies over the course of forty or so separate releases. The game takes place in a maze that is only one screen in size, and finds you attempting to destroy your opponent by the strategic laying of time bombs. The elegance of the game lies in the fact that blasts from one bomb can immediately set off another if it is within the blast radius, thus leading to massive chain explosions that leave you hoping against hope that you have found the one space to stand in that isn't about to be scorched.

If you were to analyse the appeal of *Bomberman* then you could point to the fact that everything you need to know appears on screen all at once, or you might want to dwell on the fact that it has a propensity for great natural climaxes with battles escalating to ever more destructive heights before someone eventually buys the farm. However, the best thing about *Bomberman* is the fact that on most versions you can take on up to three of your mates in a riotous battle royale. Such encounters always provoke raucous shrieks of a kind that on sober reflection sound a little bit effeminate, but nevertheless explode the myth that computer games are inherently anti-social. *Bomberman* is definitely the archetypal 'over a few pints game'.

However, don't ever try to play it in **3-D**, for as those of you who know such things will doubtless concur, any inherently two dimensional game given a 3-D makeover is always rubbish.

## Breakout
### 1976

In the history of video games there are very few titles that have managed to retain their original appeal over a number of years. **Tetris**, although unarguably benefiting from new gaming plat-forms such as mobile phones, is a prime example. However, in the main the glory games of one era are soon forgotten by the following (although titles such as *Defender* and **Spy Hunter** charitably give up their best concepts for the greater good of securing the evolution of their respective genres). In particular, the titles from the very dawn of the computer age generally ran out of steam as soon as home systems became commonplace and the novelty value of playing an arcade hit in your own front room faded.

**Atari**'s *Breakout* should therefore be hailed as one of the great survivors of that first age, and of computer games in general. Although you are unlikely to see *Breakout 2006* released for the Xbox any time soon, it did survive and prosper right through the age of the **ZX Spectrum** and on into the Nineties. It might have taken on a few bells and whistles down the years, but in principle the gaming mechanics that drove the first ever *Breakout* arcade console in 1976 were alive and well in 1997's *Arkanoid Returns*.

*Breakout* was created during Atari's first flush of success in 1975. Their title **Pong** was doing very nice business in the amusement arcades, but other companies such as Midway were starting to muscle in on their patch and multiple *Pong*-like games were starting to appear. Reasoning that the best way to stay ahead of the market was to innovate, Atari chief Nolan Bushnell encouraged his team to come up with new ideas for games. One of the fruits of this initiative was 1976's *Night Driver*, a cleverly designed driving game with a realistic look-ing behind-the-car view of the road, created by displaying only street-lights. Bushnell had another idea on the go; however, many considered it derivative of *Pong* and given it was widely believed that 'ball and paddle' games were no longer popular with the public, no one was very keen on developing the idea any further, so the job was given to a young and then lowly, pre-**Apple** Steve Jobs.

Basically, the object of *Breakout* was to dismantle a wall by bouncing a little ball off a paddle and into some bricks sus-pended above. For each brick you were able to hit you were awarded a score. If you were skilful enough to hit more than one brick per bounce, then your score would rise exponential-ly. Of course, if you failed to hit the ball with your paddle you lost a life. The physics were very familiar to those who had grown accustomed to *Pong* and graphically it looked a lot like it too. However, changing the object of the game from attempt-ing to avoid a target, to attempting to hit one resulted in an array of new gaming strategies.

Arguably it could be said that *Breakout*'s success was actu-ally attributable to the fact that it was so similar to *Pong*. A huge part of the enjoyment was derived from being able to use pad-dle skills attained from countless *Pong* sessions to enable you to deftly flick the little ball up a gap in the side of the wall, and watch it bounce away, demolishing bricks from the top down. This was one of the most effective ways to rack up the points and was damn satisfying too.

From repeated play, other subtleties and nuances would surface, like the fact that if you flicked the paddle to one side just as it made contact with the ball then you could hit some really acute angles. Similarly if you were able to make the ball hit the wall in a diagonal motion then inexplicably it would rip through loads of bricks, thus increasing your score further.

Over the years, *Breakout* clones appeared on most home systems, with the most successful being the *Arkanoid* range from Taito which first surfaced on the **NES** in 1987 and proliferated on various platforms for the next decade or so. A word too, for *Thro' The Wall* on the Speccy, which holds a special place in the affections of many computer fans, simply because it was bundled in with Psion's *Horizons* package. This collection of mainly boring software was given away with brand new **ZX Spectrum**s in 1982, resulting in *Thro' The Wall* being quite possibly the first game many of us ever played on a home computer.

## Carrier Command
## 1988

For those **Atari ST** owners previously used to the complexity of *Goldrunner* or *Bomb Jack*, Rainbird's *Carrier Command* was a mind bogging entrée into the world of strategy and resource management. The game concerned a strategic battle played out over a vast ocean between you and a malevolent computer enemy aircraft carrier, the SS *Omega*. As per the title you had control over an aircraft carrier (the SS *Epsilon*) and all the attendant resources that came with it. This meant that you could launch and pilot small planes (Mantas) scoot around in amphibious crafts (Walruses) or fire off missiles at all and sundry. The objective of the game was to take over as many islands as possible in order to construct a carefully balanced network of defences, resources and factories that you could use to provide you with the necessary payload to take on and destroy the SS *Omega*.

Undoubtedly the filled in **3-D** vector graphics had a lot to do with *Carrier Command*'s appeal. Although pretty simplistic and blocky looking, for its time *Carrier Command* offered unlimited exploration rights to a vast (albeit visually limited) world. This sense of freedom was further enhanced by the ability to switch from one viewpoint to another. This meant that at one moment you could be piloting a Manta heading towards a rogue island, whereas the next you could be on board the Epsilon watching that self-same Manta. Indeed the ability to watch your vehicles in action from any angle was pretty cool and would result in many pointless sorties in which you took a Manta out for a spin just simply to look at things.

As such, whilst the intricacy of *Carrier Command* might have put a lot of people off, because the thing looked so damn good you were content to twiddle around for hours on end, and in the process you would gradually assimilate the necessary information required to play properly.

And it was a big game; sometimes travelling from one island to the next would take several minutes. This gave proceedings a sense of vastness that ensured when you actually managed to build up a useful supply chain between the islands, you would protect it very carefully. Of course, all of this was simply a preamble to the main job at hand: to blast the hell out of the baddie carrier. This mostly unseen force quickly attained a suitable stature thanks to the fact that you spent most of the game having to deal with the consequences of its terrible actions. When you did finally clap eyes on it (usually from the cockpit of a Manta on an extreme reconnaissance mission) it was a pant-wettingly scary moment, particularly if you happened to witness it sailing straight through an island (a bug fixed on later releases of the game).

## Chuckie Egg
## 1983

Of all the gaming genres, the **platformer** is the most unforgiving. It relies on pixel-perfect positioning and split-second timing, and should you get either one of these two elements wrong, then death and the frustration of having to re-start the entire level, if not the whole game, await you. Whilst this proved tough on the player, it could also be tough on the software developer, as any dodgy collision detecting or suspect physics would be pounced on straight away and pilloried in all the best **computer magazines**.

*Chuckie Egg* (initially released on the BBC Model B and **ZX Spectrum**) is a testament to precision programming. Like most **platformers** of its time the objective was clear: you simply had to collect all of the eggs in a given time limit whilst avoiding the various hens that milled around the screen. Whereas the title could barely lay claims to originality, as **Donkey Kong** derivatives go, it was one of the best.

As one level was completed the next would prove to be slightly harder, introducing more elements (such as an extremely infuriating lift on the third level) that would require you to become an ever more accomplished player. After eight levels the whole thing went back to the beginning, except this time you were being dive-bombed by a giant duck. If you made it back round to level one again, then the hens moved twice as fast. In theory you could play *Chuckie Egg* forever, with the only real limitation being an ever-decreasing time limit. However for the experienced player, time almost seemed no object. The game moved so fast that you were able to pull off the most outrageous feints and U-turns, in the process securing your position as a *Chuckie Egg* supremo.

And that was it really. *Chuckie Egg* became a classic simply by understanding the rules of the platformer and adhering to them brilliantly. Its reward was a cross-generational appeal that eluded most games. It's probably not too far off the mark to herald *Chuckie Egg* as one of the few titles that mums ever became really accomplished at.

## Coin-op conversions
## 1979

Whilst home computer games were all well and good, there was something about them that couldn't quite match the visceral appeal of a 'coin-op' game in the local amusement arcade. Maybe it was the fact that you played home computer games on the same screen that earlier that day carried images of Mavis Nicholson presenting one of her interminable daytime shows; or maybe your home computer denied you the immediacy of sticking ten pence into a slot and cracking on; or it was simply that having to pay each time for a go, you were never able to afford to get past the novelty value of any particular game down your local amusements.

Whatever the reason, coin-ops were exciting and sexy and sort of American, whilst home computer games were friendly and domesticated and sort of parochial. Indeed it's a bit like comparing a wild cougar to a household moggie. You can imagine the excitement then, when **Atari** announced that they had secured the first ever home license for an arcade game, and not just any game either, but the big one, *Space Invaders*. From here the floodgates opened (Atari in particular were quick to secure conversions for their 2600 console). Before long you could enjoy the delights of such hits as *Frogger* and *Pac-Man* on a range of console systems, all of which were inferior to the original arcade versions.

And there was the rub. In much the same way as the cheap brand of cola that you bought in the hope that it would taste as good as the real thing turned out to be an inevitable disappointment, there was no way that home consoles could hope to be as good as their coin-op cousins. Or at least they couldn't until very recently. In fact, the margin in technical sophistication between the two grew in the Eighties as the home market bedded in the 8-bit computer range and the likes of **Sega** and Taito started to revolutionise the amusement arcades. During this time, coin-op conversions secured a strong foothold on the home market, but by the middle years of the decade it was clear that some of the home versions of popular arcade classics bore only the most cursory of resemblances with the originals. The **ZX Spectrum**, in particular, seemed to suffer a great deal. The computer wasn't really geared up for handling the colourful sprites that appeared in most arcade titles of the time. As such, whilst the **Commodore 64** or **Amstrad CPC** versions of *OutRun* could at least offer the player a red car on a grey road with a green background and a blue sky, Speccy owners had to put up with a see-through car on a see-through road (although to be fair it was able to handle the green background and blue sky).

Not that all coin-op conversions were a waste of time. Elite System's 1985 version of *Commando* was a successful transfer to the small screen and *Gauntlet*, published by US Gold the following year, was worth a look too. However, as the years rolled on, the machines that followed the 8-bit computers also struggled to make the best of their source material. But this time it was less to do with system limitations and more to do with the speed and lack of care taken when converting a coin-op to a home console. It would take until the mid-Nineties and the release of systems such as the **Sega** Saturn before home consoles could truly recreate the arcade experience. Indeed in 1994, games fans positively cooed over *Tempest 2000* for the Atari Jaguar, claiming that it had achieved absolute fidelity with the original. But given that the original was by then thirteen years old, you would have hoped that they would have got it pretty much spot on, wouldn't you?

## Daley Thompson's Decathlon
### 1984

It could be said that the Los Angeles Olympics were the first real Olympics of the home computer age. Whilst it's true that the odd household owned a **Mattel IntelliVision** or **Sinclair ZX80** back when Allen Wells was going for gold in Moscow in 1980, by the time Lionel Richie was inviting a confused Ronald Reagan to party 'All Night Long' at the 1984 opening ceremony, software publishers were rubbing their hands in expectation at the cash they could generate from the well-timed release of Olympic themed games.

Unquestionably the pre-eminent title on the block was Konami's 1983 arcade game *Track & Field*. Loosely based on **Microsoft**'s *Olympic Decathlon* (released for the **Apple** II in 1981), Konami's title featured full colour graphics and a refinement of Microsoft's control system, the infamous 'button bashing'. Indeed, the phrases 'button bashing' and '**joystick** waggling' (the term used being dependent upon the control mechanism) have long since been regarded as euphemisms for acts of beastliness. However, that is to deny these two well-practiced gaming techniques their rightful distinction as ingenious methods of control that are actually, in some small way, analogous to the effort required when participating for real in the type of events such games seek to recreate.

Of the home computer track and field games released during 1984 (and there were a fair few, including Century City's *Olympic Challenge* featuring a stick man in the title role), undoubtedly the most well known was Ocean's *Daley Thompson's Decathlon*. This was in part due to the fact that the game (which was released on most of the popular machines of the time such as the **ZX Spectrum**, **Commodore 64** and **Amstrad CPC-464**) had the nicest graphics of all titles released (with the honourable exception of Hill MacGibbon's first-person racing game *Run For Gold*, which looked absolutely great but was limited to just middle distance races). However, *Daley Thompson's Decathlon*'s biggest selling point was its association with the Olympic gold winner. At that time, celebrity endorsements for computer games were a relatively novel idea, but in retrospect, the likes of Daley Thompson made for a far more appealing cover star than a humble programmer (as was the case with Kevin Tom's **Football Manager** range).

*Daley Thompson's Decathlon* featured all ten decathlon events and stuck fast to the button bashing controls that had proved so successful in *Track & Field*. The skill level, not to mention stamina, required to secure that coveted gold medal was pretty high; however, as with most games there was always a way round. Indeed in issue twelve of *Crash* magazine one reader wrote in to reveal a loophole. 'I was making my first attempt at the long jump when I landed directly with my back level to the line,' he wrote. 'I considered this to be a pretty feeble effort, but to my delight the scoresman measured out the rest of the pit and then the track, giving me a jump of 253 metres! Is this an Olympic achievement?'

The appeal of Daley, plus his gold medal victory and ace Lucozade ad (featuring rocking music from Iron Maiden that became an essential unofficial soundtrack to any *Daley Thompson's Decathlon* sessions), meant that Ocean scored a sizeable hit. Unsurprisingly, a sequel was rushed out. However, without any significant sporting hook to hang it on, *Daley Thompson's Super-Test* was about as well received as the titular athlete's supposed insolent whistling during the Olympic medal ceremony.

## Demo Mode
### 1981

It goes without saying that 'demo' is short for 'demonstration'. The demo mode is one of the facets of computer games that is so engrained into our psyche that we seldom give it very much thought at all. It is simply the thing that will happen if you fail to press the START button. These days, its status as 'the thing your game will do if left alone' has been challenged by the full motion video; however for the seasoned gamer, a bit of back story told using graphics that are obviously going to be better than those you will get in the game itself, is no substitute for the enjoyment of catching a look at levels yet unplayed. This is what any good demo mode offers you. A tantalising glimpse of where you might be if you can ever get off level one. Who here can say that they have never tried to take control of the action when the demo happens to flick to a particularly exciting level, or studied a demo mode religiously for tips on how to circum-navigate a particularly tricky set of dissolving blocks?

The demo mode has been with us almost since the beginning of the video game age. Its initial function was to entice passing fare into foregoing a quick pee at the service station in favour of a swift *Tron* session. Of course, demos serve a different function on home systems (**Atari**'s *Video Pinball* released in 1981 was the first ever game on the Atari 2600 to feature a demo mode). Apart from the aforementioned appetite whetting for worlds yet unseen, it is a handy way of preventing a static image burning itself onto your computer monitor or TV screen and a chance for you to pretend to your mates that you have actually got past the end-of-level baddie (assuming you time it just right).

## Doom
### 1993

On 10th December 1993, the University of Wisconsin's servers were under extreme pressure. Every possible route in was jammed by expectant computer fans waiting online to get their hands on what they believed would be the greatest computer game of all time. Meanwhile id software's Jay Wilbur was desperately trying to find a way into the servers so that he could upload that self-same game. The irony of the situation was lost on the fans. Instead they moaned and complained on Internet message boards, claiming that id had promised to release this exciting new game – *Doom* – sometime that day but that it looked like it had been simply hype. Eventually though, the penny dropped and fans realised that if they ever wanted to play *Doom*, they would need to give Wilbur sufficient bandwidth to get it uploaded.

But what was *Doom*, and why was it deemed so special even before it was released? Well, taking the second question first, *Doom* publisher id had been issuing hyperbolic press releases since January and rumours had begun to take on a life of their own on the various online forums as to what might be included in the finished game. Certainly the programmers at id had an excellent pedigree (having already been involved in the creation of the seminal **first-person shooter** *Wolfenstein 3-D* in 1992), and so feeding the expectant frenzy was reasonably easy.

*Doom* was clearly going to be built on the *Wolfenstein* technology; however, whereas the earlier title had challenged the player to break out of the Nazi-controlled Castle Wolfenstein, the objectives and themes of *Doom* were to be quite different. Originally id had tried to acquire the rights to the science-fiction horror film *Aliens*, but when this was not forthcoming, programmer John Carmack looked to his experiences playing the **role-playing** game *Dungeons & Dragons* for inspiration. Apparently his most recent campaign had ended rather abruptly when demons appeared and took over the whole planet. Although this might sound like a *Dungeons & Dragons* Dungeon Master simply running out of inspiration, to Carmack here was a germ of an idea.

From these beginnings, Carmack and the rest of the id development team fashioned an incredibly **violent** game in which the objectives were extremely simple: kill everything and don't get killed. Graphically, the game moved at a frantic rate and looked brilliant, particularly when loads of blood and gore erupted when you managed to take out one of the demons with your BFG (Big Fucking Gun). However there was more to *Doom* then just thrilling graphics – a lot more. Firstly, id's attitude towards its code was markedly different from other software companies: it encouraged others to examine their work and use it as a basis to create further *Doom* levels or fix bugs in the game itself. Secondly, and most importantly, *Doom* included a multiplayer option.

This allowed several people to play directly against each other using either a Local Area Network or Internet connection. Whilst the concept of multiple users wasn't exactly new, limitations in technology and speed had ensured that such games had been very light on graphics, and usually pretty heavy on text. What *Doom* offered was the opportunity to explore a realistic looking shared online space. More importantly, it also offered the opportunity to blast the smithereens out of each other, particularly if your computer's connection to the network was faster than the other guy's.

Given that id were – at the time – a relatively small company, their way of marketing *Doom* to the masses was particularly ingenious. They simply publicised that they would make a 'shareware' version of the game available online at a given date (hence the Wisconsin log-jam), which meant interested users could try out an early level for free, and if they liked what they saw, could simply pay to get the rest.

As it turns out 1.3 million copies of the shareware version of *Doom* were downloaded, and the game went on to sell by the truckload. Yet loads of computer users have never played it – somehow *Doom* has never been able to shake off its sub-cultural heritage, and to many it is a title that has associations with over-earnest heavy-metal fans and IT administrators. Its iconography is deeply rooted in the worlds of role-playing, heavy metal and Satanism, which makes it just a little too geeky for the mainstream player looking for a quick gaming fix before heading out for a night on the foaming mead.

# Ecco The Dolphin
## 1992

On the TV show **Bad Influence**, this would have got a great review from the girls and a so-so one from the boys. Not that Novotrade's *Ecco The Dolphin* (originally released for the **Sega Mega Drive**) was intrinsically a game that only females would enjoy, rather it was interpreted as such by computer pundits. Indeed, for a spell in the early Nineties, *Ecco The Dolphin* was never off *Bad Influence*, **GamesMaster** or Sky Television's *Games World*. Perhaps programme makers felt that a game featuring nice colours and a sea mammal would help dispel the myth that computer games were inherently **violent** and evil.

The objective of *Ecco The Dolphin* was to guide the titular mammal through a series of oceanic platform levels in a quest to save the world from horrible aliens. Throughout the game, Ecco needed to keep his energy levels up by eating food and ensuring he got a good lung full of air on a regular basis. So far, so ordinary, yet there was something about the game that made you feel tranquil. Perhaps it was Ecco's dolphin song that you could use to create sonar maps, or the way you could make Ecco swim faster and faster before bringing him to the surface for a completely pointless, but nice looking spin in the air.

Not that all was sweetness and light; the game was incredibly difficult, with Ecco often finding himself lost in some deep sea tunnel or other with no access to air. However, the overall charm was enough to keep you coming back, and such was the appeal, a number of sequels were made including *Ecco: The Tides of Time* in 1995 and *Echo the Dolphin: Defender of the Future* in 2000.

\* \* \*

# Elite
## 1984

Is this the best computer game ever? A 2004 poll in Britain's *Retro Gamer* magazine certainly thought so. This epic **3-D** space trading game originally written for the **BBC Micro** and published by Acornsoft, outgunned other more famous titles such as *Tetris*, *Space Invaders* and even *Pac-Man* to be declared 'The best game ever made. Ever.' Yet for those who weren't 'there' it is difficult now to understand exactly what all the fuss is about.

You were a space mercenary equipped with a Cobra MK3 spaceship. With it you would go around destroying other ships, in between buying and selling commodities to accrue as much wealth and status as humanly possible. You started the game out with a rating of 'harmless' but if you were able to string together 6,400 killings (which would take literally hours and hours) you could attain the much-prized status of 'Order of the Elite'. And that was it, basically. *Elite*'s phenomenal appeal was derived from its awesome scale. The game consisted of 2,048 separate systems; each with their own suns, space stations and pirate ships to try and avoid.

For modern day games players this might not sound that impressive but back in 1984 it represented a quantum leap. *Elite* offered a type of computer gaming experience that would see the player embarking upon great odysseys lasting for days. *Elite*'s challenge wasn't to beat some score, arbitrarily determined by a computer, but to actually go somewhere, explore, destroy, get beaten up, regroup, re-strategize and ultimately try and better yourself.

All of these concepts were utterly alien to computer games at that time, but would later become popular in the realms of **MUD** and other interactive online **adventure games**. That two programmers (David Braben and Ian Bell), could construct something so complex and huge from such minimal resources (the routine by which all the solar systems were created was just six bytes in size) seems utterly mind-blowing today. It is unlikely that *Elite* will win over many floating voters, or even new computer fans, but its ingenuity and scale are still, in many ways, yet to be surpassed.

## First-person Shooter
## 1974

Undoubtedly the pre-eminent gaming genre of the modern age, the first-person shooter seems to become more popular as each year goes by. Today there are countless variants including 'stealth' games, where the object of the exercise is bizarrely to actually try and avoid getting embroiled in any action; and tactical games, in which you are given control of more than one character. However, fundamentally these all involve some degree of exploration and at least a smattering of killing things. Furthermore, to qualify as a 'proper' first-person shooter they must present the action in **3-D** and through the eyes of the character you are playing.

The origins of the genre are actually a little unclear. Two games released in the early Seventies wrestle for the title of the first ever first-person shooter; they are *Spasim* (released in 1974 and playable only on a network originally designed for computer-based education) and *Maze War* (developed around about the same time and similarly only originally available on private networks).

In terms of general availability though, *Tunnel Vision*, released in 1978 for the Commodore PET, may well be the first first-person shooter game that you could play in your own home. This was followed in 1981 by *3-D Monster Maze* on the **ZX81**. Over the next few years a steady stream of similar games was released, but in the main the graphics were pretty basic and so the genre's appeal was limited. It was not until 1992 and the release of id software's *Wolfenstein 3-D* for the **PC**, that the first-person shooter really began to take shape. However, just a year later the release of ***Doom*** (also created by id) changed everything. It was a massive success and opened the floodgates for loads of similarly inspired titles like 3-D Realm's 1996 title *Duke Nukem 3-D* (a somewhat bawdy first-person shooter that featured a wise-cracking misogynist who looked like Dolph Lundgren with a pair of shades and a flathead), and id's very own *Quake* (also released in 1996).

Originally, first-person shooters were the preserve of those who owned home computers. This was because the games consoles of the time weren't really equipped to handle 3-D graphics (having instead been geared up to reproduce the sprite-based games that were common in **amusement arcades**). Manufacturers such as **Nintendo**, Sony and **Sega** were quick to spot which way the wind was blowing, and from the release of the Sega Saturn in 1994 onwards, all new home consoles were far better able to handle polygon-based games.

This means the first-person shooter has been able to proliferate on almost every major system. Recent titles have continued to add additional elements to the genre (such as complex problem-solving challenges reminiscent of the traditional **adventure game**), yet the mark of a truly great first-person shooter is whether or not it contains a moment wherein having just entered a room and been confronted by a really scary monster, you furiously back pedal, fleeing for your life only to panic and end up running into a wall, allowing the aforementioned monster to blow your brains out, whilst you flail uselessly.

\* \* \*

# Flight Simulators
## 1975

Of all the computer game genres, the flight simulator, like its close cousin the **driving game**, is the one that most appeals to **dads.** Whereas just a brief bout on *Way of the Exploding Fist* is enough to make him proclaim that the whole thing is 'just silly', flight simulators are altogether different, indeed the very word 'simulator' suggests to him something more substantial and earnest.

It is said that Bruce Artwick created the very first computer flight simulator in 1975 whilst studying electrical engineering at the University of Illinois. It took him only four years to turn this simple program into the basis for subLOGIC's *Flight Simulator* for the **Apple**-II, a title that proved to be hugely successful. This early version, and those that followed, largely set the tone for flight simulators down the years. The visuals were constructed out of wire-frame polygons (initially see-through but later solid) and the bottom half of the screen displayed the various gauges and dials that most players would come to ignore in favour of simply looking out of the 'window'.

In 1982, Bruce Artwick worked with **Microsoft** on a flight simulator for the IBM **PC** and came up with *Microsoft Flight Simulator*, a dynasty that continues very successfully to this day. As technology evolved, the *Microsoft Flight Simulator* range was able to continually refine and improve upon the gameplay experience. Particular delights were the inclusion of shadowing and an external view of your own plane. Then in 1988, British flight sim fans (who were growing sick of flying around American landmarks) were at last able to take a leisurely flight up the Thames or over Stonehenge. The ability to fly over crudely delineated representations of locations that you encountered every day in real life proved to be an unexplainably thrilling experience. However, try as you might you could never find your own home in a flight simulator game.

Yet for every person who was happy to settle down for three hours to transport a Douglas DC-3 from one airport, through murky albeit realistic looking clouds to another airport (hanging around a bit on the way whilst air traffic control get their act together and give you permission to land), there were dozens more whose interests in flight simulators extended to little more than using the aeroplane as a missile to point straight at the game's technical limitations. In practice this meant seeing how high up you could fly before the computer stopped you, attempting to perform a loop-the-loop in a Boeing 747, cruising under the Golden Gate bridge and flying low through cities and then complaining when the graphical detail didn't look so impressive close up.

## Football Manager
1982

'This outstanding game of skill and strategy is now widely available and you can join the many thousands of satisfied customers who have purchased the game. This is no five-minute wonder, you will be playing this game for hours over many weeks.' This hyperbolic copy was, in actual fact, to support a title written in BASIC in which the player simply bought and sold commodities, obtained loans from the bank and then sat back and watched as the computer played out the results of your handiwork in torturously realised graphical sequences that seemed to go on forever. Welcome to the world of Addictive Games' *Football Manager*, an early Eighties computing sensation.

Although to most of us it would seem logical that a computer football game would in some way involve us actually getting to play a bit of footie, to Kevin Toms (creator of *Football Manager*) this didn't seem to matter at all. Instead he concluded that what gamers really wanted was an opportunity to control team selection, buy and sell players and attempt to achieve football management glory. So whilst you might pick the first team (each player was represented by a series of stats measuring their energy, morale, defence, midfield and attack capabilities) and even pay them at the end of each week, you had to sit helplessly on the sidelines whilst your chosen eleven headed out on to the pitch to achieve your desired result. The highlights of the game would then unfold, with the pitch shown from an isometric angle and the players depicted as little stick men. Supposedly, this would be enough to allow you to assess the performance of each player, but given the lack of detail, there wasn't much to glean and so each match became an excuse to duck out for a tea break, or an opportunity to flick the rocker switch on the back of your telly and watch a couple of minutes worth of *Nationwide*.

Once the match was completed (with the result supposedly calculated on the various strengths of the two sides with a 'random element' thrown in) the wait was still not over. Your poor old computer (*Football Manager* was available on the **ZX Spectrum**, **ZX-81**, **BBC Micro**, **Commodore 64**, Oric and **Dragon 32**) took ages to re-calculate the league tables (shown after each league match). So all in all, this was a ponderous piece of software that didn't really offer a great deal in terms of gameplay. Somehow it was hugely addictive. The snail-like pace gave it an epic feel, and there was something hugely romantic about the task ahead of you, taking your local club from the Fourth Division to the top of Division One and winning the FA Cup on the way.

Less appealing however, was Addictive Games' insistence upon including a mug shot of creator Kevin Toms on the various promotional material and, later, the actual cassette cover itself. This grinning figure with unruly facial hair and a little sweaty shine above his nose seemed an unnecessary addition to the packaging, but Addictive stuck with it right through the various re-issues of the game and its footballing sequel. Indeed Toms moved on to tackle other genres, and 1985's *Software Star* applied the same formula to the computer industry. However, without the iconic imagery, charm and excitement of football, this game proved to be far less appealing. Meanwhile, *Football Manager* went on to sell over 400,000 copies, and in 1991 was named the 83rd best Spectrum game of all time by *Your Sinclair* magazine.

## Fragfests
### 1993

In multi-player **first-person shooters** such as *Quake* or **Doom**, the art of blowing another player away is known as 'fragging'. Apparently this term originates from the Vietnam War, when mutinous soldiers would accidentally-on-purpose kill their superior officers with fragmentation grenades.

On the surface, and indeed in detail, the activity of connecting your computer up to a load of others via the Internet to play networked games such *Call of Duty* or *Hexen* would seem to have a lot in common with what is known as 'live-action laser tagging'. This indoor pursuit sees a number of adolescents, kitted out with laser guns and backpacks, set free within a gaming arena to try and shoot each other as much as possible. Whilst many people might think there is something inherently silly in this type of activity, rest assured there is a hardcore of players who take the experience extremely seriously. As such it is not surprising to turn up at your local Laser Quest and come face-to-face with a twenty-eight year old man decked out in battle fatigues and sweatband, advising a group of eleven year olds on a birthday outing with their mum, that he can help them survive the battle, but ultimately he will only take them so far and then 'no further'.

To the online fragger, the ability to brag about one's abilities, and more importantly, exude a sense of post-Vietnam world-weariness to the other combatants, is just as essential. Happily, most networked first-person shooters allow you to exchange comments either via typed-in ripostes, or (more recently) by speaking directly into the computer's microphone. Thus as you are blowing away some poor eight-year-old kid who is playing an online game for the first time in their life, you can wish them a smug 'bon voyage' as they make their way to the gaming afterlife.

If all of this makes fragfests (a term used to describe a collective of online gamers attempting to blast each other to smithereens) sound like the type of hardcore activity that you imagine would appeal to people who dress up as Klingons, then you are probably right. Certainly for the occasional gamer, an on-line fragfest can be a disheartening experience consisting of receiving taunting messages about your 'newbie' status, lots of instances of you dying before you have even been able to get your bearings, and a build-up of frustration as you attempt to understand the significance of the thing on your screen that shows your 'ping rate' (this is a measurement of the speed of your connection to the Internet and is an indication of how much lag there is between what's actually going on in the game and what you see). Yes, fragging is a complex business that like all sub-cultures possesses its own terms of reference and rules. For example, did you know that a 'gib' is like a frag but involves you making a mess of your dead opponents entrails? Similarly if someone alleges that you are a 'camper', then they mean that you generally tend to spend a whole game hidden in the same place.

The leading fraggers (who use scary monikers such as 'Thresh', short for 'Threshold of pain') can actually make a living out of their ability to be unpleasant to people online. The competition circuit, particularly in the USA, is becoming progressively a bigger and bigger business. Ultimately this will lead to the national glorification of the country's best fraggers.

Given that these people are often made up of the disaffected, picked upon and bullied of our society then regardless of what you might think of fragging itself, it is at least nice to see these often marginalized folks getting some form of a recognition for a change.

## Game Creators
## 1983

Most of us at one time or another have expressed a negative opinion about a particular game, be it to deride the poorly realised sprites of the main character or to bemoan the woeful collision detection that means you get zapped for standing on the poisonous weed even though you are clearly only standing next to it. Your mind begins to drift into a reverie in which you create your own game, free of the annoying and arbitrary limitations that riddle so many of the titles you have played in the past. Clearly at this point there are three choices open to you: forget about it and get back to negotiating those pesky weeds, learn how to program, or purchase a game creator kit and start crafting your own *magnum opus*.

The second option has some fundamental drawbacks, chief amongst them being that **programming** is difficult and requires at a minimum that you actually learn how to do it. For many creatively minded, but inherently lazy gamers, purchasing a game creator kit seemed a far better way to go. Indeed the news that such software existed was initially cause for much celebration. As with many aspects of computing, it seemed like something that would totally revolutionise your life. No longer would you need to pray in hope that someone would eventually get round to writing a **platform game** based on you, your mates and the shadowy world of your neighbourhood; now you could simply get on and make it yourself. Furthermore, you could even concoct your own home-brew games based on your favourite television shows. Anyone for a *Johnny Briggs* **beat 'em up**?

One of the earliest game creating titles was *Games Designer,* released in 1983 by Quicksilva Games. Weighing in at £15, it set the trend for all the game creator kits that followed, ensuring that for the less affluent games player this exciting opportunity would remain beyond them, at least until the software turned up at some jumble sale or other (as it always did). *Games Designer* looked promising but in truth all it really allowed you to do was to create variations on a theme, in this case **Space Invader** type games.

Over the years, this became a common complaint. Whilst their oversized and expensive packaging adorned with images of racing cars, footballers, dragons, rockets and aliens might have suggested an entrée into a vast gaming world limited only by one's imagination, the truth was that most kits allowed you to do little more than tinker with existing graphics, play around with platform level designs and compose your own music, leaving a basic underlying game pretty much untouched.

Quite apart from the fact that most of the changes you made were cosmetic, some degree of artistic talent was required, otherwise you ended up with a game featuring a smudged looking character who wore a giant hat and spewed badly realised fireballs. Happily some programs, such as Mirrorsoft's 1984 *Games Creator,* allowed you to input a musical score using standard musical notation. So whilst your game might have looked rubbish, with the help of whatever songbook you could find lying around the house, you could at least give it some decent sounding incidental music, even if the only thing you could find to transcribe was 'Annie's Song' by John Denver.

## God Games
## 1989

By the late Eighties, computer games had allowed us to manage football teams, take control of a software company, and even try at a successful career in Pop. It seemed, therefore, just one almighty leap to move from managing such operations to managing everything in the world. In 1989, Bullfrog's **Populous** gave us the opportunity to do just that, and through a fearsomely complex icon-driven control mechanism, suddenly we could raise and lower land and raise and kill people. It was great fun.

It is said that God games appeal to a specific subsection of the computer gaming community. In essence, they are much like playing a large and sophisticated board game (such as *Risk*) in that the player must gradually expand their empire through the careful deployment of their resources. It's probably fair to say that most God games are really just very sophisticated resource management challenges. However, for anyone who has ever taken a magnifying glass to an ant's nest will tell you, there is an undeniable appeal to titles such as *SimCity* (released by Maxis in 1989), or Microprose's 1991 hit *Civilisation*. Constructing or controlling a city, or world, in which its inhabitants are pretty much oblivious of your presence, means that you can indulge in your most whimsical notions, such as summoning up a tornado, or removing the very land from underneath your people. Watching those little fellas then struggling to adapt to their changed surroundings can be really entertaining.

However, it's not just about being horrible. God games offer you a world in which the inhabitants will happily get on with their lives without you (indeed it is leaving them to their own devices that often creates the problems that the game then requires you to solve). Being able to sit back and watch the consequences of your actions played out over several months or years, makes for a refreshingly different gaming experience from the instant gratification of a **shoot 'em up** or **sports game**. In truth, this is rather like that old 'foxes and rabbits' equation that you sometimes came across in computing class at school (or on the **ZX Spectrum** *Horizons* cassette), where you determined the average birth rate and lifespan for the two aforementioned species and then watched to see who (if either) became extinct first, based on the computer's calculations. In the case of most good G od games, the enactment of these carefully plotted equations usually results in something more entertaining than simply a graph on a screen. Later versions of *SimCity* even included various bits of video footage in which prominent members of your city would plead or protest to you dependent upon the actions you had just taken. Given the obnoxiousness of some of the actors' performances, making them squirm was hugely pleasurable.

Ultimately though, playing a God game is all about making moral decisions (Bullfrog's 2001 title *Black and White* makes the gaming world change in appearance dependent upon whether you do good or bad things), and it is likely that although you may start out with the best of intentions, building and nurturing your world becomes a little bit like constructing a really impressive structure out of playing cards. Unfortunately at some point the devilish notion to destroy your own creation with one deft flick of the wrist always becomes just a little too much to resist.

## Hidden Bits in Games
### 1980

Today you can buy countless books that list in minute detail all of the secrets in a particular game, but back in the halcyon days of computer gaming it was possible to stumble across all manner of idiosyncratic and bizarre elements, placed there by the programmer just to see if anyone would ever find them. These days such elements are referred to as 'Easter Eggs' but back then they weren't referred to as anything, because no one knew about them.

It is commonly acknowledged that the first computer game to contain an Easter Egg was the 1980 graphical remake of *Adventure* for the **Atari** 2600. The purpose of the game was to navigate through a series of locations, moving a cursor on the screen in the direction you wanted to go. Atari programmer Warren Robinett had been working on it on and off for several months, when he became inspired by tales of a hidden track on the Beatles' *White Album* and decided to create a secret room that you could only access if you happened to pass your cursor over a single pixel hidden on a grey wall. The room in question consisted only of the words 'Created by Robinett' in bright colours. Assuming that he would be fired if anyone else at Atari found out, Robinett kept quiet about what he had done. However, in 1980 a twelve-year old Atari fan blew the whistle, and with that the Easter Egg was born.

Over the years, hunting down secrets has become a favourite activity of hardcore gamers, and some truly bizarre stories have emerged, many of which have gone on to become urban legends of the computing fraternity. For example, it is told that on the **ZX Spectrum** motorbike game *Wheelie* (published by Microsphere in 1983), if you finally get to the end of the game you are greeted by the terrifying visage of Marvel Comic's *Ghost Rider*, who then proceeds to chase you back along the course. Similarly, it is said that there is an extra room in Software Projects' 1984 legend *Jet Set Willy* called 'April Showers'.

Or how about these ones: in the game *Impossible Mission 2025* for the **Amiga** (published by MicroProse in 1994) you could go into a room on one of the levels, sit down at a desk and play the original version of the game (that appeared on the **Commodore 64** in 1983); meanwhile in Novagen's *Damocles* (written by Paul Woakes for the **Atari ST** in 1990), you could enter the author's house, locate a bin, and in it find a ZX Spectrum. In *Kung-Fu Master* (released by Berkeley Software in 1985 for the Commodore 64), if you pressed *Ctrl* and *G* at the same time, your character would pull out a gun and shoot his opponent.

Whether any of the above are actually true or not seems

almost beside the point, gamers love to regale each other with their discoveries (even if they have just made them up), and in the process earn immense kudos for what is, in reality, nothing more than a demonstration of their ability to tenaciously examine every single dead end, waste paper basket and pixel in a computer game.

## The Hobbit
## 1982

'You are in a comfortable tunnel-like hall. To the east there is the round green door'. These were the words that opened Melbourne House's 1982 **adventure game** classic. Released for the 48K **ZX Spectrum**, *The Hobbit* would come to gain almost mythical status (indeed it topped *Sinclair User's* 1985 poll of the all-time best games), and would be considered by many as the first adventure game to feature reasonable artificial intelligence.

*The Hobbit* was a faithful retelling of the Tolkein tale, featuring most of the major characters from the book and was one of the first adventure games to feature graphics as well as text. Whilst these images were confined to simply drawn vistas, there was nevertheless something thrilling about seeing scenes actually appear on the screen in front of you as if drawn by some invisible hand. Similarly the game's (albeit limited) ability to recognize text commands excited a lot of people who boasted of *The Hobbit's* 'vast library' of 500 words (which is about the number of words in this entry – a lot less than you would think you would need to complete a complex quest).

Backed by a strong marketing campaign that boasted '*The Hobbit* is a super program that is a milestone in computer software. You will face dangers, excitement and adventure in words and graphics', Melbourne House managed to shift a hefty million copies. Given that at £14.95 it was more than twice as expensive as an ordinary title, this was no mean achievement (although bundling in a free copy of Tolkein's original book probably helped). Yet for all its popular appeal and fulsome reviews, it was a difficult game to master. One idle command to 'Hit Thorin' and you would find your skull cracked open in an instant with the message that 'you have mastered 2.5% of this adventure' ensuring you were well aware of your less than heroic prowess.

Indeed death was never very far away in *The Hobbit*, with trolls and other beasties happy to eat you as soon as your back was turned. Some of the game's puzzles were particularly tricky, with more than one player probably driven to punching the screen when they found themselves trapped in the Goblin's Dungeons. Yet few of us ever gave in. With its 40KB of machine code and four minute **loading** time, *The Hobbit* was (until *Elite* showed up) just about the most expansive and complicated computer game ever made. However, that didn't excuse the infuriating fact that when, after months of effort, you finally managed to kill Smaug the dragon, you had to make it all the way back to the beginning in order to complete the game.

## Hungry Horace
### 1982

Who or what was *Hungry Horace*? Back when computer characters were obviously not required to be any kind of specific creature, *Hungry Horace* became one of the very first British computer characters to become a star. Over the course of three games (released between 1982 and 1983), we guided Horace around a maze-like park, across roads, down ski slopes and finally through a bizarre spider-infested world.

Released for the **ZX Spectrum** by Psion, *Hungry Horace's* early success owes a lot to it being one of the very first playable games that Spectrum owners could buy. In fact, in the first few month's of the Speccy's existence, it was one of the few releases that wasn't accused of rehashing something already available for the **ZX-81**. It was however, a rehash of *Pac-Man*, but then it wasn't the only title on the home computer market that took its inspiration from what was, after all, the most successful arcade game of all time.

*Hungry Horace* offered the dedicated player four levels of maze-like madness. What made it different from many of the other maze games of the time though, was that you didn't need to clear each level before moving on to the next. So for those who were impatient you could simply flit from one screen to another via the exits. Levels three and four were particularly difficult, and on many occasions it was actually impossible to escape death as the park keepers (*Hungry Horace's* version of *Pac-Man's* ghosts) would get you trapped in a dead end and there was nothing you could do about it. To have such arbitrary deaths in computer games seems almost unthinkable now.

The object of *Hungry Horace* was to rack up as big a score as possible, with extra lives (or passes as they were referred to) being awarded whenever you passed certain scoring thresholds. This generosity could be taken advantage of in a particularly sneaky way. On each level there was a bell that, when consumed would give you extra points. Skilled players worked out that you could touch the bell for a fraction of a second without making it disappear, and then repeat the process ad infinitum whilst watching your score accumulate.

*Hungry Horace* was a huge hit and stayed atop the Spectrum charts for several weeks. A sequel was released not long after, and, as before, it drew upon a recognised arcade hit for inspiration. *Horace Goes Skiing* saw our titular hero first having to navigate a busy road – **Frogger** style – to acquire his skis, and then take to the slopes where he had to weave between flags to attain as many points as possible. Whilst still popular with the *Horace* faithful, the game seemed more repetitive than its predecessor, even though on paper it offered a greater variety of challenge. Nevertheless a third and final game– *Horace and the Spiders* – was released. Again, this didn't actually build on any of the gameplay of the previous title and instead confronted the player with a series of spider killing challenges, culminating in a quasi-**platformer** level in which Horace had to trample arachnids to death. Whilst an improvement on the previous title, by 1983, Horace was no longer the Spectrum's only loveable character, and the likes of *Miner Willy* and *Hen House Harry* were proving to be more attractive to games players than the strange purple blob that was Horace.

## Jetpac
### 1983

Released for the **ZX Spectrum**, **VIC-20** and **BBC Micro**, *Jetpac* was the first title by British software company Ultimate: Play The Game. The objective was to propel Jetman around the screen so he could collect various pieces of rocket, assemble them in the right order and then obtain sufficient fuel to take off for the next level. What made the game particularly compelling was the effects of gravity on the Jetman, which meant that manoeuvring around the levels was very difficult. The game came with a fussily metallic looking logo and a picture of two astronauts on the cassette cover (even though only one was featured in the game).

Best of all though were the torturously detailed notes on the inner sleeve proclaiming that the game featured a 'Universe of planets, Quad Photon Laser Phaser, Hydrovac JET PAC, Collect-a-pod, Hover button, Thrust control, Fly left/right, Lives left displayed, Massive every hit explosions'. Clearly, this was over-egging the pudding; however such detail became a useful weapon in persuading your parents to buy it for you – to whit: 'see, Mum, it's got "Lives left displayed" and everything'.

*Jetpac* sold over 300,000 copies, which was a remarkable figure for the time, particularly given there were only about a million Spectrum owners. But it was soon superseded by Ultimate: Play the Game's later releases such as *Atic Atac*, *Sabre Wulf* and **Knight Lore**. This is where it all started, and a welcome sequel (*Lunar Jetman*) was released in 1984. Keeping up the tradition of anomalous cover artwork elements, *Lunar Jetman* featured a little trailer that gamers spent hours and hours trying to track down only to discover that it was just a bit of artistic license, and not in any way indicative of what appeared in the game.

## Knight Lore
## 1984

By 1984 software company Ultimate: Play the Game had developed a reputation for producing cutting-edge computer games for the **ZX Spectrum.** Having paved the way with distinctive titles such as *Jetpac* and *Tranz Am,* they released their most impressive title yet, *Atic Atac*. However this was just the start. *Sabre Wulf* (also released in 1984) was just as good, but it came in a fancy box with a distinctive cover design and an enigmatic advertising campaign. **Computer magazines** went berserk and bestowed fulsome praise upon it (although some were a little sore at having to shell out £9.95 for the pleasure), and the die was cast.

So, when inscrutable full-page spreads began to appear in the press portraying what looked to be some kind of marble carving of a wolf's face, adorned with the legend 'Knight Lore', the pleasurable build-up to the release of another great game began again. Ultimate clearly believed they had something special up their sleeves with *Knight Lore,* describing it to *Sinclair User* magazine in December 1984 as 'the first step in the new generation of computer adventure simulation developments which represents the very pinnacle of software development on the 48K Spectrum'. This 'adventure simulation development' turned out to be a **3-D** isometric technique that Ultimate referred to as 'Filmation'.

Knight Lore's graphics were truly groundbreaking for their time. Whilst titles such as **Ant Attack** depicted a three-dimensional world by using degrees of shading, and simplistic looking characters, Knight Lore actually looked quite a bit like a cartoon. The characters and obstacles appeared in detailed outline, meaning that features could be properly portrayed. Colour clashes (a perennial problem on the **ZX Spectrum**) were completely eliminated by having each screen daubed in a single colour. Shading, so effectively used in Ant Attack to generate a sense of depth, was used to similar effect here. All-in-all, Knight Lore looked incredible, producing graphics that made even **Commodore 64** owners jealous.

But what of the game? The objective was to explore a castle in an attempt to locate six objects that, when dropped into a wizard's cauldron, would deliver your character (the same chap who had featured in Sabre Wulf) from his terrible lycanthropic curse. Given Ultimate's three previous titles had all featured characters having to explore a series of 'rooms', the concept seemed a bit formulaic; however, the simple fact that you were dealing with a three dimensional gaming environment meant the experience was totally different from all that had come before. For a start, as with many isometric games, the control mechanism was tricky to get a hang of, requiring you to rotate Sabreman (this was the name of your character) until he was facing the correct direction, and then make him walk. However once you had mastered it, you were able to do all manner of things such as push blocks around in order to solve problems or surmount obstacles.

Released in time for Christmas, Knight Lore was an unsurprising big seller, with every computer magazine giving it ecstatic notices (by this time no one seemed to care about the hefty price tag). 'Knight Lore has that magical ingredient which makes it exciting to play and watch' proclaimed CRASH magazine in January

1985, 'and keeps you on the edge of your seat with anxiety. IT'S SIMPLY A GREAT GAME.' Certainly it made everything else reviewed that month look prehistoric in comparison.

For Ultimate this looked like the beginning of the beginning. The company had developed great charisma (thanks in part to its team's reticence to participate in press interviews); however the development of Filmation seemed to send them into a creative cul-de-sac. *Alien 8*, released in 1985, was a rehash of *Knight Lore* and even 1985's *Nightshade* (which featured the much vaunted 'Filmation 2' technique that actually made objects and buildings scroll as you walked past them) didn't offer anything that new in terms of gameplay ('don't expect anything too out-standing' was *CRASH* magazine's warning). Finally, in 1988, *Martianoids* (again using *Knight Lore* techniques) was only able to scrape 58% in *CRASH* magazine's review, a score previously unthinkable for a games company that had produced a slew of groundbreaking and enigmatic titles.

## K-Tel Productions
### 1983

K-Tel are best remembered for their fantastic 'Hooked on Classics' and disco compilation LP series; cheapo gadgets such as the 'Brush-O-Matic' and 'Bottle and Glass cutter'; and their arch rivalry with the ubiquitous Ronco. But in the early Eighties, K-Tel took their 'stack 'em high and sell 'em cheap' philosophy and applied it to the world of computer games. Although we knew from watching satirical comedy shows that K-Tel was a company best avoided, their nascent range of titles for the **ZX Spectrum** and **Commodore 64** were nonetheless alluring, principally for the fact that most tapes came with two games for the price of one.

Their cassette covers sported a vaguely Eastern European text font giving the whole thing a sophisticated look that was fatally undermined by a background (grey with multi-colour diagonal stripes) that closely resembled the wallpaper found in **boys' bedrooms**.

Of the whole series, the most memorable release was the *It's Only Rock 'n' Rock/Tomb of Dracula* double cassette in 1984. Here the cover depicted a nicely-lit photo of some bloke dressed up as the eponymous Count, and a shot of a nameless pop star holding his guitar in the style of the bassist from *Level 42* (i.e. right up in the armpits). *It's Only Rock 'n' Roll* was a supposed strategy game in the mould of **Football Manager**. However, given that your input was restricted to little more than choosing a name for the group and planning tours, it was difficult to get too involved. Reviewing it at the time, *Sinclair User* magazine noted that apart from the occasional newsflash such as 'Government taxes pop groups' or 'Tony Blackburn likes [insert name of your group here]' not very much happened at all. *The Tomb of Dracula* was a slight improvement but was far too easy to complete.

Whilst gamers would generally find the K-Tel games to be pretty disappointing, the fact that they were affordable to those who had to rely on pocket money meant that, time and again, in desperate need of a new game to play, cash would be handed over in the hope that this next title would be better than the last. In the end, K-Tel's dalliances with the computer games market proved to be short-lived, spanning just over two years. The company went back to doing what it does best, churning out budget price music compilations that appealed to your aunts and uncles and the horrible family down the street.

## Lemmings
1991

There are certain computer games that seem to gain an appeal beyond the core audience. Generally speaking such titles eschew traditional computer gaming preoccupations such as shooting people and over-earnest back-stories, in favour of something that seems to make a virtue out of its own ultimate inconsequentiality.

Psygnosis' *Lemmings* owes its existence to some developers mucking around whilst they were meant to be working on another game. According to Mike Dailly (who worked on *Lemmings*), the original impetus came from an attempt to try and create realistic looking animations of men using only eight by eight pixels. The resultant figures (worked on by both Dailly and his colleague Gary Timmons) so amused their colleagues that the twosome realised, assuming they could come up with a good concept, they had the basis for a proper game.

In an age when software developers had finally broken free of restrictive and simplistic looking computer characters, *Lemmings* seemed to be swimming against the tide. However, those comical looking characters with their green hair set the tone and various other humorous elements were added, including amusing explosions and little cries of 'oh no' when your Lemmings plunged to their doom.

It would require more than just charming little characters to craft a hit game, and *Lemmings*, like almost every title that has broken through to the 'mainstream', had at its heart an extremely simple concept. Your task was to guide as many of the green-haired critters through each level as possible without losing lives along the way. The catch was that the Lemmings couldn't think for themselves and so would happily walk off the edge of a cliff if you didn't provide them with either some route across it, or an alternative path that they could take. This very basic concept, augmented with the inclusion of Lemmings with special attributes (such as the ability to dig holes or climb things) was enough to sustain a number of different levels of varying difficulty, some of which required the player to be able to complete multiple tasks at the same time, and others which needed nothing more than good logic and foresight.

Released initially for the **Amiga**, *Lemmings* proved such a hit that it was subsequently ported to most other major (and not so major) systems, and by 1998 the original game could be played on twenty-five or so different machines including the Philips Cdi and the **Amstrad CPC-464**. To date there have been upwards of ten or so sequels including the obligatory **3-D** version. As is typical of such games, it is only the ardent computer fans who have followed the progress of the *Lemmings* titles, with those casual players content to stick with what they know best – the original.

## Manga
### 1814

The Japanese perception of what constitutes a fun computer game has for a long time amused us in the West. Simulations based on train driving and fishing may sound pretty tedious but have proven to be extremely popular in Japan. Indeed when companies such as **Nintendo** or Sony launch new home consoles, it is notable that the release titles available in Japan are usually very different to those in the US or Europe.

To suggest though that Eastern and Western cultures do not overlap would be preposterous. You are just as likely to stumble across a McDonalds in Tokyo as you are in Tunbridge Wells, and debate regarding David Beckham's footballing prowess is as fierce in Yokohama as it is in Yorkshire.

The Japanese contribution to the Western computer games culture is particularly pronounced. Not only have most of the important gaming developments of the last twenty or so years come from the East but there is a Japanese gaming aesthetic that has become more and more popular. For many, the term 'manga' evokes images of angelic looking, kick ass schoolgirls and gung ho boys with impossibly spiky hair and angry white pyjamas.

However the term was first coined in 1814 by artist Katsushika Hokusai, and was taken to mean 'whimsical pictures'. Manga in the modern sense didn't really develop until after the Second World War, when – suddenly inundated by US comics (such as *Archie*) – a number of Japanese publishers began to produce their own titles, clearly influenced by the look and format of the American publications.

In the West, comics attained mass popularity for just a few decades before becoming a niche interest; but in Japan manga took off in a big way, evolving into a medium well suited for mythological, action-based, epic tales, with single issues often stretching to several hundred pages. Unlike their American cousins, manga had the scope to appeal to pretty much everyone, and titles such as *Shonen Jump* could shift a mind-boggling six million copies a week (this in a population of 125 million, just over twice the size of the UK).

The influence of manga stretched to other mediums, particularly films, where its epic scope and sequential artwork seemed to translate easily. Really, it was only a matter of time before the influence of manga was felt in the arena of video games. Of the many computer games that owe a debt to manga, the *Final Fantasy* series are the best known.

The original game (released for the **NES** by Square Soft in 1987) addressed a typical manga theme (that of all life on earth being represented by the basic elements of fire and water), and from this starting point, created a **role-playing** game in which you led a team of four warriors trying to rescue a princess who had been imprisoned by a dark lord in a dark temple. Although the graphics were pretty simplistic, the game did possess an epic back-story that appealed to manga lovers, and so became a bestseller in Japan. Consequently, Square Soft (who had intended *Final Fantasy* to be the company's last ever software release – hence the title) felt compelled to carry on.

But although *Final Fantasy* had proved to be a significant hit in the East, its US sales were so disappointing that Square Soft didn't even bother release *Final Fantasy II* and *III* there.

Although the gameplay evolved over each release, *Final Fantasy IV* (released for the **SNES** in 1991) marked a significant shift in the series' focus. The adventures became plot led and the epic feeling implied in the previous games' back-stories now became more explicit. By 1997, Square Soft abandoned **Nintendo** in favour of the **PlayStation** and *Final Fantasy VII* (their first release for the machine) became the biggest selling game of the year, even scoring in America (where it actually sold more copies than it did in Japan).

News of each new release is met with fervent anticipation by gamers in the East and the West alike. In general, Japanese culture seems to have become increasingly palatable over here, with films such as *The Ring* drawing big crowds; and manga in all its forms growing ever more popular. However, you can't help but think that underneath the fusion of futuristic technology, traditional Japanese art and Western comic book sensibilities, there is a deeper intellectual side to manga that we are failing to pick up on because we are too pre-occupied with looking at the neo-punk cityscapes and cutesy schoolgirls.

## Manic Miner
### 1983

Surely there can be few games from the golden era of computing as well loved as Bug-Byte's *Manic Miner*? On the surface it might have looked like a run of the mill **platformer**, but *Manic Miner* had bizarre characters, superbly eccentric level designs and a miner called Willy.

Apparently based on the **Atari** game *Miner 2049er* (also released in 1983), *Manic Miner* was arguably the better game with Miner Willy's parabolic jump proving much superior to the Atari game's triangular leap. Simply put, *Manic Miner* was more inventive and imaginative than *Miner 2049er,* or indeed pretty much any other game out there at that time.

Of its twenty levels the most memorable was 'Eugene's Lair', apparently named after Bug Byte programmer Eugene Evans. As well as featuring a big Humpty Dumpty looking character (who most presumed to be the eponymous Eugene), there were also a couple of toilets whose lids would snap up and down in a most threatening fashion. *Manic Miner* was a tough game though, and like most platformers of its time, very unforgiving. Were you to lose your life at the end of a level then the game had no compunction in starting you back at the beginning. Similarly, there was a stringent time limit to be adhered too (Willy's air supply) and should you fail to complete the level before it ran out, then a life would be have to be sacrificed.

*Manic Miner* became a big seller (particularly on the **ZX Spectrum**) and its creator Matthew Smith was pressed into making a sequel. However, whilst *Jet Set Willy* might have operated on a larger scale and featured even more invention, it was rather ill-disciplined and beset with problems thanks to being released before Smith had finished writing it. It was actually impossible to finish the game, a fact that many gamers refused to accept, preferring instead to believe that somewhere in Willy's vast mansion (which was where the game was set) lay the means to completion. So intense was the belief that some wags even went so far as to mock up screens showing hidden levels, and send them to unsuspecting **computer magazines**.

Some two decades on, whatever sense of disappointment *Jet Set Willy* might have created has long since dissipated, and Miner Willy today stands proud as the ultimate icon of retro computer cool, at least in this country.

Mario
1981

At the beginning of the Nineties, Mario was the most recognised children's icon in the world, surpassing old favourites
such as Superman and even Mickey Mouse. Whether the Italian
plumber ever achieved such widespread fame in this country is
questionable, but with a feature film, cartoon series and copious games all to himself, he remains a giant in video gaming
right to this day.

Mario's first outing might have been in the form of Jump Man
in **Donkey Kong**, but by 1983 he was starring in his own game
(not before turning evil for a spell in 1982's *Donkey Kong Jr* and
imprisoning the titular hero's father). *Mario Bros* not only introduced the world to the fully fleshed out Mario (his occupation
was now explicitly stated as 'plumber'), but we got our first
glimpse of some of the supporting cast too, such as Mario's
brother Luigi and the Koopa Troopas. However, *Mario Bros'*
most important legacy was to establish, beyond any doubt, that
*Mario* and *Donkey Kong* creator, Shigeru Miyamoto, was much
more than a one trick pony.

If further proof were needed it came in 1985 with the release
of *Super Mario Bros* for the **NES**. The game opened up Mario's
world by introducing side-scrolling levels, meaning that the
challenges that Miyamoto designed were no longer confined by
the dimensions of the television screen. Now Mario could roam
across sprawling landscapes chock full of dangers and surprises.

There is no doubt that *Super Mario Bros* is a seminal title and
earned Mario the right to become **Nintendo**'s mascot. The game
was bundled with the NES and more than 40 million copies
were sold in North America alone. Whilst aficionados might
claim that *Super Mario Bros 3* (released in 1988) is the better
title, it was *Super Mario Bros* that put in place all of the elements
of the Mario universe that have since proved to be so popular.

Miyamoto claims the secret of his success is to approach the business of designing each game as if he were a child. It is well documented that in his younger days he enjoyed exploring and claims that the experience of suddenly coming across a lake, or plucking up the courage to explore a cave, informed his level designs. Certainly the thorough explorer is well-rewarded in the *Super Mario Bros* games, with secret bonuses and locations hidden in some of the most unusual places.

It is not just the geography though that makes the Mario games so enchanting. Each one is a text book example of how to constantly increase the challenge level so that it remains just at the upper limit of our ability. It is also claimed that Miyamoto spends a great deal of time testing each game to ensure the pacing is just right. His belief is that the player needs to receive rewards at the correct frequency: if they get them too often their motivation to try harder will dip, similarly if rewards are too infrequent the player is likely to look elsewhere for gaming gratification.

Throughout the mid-Eighties and early Nineties, tens of millions of Mario games were sold, and 27 separate titles were released between 1985 and 1994 (including the epic *Super Mario World* and the addictive racer **Super Mario Kart**, both released for the **SNES** in 1992). The plumber even survived an appalling movie version made in 1993. During this period, Mario became synonymous with Nintendo and represented all that was good about the company's ethos. Indeed when Sega came up with their own mascot, **Sonic The Hedgehog**, in 1991, it was telling that both companies could be defined by their leading characters – Nintendo (and Mario) was family orientated and playful, whereas Sega and Sonic were a little bit more aggressive and cutting edge.

For a while it did look as if Sega's blue hedgehog would transcend Mario's popularity, but crucially it was Mario who found himself best able to adapt to the modern era of gaming, specifically, the leap to **3-D** (made in 1996's *Super Mario 64*). At the time of writing Mario is still Nintendo's best ambassador, and predictably the launch of Nintendo's latest system, the DS, has been accompanied by a brand new Mario game.

## Metagalactic Llamas Battle At The Edge Of Time
### 1983

Computer games today are developed by a large team of people and typically require the budget of a small feature film. So it is obviously hugely important that the eventual title sells in reasonable numbers. How strange then to think that the inspiration behind a commercially released computer game could once be as simple as attempting to come up with the silliest name possible. But this is exactly how legendary programmer Jeff Minter arrived at Llamasoft's **VIC-20** game *Metagalactic Llamas Battle at the Edge of Time*.

The game, whilst failing to live up to it epic title, was at the very least quirky and consisted of a (in the words of Minter) 'feckless' llama attempting to keep alien spiders at bay by spitting at them. Unsurprisingly, there was very little else like it in the marketplace.

However, *Metagalactic Llamas Battle at the Edge of Time* is very typical of Jeff Minter's oeuvre. Perhaps his most famous game is 1983's *Attack of the Mutant Camels* (released initially for the **Commodore 64**), which offered Minter's own unique take on, bizarrely, *The Empire Strikes Back* (it seems that Minter was inspired by a computer magazine review that likened AT-ATs to camels). During the early to mid-Eighties, Minter released a number of quirky games on his own Llamasoft label, all with similarly peculiar themes, and built up a sizeable cult following that remains loyal to this day.

But not all of Minter's output was as niche. In 1994 he produced an updated version of the arcade classic *Tempest*, and over the years he has championed visualiser software that can create patterns and colours synchronous with music. Indeed if you've ever seen anything coming out of your computer that made you think 'what were they on when they thought that up' then Minter may well have had a hand in it.

## Military
## 1980

The American military's heavy involvement in video games seems to come as a surprise to many, but given this is the same organisation that runs courses for soldiers to learn how to kill animals simply by staring at them, dalliances with computer simulations and **first-person shooters** seem pretty reasonable areas of military research.

Although for a while the army used spreadsheets to model combat situations, it was the **3-D** vector graphics and supposed realism of **Atari**'s 1980 tank simulator *Battlezone* that first got military chiefs interested in computer games, and they paid Atari to develop an even more realistic version for them to use in their own training sessions. Over time, a pattern seemed to emerge, we would get some exciting new **flight simulator** or combat game, and the army would get a souped-up version with big screens and, in some cases, helmets fitted with video visors. It just didn't seem fair somehow.

Mind you, they did give a little back. Lockheed-Martin, better known for constructing American war planes, worked with **Sega** to design the computing system that was used on the 1997 arcade game *Super GT.* Meanwhile in the Nineties the US Marines invested in a job lot of **Doom**, creating an influx of cash that was to the benefit of the game's publishers.

In recent years, the widespread use of video games in army training has been openly acknowledged. The belief is that cadets will happily play combat games for hours on end and, in the process, pick up skills (not to mention becoming desensitised to combat conditions, or so the theory goes) that previously they would have had to learn about in a dull classroom environment. More recently, the US military has released a series of games under the banner *America's Army*. These titles are being distributed for free in the hope that young kids will play them and become interested in pursuing a military career. Given that **Hungry Horace** led to no reported uptake in park vandalism you would like to think that the military is on to a loser here, but early indications suggest it is having the desired effect. But do we really want soldiers who think that if they get all their buddies wiped out in enemy fire, all they need to do is go back to the last save point?

## Mortal Kombat
1992

1992 represented the zenith year for the **beat 'em up** genre. *StreetFighter II* ruled supreme in the amusement arcades, and for those who weren't willing to suffer the queues to get to play it, there were plenty of derivative versions to attract your attention. Developers Midway had achieved some success two years earlier with their arcade title *Pit Fighter*. This slugfest of a game offered little in terms of complexity or variety, but it did feature realistic (albeit rather pixelated), digitised graphics, meaning that the character you controlled looked quite a lot like a real man.

Recognising the popularity of Capcom's *StreetFighter II*, Midway looked to develop the *Pit Fighter* technology into something more presentable. In the space of ten months they came up with a title that would briefly wrestle with the aforementioned Capcom beat 'em up for genre supremacy. This was *Mortal Kombat*. Whilst the game's digitised graphics might have ensured that it looked very different to *StreetFighter II*, the notion of allowing players to pick one of a number of distinctive characters, each with their own special moves was rather familiar. Of the various characters on offer, the ones that people seem to remember best are Raiden – God of Thunder and Scorpion – a shadowy ninja whose true identity was hidden. There was some sort of a back-story, full of cod-Eastern mythology but no one really knew what it was and it didn't seem to matter anyway because gamers immediately and instinctively understood the motivations and histories of each of the characters

Whilst graphically impressive, prolonged play revealed that *Mortal Kombat* was actually a somewhat limited gaming experience, with bouts often decided by whoever could hit the punch button fastest. The inclusion of a secret baddy (Reptile) that would only appear when something flew past the moon, was a neat idea but not really enough to paper over the cracks. Where *Mortal Kombat* definitely scored though was in the introduction of 'fatalities'. Basically these were moves that the victor could pull at the end of the bout that would result in some form of spectacular final move such as a decapitation or (if you were playing Kano) the removal of your opponent's heart. These gory scenes attracted players to machines in their droves.

Although *Mortal Kombat* was an undeniable success in the arcades, its infamy was sealed when it appeared on home systems. Announced via a much-hyped 'Mortal Monday' campaign, by the time the title was released on 13th September 1993, kids were positively stampeding shops for a copy. In addition, television programmes such as **GamesMaster** trailed and featured the game heavily as part of their weekly challenges.

Controversially, it looked like the conversions to the **Sega Mega Drive** and **SNES** had cut out the blood and gore, but it became apparent that on the Mega Drive these elements could be unlocked. Fearing adverse publicity, **Nintendo** insisted their Mortal Kombat would be gore-free. Unsurprisingly, the Mega Drive outsold the SNES version three-to-one, and in the process attracted massive controversy for its **violent** content.

Today, no one seems to look back on *Mortal Kombat* with much warmth. Most agree it was a shallow game and a bit of a cash-in; however, someone must have liked it. Indeed you can't help but think *Mortal Kombat* is the video game equivalent of the Eighties BBC comedy series *Bread,* hugely popular at the time, but impossible now to find anyone who admits to having watched it.

## Motion Capture
## 1980

Motion capture is a technique that always seems to turn up on science programmes and software companies' promotional videos. The process of sticking lots of little dots on an actual human being and then seeing their movements translated first into a little stick man on a computer screen, and finally a fully rendered figure certainly looks impressive. **Sports games** in particular make a great deal of fuss over using named sports personalities for their motion capturing, with the implied message being that because Thierry Henry has been used to generate the movements for the players in a football game, the finished title will be far more authentic.

Motion capture actually has its origins in the traditional animation technique of rotoscoping (whereby animators would trace over film footage); however, whilst rotoscoping required frame by frame examination of the source material, motion capture allows you to store sequences of movement that can be replayed or spliced together to create longer chains of action. Traditionally, motion capture involves attaching a series of LEDs or small reflective dots to the various joints on a person's body and then filming them using two or more special cameras. These cameras pick up the movement of the joints and convert them into data that can then be used to construct a **3-D** model. Games designers take these movements and align them to various commands within the computer games, such that if you move the controller in such a way as to make your character start running, a particular motion capture sequence will be used to realise that command.

Whilst motion capture might provide the developer with a stockpile of authentic movements, it does present some issues too. Firstly, the processing of the data is generally quite taxing on the computer. Secondly, and more importantly, given that the technique relies on reusing pre-recorded sequences, it is very difficult to construct improvised movement within a motion capture game. This means that if you change your mind and want to jump instead of run, you need to wait until the run motion capture sequence has completed its cycle, before the jump sequence can start. This limitation becomes really frustrating when, in a game of *FIFA*, you attempt to make a well-timed tackle on another player just outside the penalty box, only for it to turn into a gruesome hack, thanks to the motion capture delaying your move. Some computers do attempt to get round this issue by creating routines that run calculations based on the angles of the computer characters' joints to allow you to seamlessly transition from one move to another, but again, this is all very process intensive.

Still, for all its drawbacks, most players would agree that they would hate to do without that distinctive Thierry Henry canter, or that mazy Ryan Giggs dribble, and so we have long since learned to adapt to the drawbacks and limitations of the technique (although that doesn't stop us going off in a huff if that downed opposing striker is awarded a penalty and manages to slot the ball into the back of the net).

## MUD
### 1979

Of all the impenetrable online communities, the ones that align themselves most closely with the general populace's view of computer geekdom are MUDs. These groups exist within a fictional world of *Dungeons & Dragons* sword and sorcery shenanigans, where troubled teenage boys from Illinois can pose as battle weary warriors and middle-aged women from Frankfurt can pretend to be blissed out immortal elves called TwilightMother.

The term MUD was originally an acronym for Multi-User Dungeons, but today it more usually means Multiple User Dimensons or Multi-User Dialogue. The basic premise behind the concept though, remains largely unchanged. First created in 1979 by students at the University of Essex, MUDs look and feel much like traditional text-based **adventure games**. However, the crucial difference is that multiple real-life players can inhabit the same adventure at the same time. When you first enter such a game this distinction may not appear to be very significant – after all the first words that you will likely see will be a computer generated description of your character's location. Should another player be in the vicinity though then it is entirely likely that they will begin talking to you, or attacking you. Importantly, their actions will not be determined by the computer (although they will be restricted by what the computer allows them to do). In addition, although the landscape is originally defined by the computer, players can affect it by, for example, leaving an item in a particular location, or perhaps killing the troll that was programmed to wait under a bridge. Indeed advanced users are even able to create new areas of land themselves. As such, a MUD can be a highly chaotic and unpredictable experience.

The objective of these games is not to complete a particular quest or vanquish a computer generated baddy, but rather to exist in an online world and try and grow as strong and powerful as you can. Attributes are generally obtained by either finding stuff (such as gold coins, weapons and spells), or by killing other monsters and characters and gaining what are referred to as 'experience points'. These crucial merits can be used to improve your character's abilities and will allow you to win more fights, earn even more experience points and so become ever more powerful.

The obvious appeal then of such games is that much of the restrictions of traditional text-based adventure games are removed. Now when you are conversing with other characters, you no longer have to worry about getting the syntax correct, or using the appropriate terminology; assuming the person you are conversing with shares the same mother tongue as you, you can say whatever you want and be perfectly understood. As such, a number of MUDs have evolved beyond the point of being mere games, and have turned instead into 'virtual communities'. Such 'games' are often referred to as MOOs (MUD Object Orientated), and can come with their own governments, publications and even committees to approve planning permission (when a player wants to create a new bit of land). In fact, such is the complexity of social structure that can be created within these constructs that many real world issues pertaining to law and order have surfaced online (including a notorious 'rape' case in which a player acting under the name of Mr Bungle used their character to cast a spell on a female character called Moondreamer. This spell gave Mr Bungle complete control over Moondreamer, and, well, you can imagine the computerized consequences).

But for most MUD gamers the experience is far less complicated. You go through the process of creating a character (a tedious exercise that requires you to define attributes such as strength, speed and so on by assigning various scores to each), and you then enter the game in what seems to be a 'pleasant, grassy area'. Then you get killed by another, more powerful, player on the look out for easy experience points. After that it's back to generating a new character. With time and perseverance though, plus a momentary shortage of gaming vultures it is possible to obtain a foothold, and start to develop your character. Of course, the most effective method of development is to hang around at the place where you first appeared and kill any 'newbies' (the preferred term for new players in a MUD game) that happen to come along. MUDs, like life, can be cruel.

## Night Trap
### 1992

**Sega**'s *Night Trap* generated a level of publicity far in excess of its worth. Created back in the late Eighties it didn't achieve a commercial release until Sega reasoned that the game's reliance on full motion video footage would make an ideal showcase for their new Sega **Mega Drive** add-on, the Mega CD.

The objective of *Night Trap* was pretty dull. Simply put, you were required to monitor a number of cameras situated in a house in an effort to spot vampire minions, known as Augers (who were men with black stockings over their head). Once you found one you then had to spring a trap to prevent it from attacking the inhabitants of the house (predictably a group of girls having a 'sleepover' party). Later on things supposedly heated up as you then had to help the girls escape the house.

The game required little skill beyond being able to remember where and when the Augers appeared, and possessing the stamina to keep playing until your continual trial and error resulted in completion. Given it was driven entirely by full motion video sequences, a certain linearity of gameplay was always inevitable. But for a while, *Night Trap* was heralded as the future of video games (until people started playing it that is). Its lasting legacy was to be one of the titles reviewed as part of the US government's 1993 debate into **violence** in video games, and as such it can at least be said that *Night Trap* contributed to the introduction of tighter industry legislation.

## Painted-on Doors
## 1972

The earliest computer games were pretty basic. Usually the playing area was no bigger than the size of the screen, and your objectives were very straightforward. However, as the technology improved, games grew more sophisticated and the self-evident rules that had defined a **Pac-Man** or a *Sprint 2*, gave way to games in which it was no longer obvious what we were meant to do. This meant that increasingly we had to rely on our own curiosity. In particular games with **3-D** environments, seemed to compel us to explore every last nook and cranny, constantly pushing at the fringes of the computer created world. At times it felt rather like going on a school trip to a museum and skipping the prepared tour in favour of seeing how many doors you could get through with a 'not open to the public' sign on them.

For example, whilst **driving games** remained two dimensional top down affairs we never questioned what might lie beyond the road side, but as soon as we loaded up *Chequered Flag* or any other racing game that gave us a driver's eye view, it felt completely natural to attempt a little off-roading to see where else you could go. Of course, where you went was usually to the very limits of the game itself. *Chequered Flag* had no contingency plan to deal with you attempting to flee the confines of the racecourse and so would have to cheat to stop you (in this case by bringing your car to a dead halt).

But the desire to leave the 'tracks' and have a mooch around is central to our existence as games players. This is particularly true of **first-person shooters** in which the player is deposited into a world and given (what appears to be) freedom to go wherever he or she pleases. The natural urge to check behind every door and round every corner is an essential strategy in ensuring you track down all of the secret goodies that might be lying around, but it can also bring you face-to-face with the odd 'painted on door' too. At first these objects seem to promise entry to a new part of the playing area, as yet unexplored. However, on closer inspection, you find that they are only set dressing. Indeed in most games, these 'phantom doors' actually look a little different from the 'real doors', somehow flatter and less 3-D. Whilst necessary to create the illusion of a realistic looking location, they are, nonetheless, broken promises.

Whilst it is understandable that you cannot have an infinite number of rooms, it is still frustrating, particularly so when a game tries to create an illusion of a playing area being bigger than it actually is. Even in games that are able to carefully disguise their restrictions, you will still always come up against 'the end of the world', or, at best, find yourself disappearing far off to the west only to emerge on the other side of the screen marching in from the east having seemingly travelled right round the world.

'Painted-on doors' don't just come in the form of 'painted-on doors' either. Capcom's *Resident Evil* (released for the **PlayStation** in 1996), features loads of artificially enforced restrictions, such as everyday objects that can only be used for one predefined function. Equally frustrating are what seem to be easily surmountable obstacles (such as an abandoned car blocking the road) that the game won't let you pass. Try as you might, you are always forced into backtracking half a level to re-approach the thing from another side.

The most frustrating gaming restriction of them all, though, is the phenomenon of baddies coming back to life when you re-enter a room or level you have previously cleared. This is particularly annoying in the 1987 **Atari ST** title *Dungeon Master* (published by Activision). This decidedly gruelling game requires you to lead a band of adventurers through a series of dungeons populated by all manner of terrible creatures. It is inevitable that at some point in your campaign you will realise you have left an important artefact on the previous level. So off you trudge to fetch it, only to come face-to-face with the same marauding mummies that you killed about three hours ago. With the element of surprise now on their side they are able to completely wipe you out. This is the point to kick the computer, as not only have you forgotten they would be there, but you haven't saved the game since you killed them the first time.

## Platformers
## 1980

In the early Eighties, after the **shoot 'em up** had exhausted its initial appeal, but before the **beat 'em up** gained temporal supremacy, the platformer was king. It offered players tests of manual dexterity, timing and – if it was a particularly good example – problem solving.

Although many claim that **Donkey Kong** was the first ever platformer, it is possible to trace the genre back a little further. For example, the arcade game *Space Panic* released by Universal in 1980 (a whole year before *Donkey Kong*), required the player to destroy various space monsters by creating little holes in the platforms that these horrible creatures wandered around on. Although the objective wasn't to get to the end of the level (as was the case in most platformers) the layout did look very familiar (even featuring ladders connecting the various different sections together) and a number of key platformer skills were required to be successful.

However, it was the success of *Donkey Kong* that defined the genre's winning formula and whilst titles like **Manic Miner, Chuckie Egg** and *Wanted: Monty Mole* (released by Gremlin Graphics in 1984) were able to gain distinction thanks to their inventiveness and playability, they were simply variations on a theme.

Fittingly **Nintendo**, the publisher of *Donkey Kong*, were the ones to push the boundaries further, and through their *Mario* Bros series of games they introduced sideways scrolling, power ups, the ability to change a character's direction in mid-jump; as well as practically every other major element of the platformer genre. Sega's **Sonic The Hedgehog**, would also prove influential; however, its primary contribution (extreme speed) offered yet another interesting variation, rather than an integral new element.

Undoubtedly, the most significant development in the last ten years has been the move from a 2-D to **3-D** gaming plane. Again Nintendo were at the forefront, with 1996's *Super Mario 64* providing the first completely three dimensional platformer. This move introduced a number of new design problems which in the main Nintendo were able to successfully resolve; however the precision jumping, so long a hallmark of the genre, was an attribute that proved difficult to recreate in a gaming world where the player's view was always slightly at an angle. Indeed battling with the positioning of the in-game 'camera' has now become an integral (albeit unwelcome) part of many modern day computer games.

Although *Super Mario 64* deliberately reproduced many of the much-loved elements of its two dimensional predecessors, the obvious hallmarks of traditional platform games such as, well, platforms, are becoming increasingly scarce in today's titles, such that it is very difficult to assess whether something is actually a platformer, or rather a 'Third person action game' (like **Tomb Raider** or *Grand Theft Auto*). It is still possible to get hold of the odd traditional 2-D platform game (particularly for download on mobile phones), but regrettably, it does seem as if the age-old skill of the well-timed parabolic jump is gradually being lost in favour of free-style marauding around a 3-D world.

## Pokemon
### 1996

The chances are that *Pokemon* represents the moment in your life when you started to feel a bit old. This bizarre Japanese fad passed a lot of aging one-time **BBC Micro** users by, and although we knew it was creating a kafuffle, for once we weren't on the inside, and were left to watch with disbelief from the sidelines as kids went berserk for these strange computer monsters. Creepily, standing next to us with equal bemusement were our parents.

The original *Pokemon* (which by the way is a contraction of the phrase 'Pocket Monsters') was released by **Nintendo** for the **Game Boy** back in 1996. The objective was to collect as many of the 151 little pocket monsters as possible and then train them up to fight each other. The game came in two versions, *Pokemon Red* and *Pokemon Blue*, each containing different creatures. The idea was that players would only ever buy one version, but would be able to get their hands on the monsters that appeared on the other by entering into swaps (using the Game Boy's Gamelink cables to transfer data).

Initially envisaged as a title with only limited appeal, *Pokemon* became a big craze in Japan (where the game was first released), and in just a couple of years had spawned all kinds of merchandising such as trading cards, clothing and, most importantly, a top rated cartoon series. The game hit the USA in 1998 where, with all the additional merchandise and spin-offs already in place to support it, it became a monster hit, selling somewhere in the region of twenty million copies in two years (indeed *Pokemon* titles constituted a whopping ten per cent of all software sales made in 2000).

To this day, *Pokemon* still generates cash for Nintendo; its cutesy characters effortlessly appealing to each new generation of young gamers. However, for those of us who were simply too old to get on board that particular fad, it remains a curiosity that we will likely never fully understand.

\* \* \*

## Pokes and Cheats
1980

Whilst all of us enjoy using our wits to overcome a decent challenge, there are times (for example if you've only got a lend of a game for an afternoon) when all you really want to do is take a look at each of the levels and find out what happens in the end. It is at these moments that the temptation to cheat becomes overwhelming. Happily, almost every computer game is cheatable if you happen to know how.

The phrase 'pokes and cheats' (a 'poke' is a computer language command) became popular in the computer press in the Eighties. It referred to little codes or passwords hidden in games that could be input by the user to obtain infinite lives, unlimited bullets, super speed or other attributes that would turn a previously **really difficult game** into a walkover. Whereas the function of a poke was to actually change one of the attributes of the game as defined in its **programming**, a straightforward cheat was usually a command to give you access to an element in the game that was always intended to be there, but simply kept hidden from the player.

Actually, most cheats started out as an expeditious way for a programmer to play-test their game without having to possess the skill required to actually play it properly. These cheats therefore required the player simply to type in a particular phrase or sequence of numbers, or input a string of commands via the directional buttons on their controller. Conversely, a poke often required you to actually interrupt the **loading** process and infiltrate the game's program. For example, if you wanted infinite lives in **Manic Miner**, you would begin the loading process as normal; however, when the loading picture first appeared you would stop the tape, use the 'break' function to enter the code, and then type in '25 POKE 35136,067/8'. You would then select the 'run' command, and start the tape again to complete the load.

Other games demanded more complex poking to yield any benefits. For instance, it is mooted that the 1984 Ultimate title *Sabre Wulf* required fifteen lines of code in order to make your character invincible (and it made him run faster too).

But did all of this underhand activity enhance the games, or simply ruin them? Some gamers wisely restricted their use of cheats, employing them only once they had completed a title to see if there was anything they'd missed. For most of us though, pokes and cheats were just too tempting to resist; they were rather like turning to the last page in a whodunit novel, it ruined the whole thing, but for a brief moment it was immensely satisfying.

## Pong
### 1972

Undoubtedly one of the most influential video games of all time, *Pong* actually started out, not as an inspirational money-making idea, but simply a concept to test out the **programming** prowess of one of **Atari**'s first ever employees. The employee in question was Allan Alcorn, and his boss at that time, Nolan Bushnell, duped him into thinking Atari had received a commission to make a video game based on table tennis. In truth, no such commission had been made, but Bushnell (inspired by a recent demonstration of a table tennis game running on the **Magnavox Odyssey**) wanted to get Alcorn up to speed with programming before assigning him a proper game.

Indeed, Bushnell didn't think that computerised ping-pong had any real merit at all, and was convinced that what the market was looking for was a more advanced version of his 1971 game **Computer Space.** However, Bushnell didn't reckon on a number of crucial enhancements made to the initial design brief. Firstly, Alcorn made it so that the direction the ball would take when hit would be largely dependent upon which part of the bat it struck. If it was dead centre, then it would take a more-or-less straight course back towards the opponent. However, if you managed to nick the ball with the corner of your bat, you could send it ricocheting off in all sorts of peculiar angles. Secondly, the ball would speed up in the middle of rallies adding increasing intensity to long drawn out duels. Suddenly, a mundane idea, only lightly tweaked, had become an addictive masterpiece that required some actual skill to master.

Finally recognising its appeal, Bushnell installed a *Pong* machine in Andy Capp's tavern, a rundown bar in California, and straight away the game proved to be popular. From that point on Atari's future was secure and *Pong* machines sprung up all over the place.

Ironically, so did third-party imitations. Between 1974 and 1983 there were over three hundred versions of *Pong* or *Pong*-type games created for around two hundred different machines, and that's not counting the games that were simply variants on the *Pong* theme (such as countless hockey and football titles).

Even today, *Pong* can still be an addictive gaming experience and its importance and longevity can be ascribed to the fact that it showed computer game designers that the most popular games are those where the objective is self-evident (in *Pong*'s case 'avoid missing ball for high score'), and the control mechanism is incredibly simple, yet able to support multiple strategies and techniques. Defined in these terms, *Pong* is a work of genius.

## Populous
### 1989

Although **God games** have never enjoyed mainstream popularity they are highly regarded amongst the hardcore computing fraternity. Curiously the game that started it all though, was something of an 'overground' hit. Released in 1989, Bullfrog's *Populous* was unfathomable, massively complex, without precedent and quite brilliant. So brilliant in fact, and original, that it attracted a legion of computer fans that would later ignore God games completely. There was just something about *Populous* that compelled you to investigate further.

Like many innovations, *Populous* was the result of a happy confluence of luck, inspiration and evolution. Primarily created by just two men, Peter Molyneux and Glenn Corpses, the game grew out of attempts to create a **3-D** landscape that resembled the impressive patchwork graphics of the **Archimedes'** title *Zarch*. Sensing that the work was the start of something interesting, Molyneux and his small team of developers started to think about what kind of game they should make with this technology. The process they followed was based as much on whim as anything else, and began with Molyneux deciding that the landscape should have little people living on it, and then coming to the realisation that these little people would need houses to live in.

Here then lay the seeds of *Populous'* central concept: by terraforming the land into flat plains, the inhabitants would be able to build houses, and would then begin to grow in number. The larger the area of flat land, the greater the concentration and complexity of houses and the greater the population. Therefore, the objective of the game was to build up as big a population as possible.

To spice things up there needed to be some form of opponent attempting to achieve the same goal on the same land mass. At first, the team toyed with turning *Populous* into a two-player game, but after a while they were able to create a sufficiently challenging computer adversary. However, additional gaming elements were required to ensure things didn't get monotonous. In came the 'Acts of God', various terrible natural disasters (such as volcanoes) that you could inflict upon the computer once you had attained sufficient power. Although they didn't realise it until a journalist put it to them, Molyneux and the team had effectively cast the player in the role of a deity.

It's to the computer community's credit that when *Populous* was first released for the **Amiga** it was greeted with universal acclaim even though it was almost without comparison. Buoyed on by positive reviews (and the fact it happened to be a brilliant game), *Populous* sold by the truckload, particularly in Japan where Western games generally fared poorly. It spawned countless variations and imitations and proliferated across multiple platforms (even appearing on machines as unlikely as **Nintendo's SNES**). Unfortunately, no one outside the computing hardcore ever got quite as excited about a God game ever again.

## Puzzle Games
## 1985

Stripped of much of the visceral graphical thrill of other gaming genres, the puzzle game has to rely on the strength of its core attributes to attract players. This means that if the objective of the exercise is not immediately apparent, or isn't sufficiently engaging then there is no visual candy to sidetrack the player from realising how crap it is.

Unsurprisingly then, those puzzle games that succeed in holding our interest are amongst the most addictive games of all; whether it is *Minesweeper* on your office **PC** (which feels as though it has been around forever but was actually first invented in 1989), or Taito's 1994 arcade hit *Puzzle Bobble*, with the distractions of unnecessary graphical window dressing set aside and the subconscious comparisons between the on-screen images and their real world counterparts extinguished, puzzle games seem to offer pure experiences that tap right into our addictive personalities.

At its heart, a good puzzle game consists of a simple premise (for example in the aforementioned *Puzzle Bobble* the objective of the exercise is to group together identically coloured balls) that can withstand prolonged playing and provide the player with a satisfying learning curve. Psygnosis' **Lemmings** (released in 1991) consists of the same challenge (that of getting your lemmings successfully across the level) played out multiple times. Our interest is maintained by the well-timed introduction of obstacles that challenge our previously successful strategies.

Of course, the greatest of all puzzle games – **Tetris** – adheres to this principle, but there is also a gradual increase in the difficulty level that simply comes from playing it for a prolonged period of time. As the blocks become increasingly complex in their shape and begin to stack higher and higher up the screen, the time we have available to make our next decision decreases.

Puzzle games are especially popular with the non-computing fraternity, and in particular females. Maybe this has got something to do with the fact that, in the main, they don't come with a load of assumptions as to what the player thinks is and isn't cool (and let's face it most hardened computer games think a 'BFG' is the last word in cool whereas the rest of the population see it for what it really is – a little bit adolescent and embarrassing). Whatever the reason, trying to get grandma, or your girlfriend to relinquish the controls of *Tetris* can be its own intensely difficult intellectual challenge.

## Really Difficult Games
### 1983

Although computers games are often derided for their negative influence, it is easy to overlook some of the genuinely exemplary lessons that prolonged computer gaming can teach you. For those who have ever attempted to learn to drive, cook or acquire any new skill, years of experience bashing away at the likes of *Super Mario Bros* teaches you that what at first seems impossible can, with enough practice, not only be conquered but actually become incredibly simple. Yes, there is nothing better than sitting down for a quick session on a game that you long ago vanquished and reflect on how difficult it once seemed, compared to how ruddy easy it now appears.

This, of course, should be the ultimate purpose of any game – to provide you with a challenge that with skill and practice you can one day master. You can imagine then, how frustrating it is when you come across a title that no matter how much time or effort you commit to it, never succumbs to your gaming mastery. Sometimes this is simply because the game itself requires no skill at all, rather success relies purely on luck (step forward **Dragon's Lair**); or perhaps it has been programmed in such a way that it is literally impossible to complete (*Jet Set Willy* bow your head in shame); or, worst of all, the game controls are rubbish and the camera angles appalling (we're looking at you *Alone in the Dark 4* released for the **PlayStation** in 2001). But then there are also those games that are simply too damn hard.

Games that fall in to this latter category have, down the years, developed reputations akin to East End gangsters. Eidos Interactive's **Tomb Raider** series established itself as something of a bruiser; although *Tomb Raider* 1 and 2 were pretty tough, the third game in the series was insanely difficult. Even the first level (set in the jungle) was torturously hard and things only got worse the further you progressed. Similarly, Melbourne House's 1983 **ZX Spectrum** title *Penetrator* was an impossibly difficult **shoot 'em up** that can still provoke grimaces on the faces of those who played it; so too Probe Entertainment's 1988 **platformer** *Trantor: The Last Stormtrooper*, and not to mention *Beach Head* released for the **Commodore 64** back in 1983. There are countless games out there that still exert some strange mastery over us. What makes it worse is that every now and then we will dig one of them up and load it, certain in the knowledge that its now rudimentary looking challenge will be no match for our gaming aptitude finely honed from two decades worth of play. But the opposite is the case: not only can we still not get the better of it, but modern day games with their save points and generous credits have made us even less able to endure the stark one-wrong-move retribution of a really difficult vintage **platformer**.

## Rise of the Robots
## 1994

Computer game fans are generally a discerning lot, but there is the odd release that demonstrates that gamers can be just as susceptible to flagrant hype and a bit of fancy window dressing as anybody else. Time Warner Interactive's 1994 title *Rise of the Robots* stands as lasting testimony that you can fool all of the people some of the time.

Touted as a revolutionary **beat 'em up**, *Rise of the Robots* promised 'up to 100 frames of animation', '**3-D** visual contouring [that] allows robots to exist in a realistic environment' and a 'sophisticated punch detection matrix [which] enhances playability'. Clearly this was all just confusing hyperbole proudly touted on the back cover. However, if Time Warner Interactive's technobabble had you wondering whether the game was actually any good or not, the news that curly-haired rock legend Brian May was providing the 'original score' was surely a deal breaker.

Yes, one thing *Rise of the Robots* wasn't short on was hype. With plans to release the title on multiple systems (including the **Amiga**, **Game Boy** and **SNES**), Time Warner Interactive were quick to issue press releases regarding the game's state-of-the-art graphics (apparently they were 'film quality, controllable 3-D graphics') and supposed hugely sophisticated Artificial Intelligence. The game was featured heavily on television programmes such as *GamesMaster* and received a number of effusive reviews in the computer press.

But, whilst the back-story consisted of some torturous tail of a future world of mad robots and behavioural programming, *Rise of the Robots* was a run-of-the-mill beat 'em up, enlivened by some admittedly lovely looking metallic graphics. Time Warner Interactive might have you believe that *Rise of the Robots* was 'the most talked about game in years', but those who actually bought it didn't waste time in giving it short shrift. Opponents could be dispensed with simply by repeating the same move over and over again (surely a cardinal sin in a beat 'em up) and there was no ability to turn around, meaning that you had to spend the entire bout faced in one direction.

In the same year, Time Warner Interactive released a Director's Cut version (which included some background information) and against much public hostility even put out a sequel in 1996 (*Resurrection: Rise 2*). However, if there had been any thoughts of building a franchise off the back of *Rise of the Robot* they were short-lived. No one was going to be fooled twice.

## Skool Daze
### 1984

With a title spelled out as if it was a Slade song, and a setting as far away from abstract mazes, dreary dungeons or deep space as it was possible to get, Microsphere's **ZX Spectrum** title *Skool Daze* (released in 1985) was quite unlike anything that had come before. It was a game that seemed to speak directly to the frustrations of its audience, allowing them to exact revenge on their everyday hate figures from the comfort of their own homes. Indeed most *Skool Daze* fans probably felt as if they were playing something that they themselves would have written if only they knew how.

Set in a pleasingly busy comprehensive, the objective of *Skool Daze* was to extract the school report of the main character, Eric, from a safe before the Headmaster had a chance to read it. In order to do this you first needed to get the safe combination from the teachers, and in order to do that you had to complete a complicated exercise involving hitting the school shields with your catapult. Yes – it was a complex plot and one that was by no means self evident. For those who received a copy of the game sans instructions it was impossible to work out what the hell you were meant to do.

Not that it really mattered. *Skool Daze* was one of those rare games that was brilliant for mucking around with. Not only could you write on the blackboards, but you could give teacher a good whack with either your fist or your catapult. Such activities were made even more pleasurable thanks to the fact that *Skool Daze* allowed you to rename all of the characters, so that you could deal out some swift retribution to those who had crossed you at school earlier that day.

In 1985, a sequel, *Back to Skool,* was released which basically dished up more of the same much to the delight of *Skool Daze*'s fans. Today, both titles are remembered with fondness, harking back to, not only the happy computing days of our youth, but also a bygone schooling age when teachers' nicknames didn't necessarily have to include a swear word.

## Sonic The Hedgehog
### 1991

Fascinating fact: the 'The' in 'Sonic The Hedgehog' should be written with a capital 't' as it is the titular hedgehog's official middle name.

Sonic came about as a result of attempts made by **Sega** in 1991 to come up with ways to increase sales of their new console, the **Mega Drive**. Recognising that **Mario** acted as an effective brand symbol for **Nintendo**, the obvious thought was to invent an equivalent character; however, Sega's figurehead would represent their core values: it needed to be anarchic, forward looking and energetic. A competition was arranged amongst the company's Japanese staff, and the winner picked by Tom Nilsen – the company's head of marketing. However, Nilsen was unimpressed with the quality of the entries and in choosing Sonic he felt he was selecting 'the least objectionable' attempt.

But whilst on paper Sonic The Hedgehog might not have looked like very much, once animated on a computer screen, he was an entirely different matter. The first Sonic game (named after the hog himself) was released for the Mega Drive in 1991 and managed to pull off the difficult trick of being both extremely similar, and completely different from Nintendo's Mario games. Whilst the objective (to collect as many gold rings as possible and make it to the end of the level) was pretty much indistinguishable from the kinds of tasks that Nintendo routinely set their famous plumber, *Sonic The Hedgehog*'s execution abandoned the sedate pace and clever platform design of the Nintendo title in favour of never before seen high speeds and manic loop-the-loops. Its entertainment value was purely visceral, an attribute not usually associated with a **platformer**.

It was a smash, with many pundits proclaiming it to be amongst the greatest games of all time. Recognising a good thing when they saw it, Sega shamelessly marketed their new brand leader for all he was worth, resulting in cartoon and comic spin-offs (including a British fortnightly published by Fleetway that ran successfully from 1993 to 2002 – well after the initial craze for Sonic had died down).

In addition, there were the inevitable sequels (*Sonic The Hedgehog 2*, released in 1992, was the best selling Mega Drive game ever), and by 2005 there were somewhere in the region of one hundred Sonic computer games available across a diverse range of platforms ranging from mobile phones to **PC**s. Although many of these games proved to be entertaining in their own right, the general consensus is that whilst Sonic operated brilliantly in the largely two dimensional world of the consoles of the early Nineties, his transition to **3-D** hasn't been totally successful. In addition, the travails of Sega itself have reflected badly on the character who, after all, is meant to be the company figurehead. So, whilst competitor **Mario** still stands apart from the rank and file of computer characters, in recent years poor old Sonic has lost a lot of his iconic significance and has had to take his place (albeit still near the front) amongst the pack.

## Spacewar
## 1962

Built to run on a computer that cost $120,000, it is clear that Steve Russell never intended his computer game, *Spacewar,* to be a mass-market title.

Created in 1962, *Spacewar* is generally credited with being the first ever video game (although some claim that this honour should be bestowed upon Willy Higinbotham and his 1958 *Tennis for Two* game). In the early Sixties, Steve Russell was studying at the Massachusetts Institute of Technology (MIT). There he became a member of the Tech Model Railroad Club, a co-operative of like-minded students that liked nothing better than to tinker with machinery and electronics. Having investigated most of the machines on MIT's campus, the group came across a free IBM 407 and tried to figure out how to make it work.

Then in 1961, MIT acquired a new computer, the Programmable Data Processor-1 (or PDP-1 for short). It was far smaller than the IBM 407 and easier to work with. Almost immediately, Russell began to think of ways that the group could try out the new machine's abilities. Inspired by science fiction heroes such as Doc Savage and Flash Gordon, he began to formulate a simplistic space game.

After six months of work, the result was *Spacewar*, a simplistic game in which two rocket ships slugged it out firing torpedoes at each other. Over the next few months, various members of the Railroad Club helped to refine the game, adding Newtonian gravity, a realistic star map, a hyperspace function (which made your ship disappear and randomly reappear somewhere else on the screen) and a couple of rather crude game controllers.

The group became addicted, and *Spacewar* gaming sessions stretched long into the night. Though the game's reputation spread, it seemed clear to Russell and the others that given the cost of the equipment required to run it, there was no money to be made. As such, *Spacewar* ended up being used as a diagnostic program for PDP-1s. Nevertheless, *Spacewar*'s legacy is vast and profound, directly influencing the world's first video arcade game and, of course, planting the seeds from which every form of computer game that has since followed would grow.

## Sports Games
## 1972

Of all the gaming genres, sports games are the most sociable. Not only do most sports require more than one person to play them, but those unaccustomed to computer gaming don't need to learn what it is you are meant to do in the way they would were they trying to get to grips with a **platformer** or a **God game**. If you know how the rules of tennis work in real life, all you need to work out is which button you press to serve and you are up and running. Similarly, for the spectators, it is always apparent who is winning, who is losing and what stage the game is at. This does mean though, that if it is you that is losing there is no good way to disguise the fact from your peers.

Computer sports simulations are almost as old as computer games themselves, arguably with *Pong* kicking off the whole genre. Down the years, we have had games that rely on button bashing, and those that have required tactical acumen; however, for as long as there have been sports games there have been people decrying why anybody would want to play a game of computer football when they could go outside and play the real thing. But whilst that argument may have held some water twenty or so years ago, to suggest as much now is to misunderstand the key element of any good modern-day sports title.

Early efforts such as *Pong*, and Konami's 1983 arcade title *Track and Field*, focused on attempting to recreate the particular challenges of the sports they were trying to emulate; today's titles go far beyond that modest, if noble aspiration. Ever since the emergence of decent **3-D** gaming technology and increased storage capacity, sports games have attempted to recreate, not just the on-pitch action, but the whole spectacle of the event as mediated through a television broadcast.

This means that whilst games such as Konami's *International Superstar Soccer* may be able to reproduce the beautiful game that is football with far more fidelity than Electronic Art's *FIFA Football* range, historically the latter series has outsold the former because its presentation far more closely resembles the football coverage that you would expect to see on Sky Sports or *Match of the Day*. Indeed the ability to replay your mazy dribble past your mate's defence from multiple angles is an important part of the enjoyment; as is meticulously and volubly providing your own pundit-style analysis deconstructing exactly why you are so good and they are so rubbish.

This holds true not only for football, but for other titles too. It seems that for us to become truly immersed in a computer sports game we must be able to feel, not so much that we are actually there on the pitch playing the game itself, but are watching our performance unfold as it would appear if broadcast via TV.

The downside of this is that it actively encourages your mates to speak in hugely irritating faux John Motson voices as soon as you switch the computer on.

## Strategy Games
## 1980

Can there be any greater thrill than leading your mighty empire to world domination, crushing all that comes before you with your superior intellect and strategic brilliance? For those who enjoy strategy games, there are few computing moments quite as sweet. But for the rest of us, as of yet unable to get to grips with the subtleties of Command & Conquer, strategy games remain a mystifying and overly complex genre.

Actually, when you think about it, with the exception of what are called 'real-time' strategy games, most strategy titles are quite different from other kinds of computer games: there are no demands made on your manual dexterity and the challenge is almost purely cerebral, requiring you to effectively resource manage, as well as come up with creative solutions to wrong foot your enemy.

In effect, most computer strategy games are simply far more complex versions of the tabletop battle games that were popular in the Seventies (and which in themselves are really just variations on more traditional board games such as chess). Indeed, the earliest computer strategy games (such as Strategic Simulations' 1980 release Computer Ambush) adhered so closely to this formula that the player had to wait for their turn before they could make a move.

In 1990, Microplay released Command HQ, which whilst adhering to all the basic tenets of the strategy game, allowed players to make their moves whenever they liked. These 'real-time' strategy games (as they were called) attracted some sniffy comments from pure strategy game aficionados who felt that they disregarded strategic and tactical planning in favour of manic button clicking. Certainly it is true that real time strategy games require you to make and enact decisions before your opponent gets there first, and so undeniably there is an element of physical dexterity added to the mix; however one suspects that in real life General Custer or Napoleon recognised the need to factor timing issues into their strategic thinking, and so the various grumblings do seem a little silly.

Over the years all manner of strategy games have hit the market, some truly epic in scope, and some less so (Electronic Arts' 2002 title *Sid Meier's SimGolf* confines itself to merely 18 holes). Few have attained the popularity of Westwood's long running *Command & Conquer* series. Launched in 1995, but set in the near future, the first instalment sold over a million units. This was in part due to its full motion video cut scenes that magnificently complemented the theoretical strategic campaigning of your game with an element of physicality and consequence that the genre had previously lacked.

From 1996 onwards, a number of *Command & Conquer* clones have emerged, some of which are awful and others pretty good. To this day, strategy games remain a popular element of the computer gaming scene, particularly amongst a certain subsection desperate to pit their wits against great leaders both historical and fictional, and emerge as the most cunning strategist since old Boney himself.

# Street Fighter II
## 1991

Of all the games, *Street Fighter II* is the one that you didn't want to play when you went round to your mate's house. Inevitably he would have been practising for hours – perhaps days – before your arrival, and would extract the maximum amount of pleasure from kicking your computerized head in, whilst you were still trying to work out which character on screen was meant to be yours. Yes indeed, of all the **beat 'em ups**, Capcom's *Street Fighter II* (first released in the **amusement arcades** back in 1991) was the one that separated the dedicated gamers from the casual toe-dipper (or 'men from the boys' as those committed gamers would doubtless put it).

As is evident from its name, *Street Fighter II* is a sequel. The first game was released some four years earlier; however, it was far less impressive. It only featured two characters (Ryu and Ken), and it employed a pressure sensitivity control that, although sensible in theory (basically the harder you hit the punch button the harder your character punched at his opponent), proved in practice to be counter intuitive, not to mention hugely damaging to the arcade machine.

In crafting a sequel, Capcom took a great deal of time to ensure their new title would consist of a perfect balance of complexity, difficulty and visual appeal. Recent beat 'em up titles had relied too heavily on simple button bashing and although this technique provided some level of enjoyment, there was no scope to hone your skills and therefore no reason to come back for more. To that end, Capcom spent a lot of time play testing and tweaking *Street Fighter II* before its release. In the process they recognised that if they wanted their game to attain real popularity they needed positive word of mouth to spread the news amongst amusement arcade dwellers. To achieve this, they came up with some killer special moves for each character, guaranteed to set tongues wagging.

Whilst *Street Fighter II* was not the first game to feature this technique, it redefined the concept, aligning spectacular roundhouses and upper cuts to complicated **joystick** and button combinations. Those players able to master a character's suite of spectacular attacks would be feted by their mates, and as a result *Street Fighter II*'s fame spread thanks largely to those experts showing off their prowess at every given opportunity.

Inevitably, home conversions followed, most of which were pretty good, and countless sequels and special versions were released in the arcades. The game even spawned a spin-off film in 1994, which most people didn't seem to like very much.

Whilst the basic look of the game is now rather antiquated, many players still harbour residual affections for what once was the king of the beat 'em ups. Even today, should an unsuspecting hard-bitten friend or relative happen to visit a *Street Fighter* fan, they may well find themselves coerced into a one-sided computer blood bath, but just for old time's sake of course.

## Super Mario Kart
## 1992

Although **Mario** had been dominating the **platform** genre in the early Nineties, **Nintendo** weren't content to let matters simply rest there. In 1992 they released one of the most sublime **driving games** ever created. *Super Mario Kart* for the **SNES** has been much imitated but never bettered (although UBI Soft's rather derivative 1994 title *Street Racer* wasn't a bad attempt). Combining Nintendo's core strengths of cutesy graphics and finely honed gameplay, *Super Mario Kart* was somehow much more than the sum of its parts.

This was a game that managed to get everything just right. So right that it even got gaming elements that you couldn't articulate or even pinpoint completely right – that's how inherently *right Super Mario Kart* was. The various racing challenges (broken down into cup competitions taking place over different stages) were perfectly pitched, and the racing tracks elegantly designed, such that for a beginner it was possible to get round in one piece (save for Rainbow Road), yet the seasoned driver could endlessly experiment with subtle variations in timing and positioning. The competition was stiff but not formidable, but even if you were able to lap all of the computer controlled characters, *Super Mario Kart* would allow you to race against a ghostly apparition of yourself, recorded whilst you were clocking up your best lap times.

Undoubtedly, *Super Mario Kart* was at its majestic peak in

two-player mode. Pitched against another equally fervent player it became a pursuit for perfection. If you failed to start the race with a super boost then the game would have to be abandoned; similarly it became standard practice to restart whenever your opponent attained an unassailable lead. It was in the two player game too that *Super Mario Kart*'s choice selection of weapons and power-ups really came into their own. Items such as green shells and feathers could be picked up by running over squares with question marks on them and then used against your opponent. Particularly formidable were the red shells (which acted like heat-seeking missiles) and lighting bolts (which would miniaturise your opponent, allowing you to run them over). Both acted as useful levellers if the ability of the two players were unevenly matched, and added a welcome element of randomness into races between two experts.

Nintendo have produced a number of *Super Mario Kart* sequels, including *Mario Kart 64* which when released in 1996 for the Nintendo 64, sounded as if it was going to be brilliant (largely because it featured a four player option). Crushingly though, none have been able to recreate the majesty of the original game. Why this is the case is difficult to pinpoint, but then that is reflective of the overriding characteristic of the original SNES game – there is just something indefinably brilliant about it that makes it one of the all-time greats.

## Tetris
### 1985

Some games go beyond addictive and get inside your brain. Some go even further still and become a medically recognised form of insomnia. Some (well, one actually) are so bloody annoyingly compulsive that they can even spawn a hit record based on their in-game music. Today, some twenty years after its creation, *Tetris* retains a vice-like grip on the consciousness of millions. Now available to play on your mobile phone, it seems that there is no way to escape 'just one more go'.

Yet the puzzle game that launched the best selling games machine of all-time, not to mention provided fodder for stand-up comedians up and down the land (usually along of the lines of 'playing *Tetris* as a child helped me in later life when I was moving house and had to pack boxes really efficiently. I saved a long box for when I really needed it'), came from very humble beginnings. Its creator, Alexey Pajitnov was a Russian researcher working at Moscow Academy. In his spare time he used to come up with simple **puzzle games** on his Electronica 60 (an antiquated Russian computer). Drawing inspiration from a Greek puzzle game called Pentominoes (which involved trying to arrange different shaped pieces so that they would all fit in the game's box), Pajitnov came up with a simplified computer version. The challenge the game set was incredibly straightforward: different shaped blocks fell from the top of the screen, and by rotating and moving them you had to pile them up such that they would form unbroken lines. For every unbroken line you were able to create, a score was awarded and the line removed, allowing all the blocks resting upon it to fall down one place. The game continued until the screen became full.

The preliminary version didn't feature any graphics at all, and the blocks were denoted by bracket signs. However, even at this stage it was entertaining enough to cause Pajitnov to spend the time he'd set aside to finish the **programming**, simply playing it. Eventually though, he completed his work and, with the help a young schoolboy prodigy, managed to write a version of the game that would run on a standard **PC**. From this point on, things began to snowball.

The game's fame spread beyond its homeland, and soon

computer software companies in the West were haggling over the rights to bring *Tetris* to their systems. The first Westerner to get wind of it was Robert Stein, who in 1986 attempted to secure the rights to sell the game in the UK and the USA. However, the most significant deal was struck in 1988, when an affiliate of **Nintendo** recognised *Tetris'* potential as a title for the company's then still-to-be-released **Game Boy**. A deal was struck in March of that year and a copy of *Tetris* was eventually bundled in with each Game Boy sold.

The rest is computer gaming history. *Tetris* was the perfect title for a **handheld gaming** system and positively drove sales of the Game Boy. Its graphics were simple and easy to discern when on the move, but more importantly it was a game that you could dip in and out of, say, between classes or appointments. By the early Nineties, *Tetris* was everywhere, and its catchy music could be heard on trains and buses throughout the land (which seemed especially inconsiderate given that the **Game Boy** came with an earphone socket). Even more annoyingly, in 1992, a dance track was released based on its in-game music. Somewhat predictably, the artiste, Doctor Spin, appeared on *Top of The Pops* with a costume that had loads of different blocks stuck on it.

The appeal of *Tetris* seems to cross all borders with young and old, men and women all equally susceptible. Pajitnov believes that the game's appeal has a lot to do with bringing order to a chaotic environment – in short it is a game about tidying up (and for Pajitnov at least, that explains its appeal to womenfolk). It has been proven to increase your IQ too – presumably those spatial awareness questions become a little bit easier after a marathon *Tetris* session; and one must concede that it probably does make moving house a little easier, although whether that really forms the basis of a good stand-up routine is questionable.

## 3-D
1979

For a while in the Eighties and Nineties, 3-D graphics were the next big thing. These days barely anyone talks about them, but this is not because they have gone away, quite the opposite in fact; now so many games are rendered this way that it is worthy of mention when a new game is released that is not 3-D. But why the big song and dance about games that allow you to look at a wall from an isometric perspective? Well actually it is probably as much to do with how those images are created, and what that means in terms of gameplay as it is to do with what they look like.

You see, whereas the graphics that appear in a 2-D game consist of a series of simple pictorial representations (such as sprites), true 3-D games require that each of the objects that appear are first 'modelled' in the computer. This means that instead of showing you one of a series of pre-prepared images, the computer can calculate exactly which parts of the object you will see and how they will look, dependent upon where you are viewing it from. The upshot of all this is that the player is able to view the object from any angle with the computer simply calculating on the fly how its appearance will change as you move round it. This means that 3-D games can offer the player far more freedom than a traditional 2-D game (that is restricted to showing you only those images it has already pre-prepared).

However, some of the earlier 3-D games weren't actually proper 3-D all. Cinematronics' 1979 arcade title *Tail Gunner* is generally considered the first game to feature anything approaching 3-D graphics (in this case see-through skeleton frame representations of objects). However, *Tail Gunner*, like many 3-D games that followed in its wake was 'on-rails', meaning that you followed a predetermined route on each game and couldn't move freely around the environment.

Things began to hot up a little in 1982 when **Sega** released the three-quarter view **shoot 'em up** *Zaxxon*. But, whilst the graphics looked sensational, it was clear that the move to three dimensions was pretty cosmetic and didn't actually add an awful lot to the game. But nonetheless, here was another take on 3-D – the player was no longer looking straight down the barrel of the gun at the gaming world, but viewing it from an angle. This 'isometric' view was popular on the home computer scene too, where the whole thing was kicked off back in 1984 with Quicksilva's *Ant Attack*.

In fact, the Speccy turned out to be quite good at handling 3-D images, or at least 'pseudo 3-D' images. Although titles such as Vortex's 1984 games *Android 2* and *TLL* presented an isometric view of the world, there were no allowances made for perspective, or indeed the simple fact that when your android or plane moved to the far side of the screen it should by rights look smaller as it is further away from the 'camera'. This was a limitation that affected pretty much all isometric games of the Eighties. At the time it seemed like a minor quibble.

In 1987, 'proper' 3-D graphics came along in the shape of Incentive Software's *Driller*. The game used a system called Freescape that enabled the player to roam freely, viewing objects from any angle. Whilst isometric games had afforded the player some notion of freedom, here at last you could truly poke around each and every corner of the gaming environment. Unfortunately, the computation required to generate the on-screen images was such that *Driller* and other games of its ilk (such as Incentive's next game *Dark Side*) were very slow and rather ponderous. Besides, the actual objects that made up the gaming environment were very basic, untextured shapes.

As the **first-person shooter** became increasingly popular in the early Nineties (initially amongst **PC** owners), the sprite-based graphics still prevailed. However, it was becoming apparent that constructing games entirely out of polygons was the way to go. The only snag was that it would require a lot of computational power to be able to generate sufficiently interesting looking, textured polygon objects. As such, dedicated 3-D graphics cards were developed that could support complex number-crunching. These paved the way for the first generation of aesthetically successful 'true 3-D' games. Id's 1996 title *Quake* took advantage of this technology, introducing not only characters and objects generated purely out of polygons, but texture and dynamic light sources too.

Since then, much of the development of gaming graphics has been focused on refining and improving 3-D techniques. Indeed, over the years almost every game genre has been dragged into the 3-D world, and whilst this has proved to be the making of **sports games**, other genres such as **platformers** and, in particular, **puzzle games** have struggled to make the transition, and it remains a fact that to this day, no one wants to play 3-D versions of **Bomberman** or **Tetris**.

## Tomb Raider
### 1996

For some reason Lara Croft and the *Tomb Raider* series have become the mainstream face of computer gaming. In fact, she is probably the only computer character in the last ten years to attain a level of public recognition comparable to those old stalwarts **Mario**, **Sonic The Hedgehog** and **Pac-Man**. However, Lara is totally different from her illustrious bedfellows. For a start she is a she. Indeed much of the initial publicity surrounding the first *Tomb Raider* title (released by Eidos Interactive in 1996) was centred round the fact that you spent most of the game looking at a female backside. For those able to get passed that distraction, there was a genuinely innovative and cinematic experience to be had.

Cast in the role of a female Indiana Jones, Lara Croft was an explorer extraordinaire. The title was released at a time when new **3-D** worlds were just beginning to appear on our computer screens, and her profession seemed remarkably apposite; indeed, much of the game's appeal derived from simply guiding Lara through a number of beautifully realised caverns.

*Tomb Raider* was an innovative title, that eschewed the traditional first-person perspective of games such as *Quake*, in favour of bringing you a third-person view of the world. This allowed Eidos to play around with viewpoints and introduce directorial flourishes such as pans, static camera shots and over-the-shoulder views, all of which added a sense of dynamism and scale. Similarly, the way Lara moved was quite different from anything seen before. Eidos didn't actually employ any **motion capture** techniques, but there was something elegant, but rather human, about the way Lara ran, jumped and climbed.

The compound effect was to create a title that felt strangely real, thus heightening the gaming experience. You really didn't want to send Lara careering over the edge of a cliff because it was an ungentlemanly thing to do to a lady, even if she was just a collection of polygons.

The first game was a big hit, particularly with **PlayStation** owners (who fell well within Eidos' target demographic), and soon every student fancy dress party had to contend with someone running around with cropped jeans, sunglasses and a vest pretending to be Lara Croft. Sequels appeared; however, somewhere along the line things seemed to go a little awry, and the third game in the series was almost impossible to complete. A *Tomb Raider* film was released in 2001 starring Angelina Jolie, but by then Lara's best years were behind her. Back in 1997 it was nigh on impossible to pick up a Sunday supplement without reading something about how Lara's tits were bigger than her head, whilst today months can go by in the popular press without somebody making that same observation.

## Uridium
## 1986

'Truly arcade quality' gushed reviewer Julian Rignall, back in issue eleven of the **Commodore 64** magazine *Zzap! 64*. This was a little over the top – even in the mid-Eighties, but there is no denying that, for its time, *Uridium* was a class piece of software.

Released by Hewson in 1986, *Uridium* captured the hearts and minds of Commodore 64 users. Constructed in the mould of a standard horizontal scrolling **shoot 'em up**, *Uridium*'s appeal relied on a formidable combination of superb graphics and excellent gameplay. Your craft – the Manta Fighter – was a particular delight. Able to turn on a dime, this classy little ship could also perform stunts such as spins and 90-degree rolls, allowing you a sense of freedom that most other shoot 'em ups could only dream of. Best of all, as it flew across the giant alien spaceships that constituted each level ('the dreadnoughts'), your little Manta Fighter would cast a shadow over the enemy hull. Whilst only a small detail, it was an important flourish that contributed to the game's aspirations to transcend its home computer bedfellows and seek comparison with amusement arcade blasters such as **Zaxxon**.

The thing most people remember about *Uridium* though, is how phenomenally frantic it was. Each level required you to do nothing more than attempt to inflict as much damage as possible, whilst staying out of harm's way. Unlike a lot of shoot 'em ups, there was no progression through each level. Instead you were forced to keep making sorties amongst an increasing volley of alien fire until a 'land now' signal appeared. These end-of-level respites would allow you to refuel your Mantis Fighter whilst taking stock of what you had achieved, and most importantly, take a moment to catch your breath before the next frenetic level kicked in.

## Xenon
### 1988

Not only was it an ace game in its own right, but Mastertronic's *Xenon* provided the first hints that computer games could appeal to more than just the socially reclusive stereo-typical player. Created by the mysteriously named Bitmap Brothers (they weren't brothers), *Xenon* was a traditional vertical scrolling **shoot 'em up**, albeit superbly realised for the home computer market. It offered only one gameplay innovation: the ability to transform your spaceship into a tank and vice versa, via the quick, but frantic, waggle of your **joystick**. In tank mode you were able to roam the terrain, unencumbered by the traditional requirement to keep moving forward in time with the scrolling screen. However, the rub was that sooner or later some kind of obstacle would appear that couldn't be driven over, thus forcing you to switch back into spaceship mode.

What made *Xenon* stand out from the rest of the **Amiga** and **Atari ST** games though, was its visual sheen. Graphically, it was a slick and shiny little number, with levels constructed from geometrically shaped blocks complete with nicely realised shadow and lighting effects. The look of the game even extended to a beautiful chrome logo and an ever present control panel picked out in a fetching cyan and metal finish. Add to this an impressive soundtrack that sounded appropriately sci-fi, yet also a little bit hip, and, in an era when presentation mattered little, *Xenon* made for an innovatively trendy overall package.

Picked up by the media at large, and the kids' Saturday morning television programme *Get Fresh* in particular, *Xenon* managed to shift an impressive 100,000 units, making it the first Amiga title to enter the all-format computer game Top 40.

In November 1988, the Bitmap Brothers released *Speedball,* which looked even more fantastic than *Xenon,* and in 1989 came the coolest game yet released for the home computer market, *Xenon 2: Megablast.* Since then the brothers have continued, with much success, to create hip looking titles that not only look utterly cool, but also deliver adrenalin-pounding gameplay.

# Amusement Arcades

Let's face it, amusement arcades were exciting, if a little shabby. There was a frisson of danger in the air, half-whispered tales of the local loony using the Gents toilets as his personal hunting ground and stories of lads sniffing glue in the manager's office. These places were invariably down at heel, threadbare and no matter how high the ceiling, always felt cramped and enclosed (thanks, in part, to the necessity to keep lighting at a low level). They were also rich with the smell of teenage sweat.

Once you had entered into the backroom (past the fruit machines and bingo with the obviously bored-out-of-her brain caller) you were faced with loads of hard lads who looked like they should be working on the Waltzers at the local funfair. You knew they might beat you up at any minute simply because you were a nerdy brainiac or a posh kid, and should you dare to topple their high score on **After Burner II** there would definitely be serious repercussions. Indeed, there can be few things more frightening than pumping your 50ps in to the slot for a peaceable game of *Ridge Racer*, only to find yourself unspokenly challenged to a two-player race by a strange lad wearing grubby leisurewear. Generally their approach would be systematic, ruthless and joyless, disposing of you much like the purse, now stripped of cash, that they had thrown over a wall having nicked it from some unsuspecting granny just ten minutes earlier. However, what made the whole experience even more alarming was the fact that no sooner had they begun the process of trouncing you then their friends would begin to congregate round the unit just in case you happened to edge into the lead. No words would be spoken whilst the contest was played out, just simple grim determination on your part to get out alive. However, as soon as you had been thoroughly thrashed your new companion would nonchalantly ask whether you fancied a re-match. Generally speaking this proved to be a less tricky moment then it might appear. Your decision to retire would be greeted with little more than a studied bored nonchalance. OK, so you got the message that you were simply grist to the mill of these seemingly full-time, professional arcade dwellers, but more importantly you escaped with your life.

But it wasn't always like this. For decades, amusement arcades were video game free zones and housed only vending machines, mechanical games, mutoscopes (which in the early years of the twentieth century offered the general public their first glimpse of cinematography) and most ubiquitously, gambling machines. Over the years it has been these gambling machines that have dominated the amusement arcade, tempting passersby in with their bright lights, jaunty music and promise of easy cash. When video games first appeared in the early Seventies, they quickly moved from occupying space in local bars to what seemed be their natural home in the amusement arcade. However, in so doing, these new contraptions were lining up beside some pretty shady bedfellows. Gambling machines had been the cause of consternation for a number of years, enduring several bans, pieces of legislation, and accusations that they were a corrupting influence on society at large. Specifically, the finger of suspicion was pointed at the fruit machine. These simplistic yet colourful gambling contraptions had evolved from the original nineteenth century wall-mounted machines that featured mechanical versions of popular gambling games. The fruit machines used the same gaming mechanisms, but swapped the iconography of playing cards for cherries and pineapples. The rationale was that lining up combinations of fruit would be far more palatable to the general public than an out-and-out gambling game. However, no one was fooled, and fruit machines (often dubbed 'one-armed bandits') came in for just as heavy criticism.

Although many now view video games as tainted by their association with these contraptions, the arrival of titles such as *Asteroids* and *Galaxian* had a temporarily uplifting affect on the amusement arcade's reputation. In fact, for a time in the late Seventies and early Eighties, amusement arcades were benign places where a film crew from *John Craven's Newsround* would regularly pitch up to do a piece on the latest 'electronic craze' to grip the nation. In those early days we seemed to be positively encouraged to have a bash on the latest **Space Invaders** clone or take on granny at **Pac-Man**. Yet as the games grew more immersive and, in some cases, **violent**, there seemed to be a palpable shift in the public perception. No longer was this a place where youngsters shared in a fun activity that was a bit like hula-hooping but for over-intelligent kids with minimal physical co-ordination; now it was the last refuge of the bone-idle social reprobate. By the time games such as **OutRun** were doing the rounds in 1986, the clientele had taken a notable nose-dive. Whereas camera crews might once have turned up to film a group of wholesome kids admiring the awesome sprite-scaling in the aforementioned *OutRun*, or the parallax scrolling in *Space Harrier*, these days they were more likely to pitch up at the local arcade to shoot a scene in which *Grange Hill's* Zammo Maguire took a load of smack and had a fight with a gang of lads in front of the *Double Dragon* machine.

But what finally did for video games in the amusement arcade was the release of games consoles such as the **PlayStation** and **Nintendo** 64. These machines effectively brought arcade-quality action into the home. Suddenly there was no need to frequent the less salubrious end of town, or risk a feel-up from Benny the Nutter, and so the fruit machines began to dominate once again (helped in no small part in the UK by the introduction of a National Lottery and the subsequent relaxation of legislation surrounding the maximum value of cash prizes that could be paid out on gambling machines).

Yet, whilst the common-or-garden amusement arcade may once again be ringing with the sound of punters frantically smacking the hold button whilst simultaneously feeding twenty pence pieces into the coin slot, we still have our memories of the great video games of yore and rejoice in mentally replaying our moments of glory on those long since scrapped coin-op classics. Or failing that, we can always pop into our nearest motorway café, where some decrepit old machine is doubtless still being pressed into action for the purposes of enticing young children into spending all their pocket money on *Virtual Racer.*

## After Burner II
### 1987

Along with **OutRun,** *After Burner II* is the quintessential late Eighties arcade game. Somehow it seemed to tap in to what can only be described as a 'Glen A Larson' vibe that afflicted boys of a certain age back when *Street Hawk* and *Knight Rider* were the last word in 'outside play' cool. In part, the appeal of *After Burner II* was that, like those aforementioned Saturday tea-time action series, it featured a souped up vehicle wreaking merry havoc (here it was a fighter plane that over twenty-three Super Sprite scalered levels was charged with blasting anything and everything out of the skies).

However, there were two factors in particular that really made *After Burner II* compulsive. The first was the inclusion of a throttle control. This meant that when you were really up against it you could simply power out of trouble, leaving a hugely satisfying exhaust trail behind you (this was a feature that was not included in the original *After Burner* game). The second and most important element was a sit-down cockpit cabinet that rocked about in accordance with every dive and emergency manoeuvre you pulled. Add to this a high energy rock soundtrack that sounded a bit like something from *Top Gun* or *Iron Eagle*; and it no longer mattered that *After Burner II* the game was actually a bit repetitive and graphically unexceptional. Who cared about such trivialities when there was a whole world of bragging rights on offer for the first person to make it through the canyon level alive?

## Computer Space
### 1971

The world's first video arcade game was not **Pong** (which was the world's first successful video arcade game), but a space game released in 1971 and appropriately enough, based on the first computer game ever – **Spacewar**. However, whereas *Spacewar* had been created to run on a computer that cost in the region of $120,000, *Computer Space* creator Nolan Bushnell (who would go on to found **Atari** the following year) realised that if there was any money to be made out of computer games then you would have to be able to run them on considerably cheaper hardware.

In resolving this problem, Bushnell abandoned any thoughts of using existing computer equipment and instead built a completely new, custom device. With the aid of Bill Nutting (who already had some experience of the arcade industry), Bushnell determined that the box that would house *Computer Space* had to look damn cool. To that end, he designed an impressively futuristic looking fibreglass cabinet that swapped hard edges and corners for enticing curves, finished off with a suitably garish metallic finish. Indeed the cabinet looked so ahead of its time that it was featured in the 1973 science fiction film *Soylent Green*.

Surprisingly, and rather unfortunately, the game was extremely complicated to play (even though the objective was simple enough – you either had to try and shoot down two computer controlled flying saucers or one player controlled ship) and came with several pages of instructions that detailed the finer points of controlling and manoeuvring the ship, as well as how to deal with gravity and hyperspace. Consequently, Bushnell and Nutting didn't actually sell many *Computer Space* games and it is claimed that they only made $250 profit from the whole enterprise.

However, the notion of sticking a video game into an **amusement** arcade was definitely a winner; and with his next release Bushnell would address the thorny issue of complexity – with devastating results.

Death Race
1976

Released in the USA by Exidy Games, the arcade title *Death Race* holds a special place in the history of video games by being the first title to be widely criticised for being too **violent**. The object of the game was to drive your car over little stick people that were supposed to be demons, but to all intents and purposes looked like little stick people. The player was awarded a score for each demon they were able to flatten and their progress was measured on screen by the appearance of a little cross beside each carcass.

Apparently based on the 1975 movie *Death Race 2000* (in which Sylvester Stallone and David Carradine take part in the futuristic national sport of running people over), *Death Race* was actually a revision of Exidy's earlier title *Destruction Derby* (not to be confused with the Psygnosis game of the same name published in the mid-Nineties). In that game, players were invited to try and run down, not little stick people, but other cars. Although graphically rather quaint, the content of *Death Race*, plus its gruesome livery (the arcade consoles featured drawings of evil looking skeletons, crosses and cars all swathed in flames), ensured that it soon came to the attention of an outraged American moral majority. The fact that the game tried to make it clear that it was monsters, and not people, being mown down did little to pacify parents, who seemed to be none too plussed with *Death Race*'s proclamation that 'It's fascinating! It's fun chasing monsters.'

Inevitably, parental concern spilled over into the media and local television stations began to pick up on the story, eventually culminating in *Death Race* being discussed on CBS' prestigious *60 Minutes* news programme. Whilst Exidy allegedly received bomb threats as a result of the adverse publicity, it is also believed that the game became increasingly popular on the back of the media furore. Here was an early lesson that those who would later campaign against violent or sexually explicit computer games would have done well to learn.

But whilst the moral majority might have been outraged by *Death Race*, others in the computer industry were also disgruntled, but for different reasons. Companies such as **Atari** had practiced a policy of ensuring that no recognisably human figures were killed in their games. Their fear was that titles such as *Death Race* would result in the whole video game industry being banned (after all it was only in 1976 that the ban on **pinball** machines in New York City, in place since 1942, was finally lifted).

Although Exidy did release a sequel, without the accompanying furore it didn't perform nearly as well, and the video games industry tried to pull a discrete veil over the whole issue, at least until the next uproar. Meanwhile, in the UK, comics writer John Wagner was drawing similar inspiration from *Death Race 2000* and the fruits of his muse would result in a comic character that over the years would attract far more criticism from concerned parents than *Death Race* could ever hope to muster. This character was *2000AD*'s Judge Dredd.

## Donkey Kong
### 1981

If you were to ask the average man on the street to name three arcade games, incredibly they would probably come back at you with three titles, of which the youngest was almost a quarter of a century old. Inevitably the titles in question would be **Space Invaders**, **Pac-Man** and **Nintendo**'s **Donkey Kong** (probably in that order). To this day, there has been nothing as domineering in amusement arcades, or in the media's coverage of computer games (**Tomb Raider** included). This is probably because between them, this holy trinity of coin-op classics pretty much defined the basic tenets of the video game. *Space Invaders* put them on the map, *Pac-Man* gave them character, and *Donkey Kong* gave them narrative. Indeed trying to come up with the 'first video game to have a story' was the primary motivation of *Donkey Kong* creator Shigeru Miyamoto.

Miyamoto is one of the most important figures in computer games (he went on to create a number of titles for Nintendo including countless Zelda and **Mario** games); however, he was initially employed as an artist, and his first sales pitch at Nintendo was for a range of children's clothes hangers. Nevertheless, Nintendo boss Hiroshi Yamauchi saw something in Miyamoto and in 1980 ordered him to design a new arcade game. At that time Nintendo were experiencing serious problems cracking the US market. Whilst their titles were selling in their homeland of Japan, for some reason they just didn't travel well. In particular Nintendo's *Radarscope* (a simplistic **shoot 'em up**) had been a huge flop in America and had left the company with two thousand of the three thousand machines still sitting in their US warehouse. Yamauchi realised that the most practical solution was to create a new game that could be run on the *Radarscope* machine.

With thoughts of grand narratives such as *Macbeth* and *King Kong* buzzing round his head, Miyamoto set to work. Whilst he was a keen artist, luckily for Nintendo, Miyamoto also understood the intrinsic limitations of the medium he was working in. The characters he created were distinctive but realisable on the available technology. Initially inspired by *Beauty and the Beast*, Miyamoto eventually arrived at a back-story in which a big-nosed carpenter (referred to as 'Jump Man') had to try and rescue his girlfriend (Pauline) from a giant rogue gorilla that had once been his pet. The format of the game was very simple: Jump Man had to negotiate his way past barrels, fireballs and cement pies to get to the top of each level. All pretty straightforward; however, the cleverness of the game's design, and in particular its difficulty curve, made it enormously addictive: various obstacles were launched at you by Donkey Kong from the top of the screen, which meant that as you progressed up the level, the time you had to prepare for each new obstruction decreased.

Looking for a suitable name for his masterpiece, legend has it that Miyamoto looked up 'stubborn' and 'gorilla' in an English dictionary and alighted on the words 'donkey' and 'kong'. Yamauchi recognised the appeal of Donkey Kong straight away, but Nintendo's American employees were less enthusiastic. This was an age in which arcade games were generally given menacing and excitingly futuristic names, and here was Nintendo attempting to storm the market with a game whose title was not only odd, but completely failed to evoke any kind of stimulating mental image. But after an initial test period in which Donkey Kong arcade machines were installed in two bars in Seattle, it became apparent that Nintendo had a real hit on their hands.

Eighty thousand machines were sold in the US alone, making Donkey Kong the second best selling arcade game of all time (behind Pac-Man and its various spin-offs). For Nintendo, this was a triumph, and they quickly looked at converting Donkey Kong into as many different formats as possible. One of the most memorable was undoubtedly the **Game and Watch** version. This **handheld game** found its way into innumerable British playgrounds and was the cause of many a schoolyard scuffle.

Nintendo's success was challenged in June 1982 when Universal Pictures (who released a remake of the King Kong film in 1976) filed a suit against the computer games manufacturer for breach of the movie company's King Kong licence. During the subsequent trial it emerged that some years earlier, Universal had taken RKO (the producers of the original King Kong film in 1933) to court and had proved that as the original film was more than forty years old, King Kong was public domain, meaning no

Launching Manta 1

PAUSE

MANTA FIGHTERS:
1 ............... LAUNCHING
2 ............... IN HANGER
3 ............... IN HANGER
4 ............... IN HANGER

ABORT

A Manta takes to the air in Rainbird's fearsomely complex *Carrier Command*.

Daley (or someone) celebrates a spectacular long jump in *Daley Thompson's Decathlon*.

Dirk the Daring faces certain death…again, in *Dragon's Lair*.

© PRISM LEISURE CORPORATION PLC

**GOAL!**

Aston V.    0    Blackpool    1

Blackpool go one up against the Villa in the classic ZX Spectrum game *Football Manager*.

Synonymous with video games for over twenty years,
Mario and Nintendo remain giants in the industry to
this day.

The front cover of Bullfrog's seminal God Game
*Populous.*

# STOS
## The Game Creator

MANDARIN
SOFTWARE

ATARI
ST

Games Creators such as *STOS* seemed to offer the promise of an unlimited world of gaming fun. Unfortunately they didn't always deliver.

The hit arcade game *Zaxxon* makes its way onto the home console market.

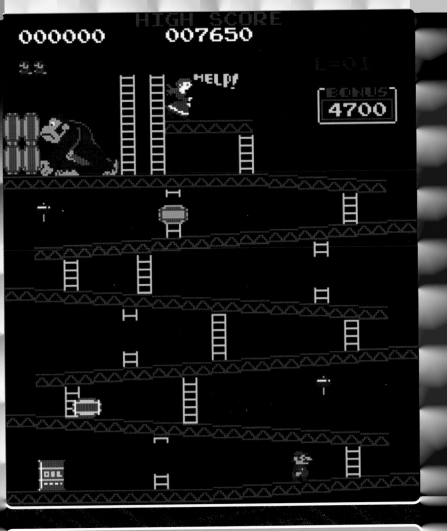

The granddaddy of all platformers. Jump Man prepares
to take on the mighty Donkey Kong.

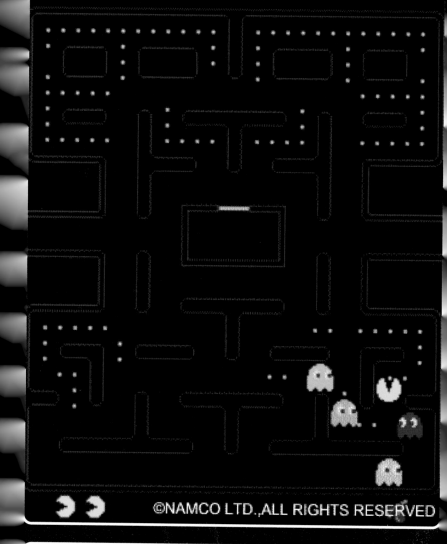

Quite simply – the guv'nor of video gaming.

These days, more often found on retro T-shirts, the Atari logo is one of the great icons of video game history.

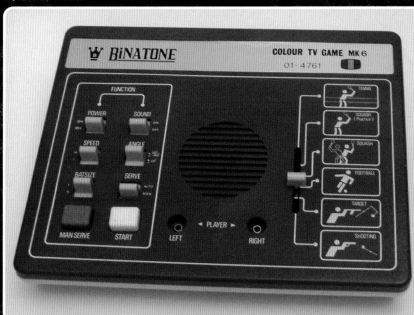

Cheap-and-cheerful, *Pong*-derived entertainment, Seventies-style, courtesy of Binatone.

Is this the best-loved British computer of all time?
Sinclair's mighty ZX Spectrum.

The home computer that kick-started the UK computing
scene - the Sinclair ZX 80.

The successor to the popular BBC Micro, and home of the 1986 Domesday Project - the BBC Master.

Amstrad's deliberately 'chunky' looking computer - the CPC-464.

The world's most popular games machine alongside the world's greatest puzzle game – GameBoy and *Tetris* (© *Nintendo*).

Mattel's would-be Atari 2600 beater – the IntelliVision.

A breakthrough in computing technology – Atari's Mindlink allows you to control the on-screen action via the waggling of your eyebrows.

Prestel – British Post Office technology at its videotexing best.

A selection of magazines from the glory years of
computing.

one owned the rights to it. Not only did it put Nintendo in the clear, it left Universal in the unpalatable position of having to answer to all the other companies it had made similar demands and legal threats too in relation to *King Kong*.

The lasting legacy of *Donkey Kong* is not the realisation that anyone can market *King Kong* merchandise, or even the seriously red faces at Universal Pictures, but the subsequent evolution of Jump Man, who with a change of name and profession would go on to become one of the best-loved computer characters of all time.

## Dragon's Lair
### 1983

Generally speaking, back in the Eighties an occasional visit to the amusement arcade was enough to keep you appraised of the latest developments in video games. Through the evolution of, for example, *Speed Freak*, **Pole Position, OutRun** and *Daytona Racer*, we could see the gradual increase in detail, realism and speed of **driving games**, and although these advancements weren't exactly happening at a snail's pace, it was clear to see how each title built on the technical achievements of its predecessors, creating, if you will, a video game family tree.

Then one fine day, and completely out of the blue, came Cinematronics' *Dragon's Lair*. Here was a game that seemed to have no antecedents of any kind, yet arrived on the arcade scene in 1983 with jaw-dropping visuals that made it look as if it had fallen through a wormhole from twenty-years in the future. What you were staring at was literally Disney-quality animation. Unsurprisingly, *Dragon's Lair* was hugely expensive to play; whilst all the other games cost twenty pence for one credit or fifty pence for three, fifty pence got you only one go, not that this seemed to be any impediment to the game's success. In those first few weeks, gangs of awestruck video game players surrounded *Dragon's Lair* cabinets, each one asking 'how is this possible?'

The answer was actually pretty simple, *Dragon's Lair* was the first laserdisc-based coin op. This meant that instead of relying on the hardware of the arcade system to generate the sound and graphics, it used conventional animation sequences that were stored to laserdisc as discrete scenes. It then simply threaded the appropriate scenes together depending upon the decisions you made during the course of the game. Ah yes, the *game*. You played Dirk the Daring, the dashing knight who attempted (usually in vain) to vanquish the fair maiden Daphne (not the most conventional of names for a fair maiden but there we are). The premise was to work through Mordread's Castle overcoming various challenges and foes along the way. In reality this took the form of watching a snatch of beautiful, albeit poorly voiced animation (the producers of the game weren't willing to hire voice actors so they did it themselves), whilst waiting for the briefest moment in which you had to direct Dirk to overcome the current challenge. If you happened to hit the right **joystick** combination at the right time, you would sit through yet another animated sequence (there was twenty odd minutes worth in total) at the end of which you would be asked to make another choice. More often than not, for what seemed like no good reason, you would usually end up sending Dirk plummeting to his death off the side of a cliff or straight into the gaping mouth of a dragon; all of which meant your game was over and another fifty pence was required. Not really the gaming experience you had anticipated when you'd slotted your hard earned money into the machine.

The problem with *Dragon's Lair* was that its basic design meant the gameplay was restricted to linear paths. In essence what you were playing was an animated version of a **Choose Your Own Adventure** book, with all the attendant limitations of that format. Whilst laserdiscs proved to be a good way of storing and accessing scenes, what it didn't allow you to do was actually interact with your surroundings. Instead you had to wait for a gap in proceedings during which you could then make one of a few predefined choices.

However, such was the impressiveness of the graphics that it didn't seem possible that a game this good looking could be anything other than ace to play. As a result, most gamers ended up a few quid lighter before they realised they weren't actually having any fun.

## Driving Games
## 1974

Most computer games put you in a position that you are extremely unlikely to experience in real life (such as being stuck in a dungeon with a horde of demons). The driving game is one of the few genres that in the main attempts to provide you with an experience that is as close to real life as possible. Whereas an early demise in a **shoot 'em up** can be blamed on a faulty **joystick**, the computer cheating or simply the computer not liking you, those who come a cropper at driving games tend to say things like 'on a real Ferrari F355, the clutch doesn't behave like that at all', or 'by rights the computer car's suspension should be totally gone by now, so it's a cheat that its still going'.

Driving games have a long history, with the first dating back almost to the dawn of video games themselves. However, **Atari**'s *Gran Trak 10* released into the arcades in 1974, is in many ways untypical of the kind of driving games we know and love today. Admittedly, it did allow the player to control the vehicle via a steering wheel, gear stick, brake and accelerator pedals, but the view provided was overhead, meaning that it had more in common with a game of *Pac-Man* than driving a real car. It wasn't until *Night Driver* in 1976 that a from-the-car view was offered to the player, and even this consisted of little more than road-side lights on a pitch black background (hence the game's name).

Vectorbeam's 1979 *Speed Freak* was altogether better, featuring a see-through skeleton frame representation of the world. Whilst this might have meant sacrificing all elements of colour, it did make for a plausible looking three dimensional environment and, crucially, meant the game was able to feature other cars – suddenly you were no longer alone on that road. However, within just a couple of years the seminal **Pole Position** had superseded this. From this stage on there was a rapid succession of titles, each one improving on the last (although too many used the trick of stripy coloured roads as an easy way to show movement).

Then in 1989 came Atari's *Hard Drivin'*, a true **3-D** driving game with filled-in vector graphics, offering supposedly the most realistic driving experience to date. Indeed *Hard Drivin'* looks a lot like those simulators professional driving instructors use today. Unfortunately though, it was not as exciting to play as, say, **OutRun**. Somehow the graphics seemed a little too pedestrian and slow-moving. Thankfully, **Sega**'s *Virtua Racing* (which hit the arcades in 1992) got things moving on the vector graphics front and offered up a genuinely entertaining gaming experience, as well as the nifty trick of allowing the player to seamlessly change camera view.

By 1994, two dimensional racing games were all but obsolete and even standard 3-D racers with coloured polygons were *passé*. Games such as Namco's *Ridge Racer* (released in 1993) and **Sega**'s *Daytona USA* (1994) featured not just coloured polygons, but *textured* coloured polygons, producing an even greater level of detail. From this point on, such was the sophistication of driving games, it became increasingly difficult to produce new ones that looked appreciably better than those that had come before, either in the arcades or on home systems. In fact the driving games of today don't look a whole lot different to those ten or so years ago. Doubtless though, they still haven't got the subtle nuances of the clutch control of a Ferrari F355 quite right yet – particularly when you send one careering off the track and into a crash barrier.

## Frogger
1981

Nestling just behind **Space Invaders**, **Pac-Man** and **Donkey Kong** as the best known arcade game in the world, sits *Frogger*. Developed by Konami and released in America in 1981 by **Sega**, *Frogger* took its inspiration from a relatively mundane real-life challenge, and somehow managed to turn it into a popular and addictive game. The task at hand was to guide the eponymous amphibian across a busy street, over a river filled with alligators and to his home, a lily pad. Perfunctory sounding as this might be (and the graphics were no great shakes either), there was something undeniably enticing about the game. Perhaps it was that, almost uniquely for that time, you were given control of a real character (albeit a frog) that had an objective to achieve that you could relate too.

*Frogger* also offered hidden depths in terms of gameplay. For example, although the objective of the game ultimately required you to move forwards, on occasions it actually benefited you to go backwards in order to achieve a successful crossing (an obvious stratagem, but one that seldom reaped rewards in other arcade games). However there was nothing to beat that occasional caution-to-the-wind moment when you simply made a dash for it and actually made it all the way to the lily pad.

The game got harder the further you progressed, with the vehicles and the river current moving increasingly faster. Indeed if you played *Frogger* for long enough you would eventually come up against a level that was impossible to beat (these were referred to as 'kill screens'), so that the game could be brought to some kind of conclusion. However, on the bright side, there were numerous secret passages and tricks that the player could invoke (usually exploiting some bug in the game) to help rack up an impressive score.

Having been converted to almost every popular home format, *Frogger* is still with us today, although you would have thought someone would have built a bypass by now.

## High Scores
## 1979

One of the most annoying things about lending a game to one of your mates is when you get it back and find they have wiped all your high scores off the game's leader board, and have used the name field on each of their high entries to make some catty remark about your gaming prowess, such that the top of the table reads something like 'U-SUK – 15,000,923'.

The concept of scoring is so closely tangled up with our perception of computer games, that it is difficult to mentally prise the two things apart. Even the earliest commercially released games such as **Pong** allowed players to keep tally of who was beating who.

It wasn't until the release of **Atari**'s arcade game *Asteroids* in 1979 (the first game to feature a high score board) that the opportunity for real computing immortality was offered to players. Whereas previously high scorers had to make do with scoring their initials into the arcade cabinet and thus run the risk of eviction from the **amusement arcade**; now their prowess could be immortalized on screen for all time (or at least until someone was able to beat them). This added a new edge to arcade gaming, meaning that not only could you prove that you were the best out of your peer group at *Star Wars*, you could actually take on the entire clientele of the amusement arcade and discover that beating a complete stranger's score was even better than beating your mates'.

OutRun

1986

Here was a game that made you roll your sleeves up whilst slotting in your fifty pence pieces. Not because you were expecting to get seriously stuck in, but because just a whiff of *OutRun* was enough to make you want to adopt even a vague approximation of the *Miami Vice* look.

*OutRun* was a game that was made for its time. Its flamboyance, fast cars and funky music summed up the decadence and excess of the decade it came from. Released into the amusement arcades by **Sega** in 1986, you could almost feel the cool Miami sea breeze when you stepped up and slotted in a few coins. Other **driving games** had mainly focussed on traditional racing cars and race tracks, but *OutRun* was far more aspirational and placed you in the driving seat of a Ferrari Testarossa, on a road lined with palm trees and with a blonde girl at your side.

In almost every respect the game was impressive. Thanks to Sega's exemplary sprite-scaling techniques (which enabled oncoming objects to grow larger in an authentic looking way), the bright colourful graphics and strip-shaded roads flew by at remarkable speeds. Unlike other driving games there were also highly detailed backdrops to admire and other cars to avoid.

The mid- to late Eighties was probably the time when the gap between arcade and home computer technology was at its greatest and when it was announced that *OutRun* was coming into our homes, it was obvious that there was simply no way that systems such as the **Commodore 64**, **Amstrad CPC-464** or **ZX Spectrum** could cope – indeed the Spectrum version couldn't even replicate the basic colour scheme.

*OutRun*'s popularity endured long after its 2D sprite-scaling was made redundant by the likes of Namco's *Ridge Racer* (1993). Quite simply, the game has a brash charm that has seldom been replicated and remains to be bettered. Whilst now a museum piece, it is a game that can still have you reaching for your luminous socks and grey slip-ons.

## Pac-Man
## 1980

Who's the daddy? Undoubtedly it's *Pac-Man*. The single most recognised video game icon, *Pac-Man* bestrides the computing scene like a hungry pizza-shaped colossus. Whether he is a Neo-Marxist critique on capitalism, a satirical broadside at modern day consumption or just a round yellow thing, one senses that *Pac-Man's* influences has long since seeped beyond the confines of the **amusement arcade** and has altered the very world in which we live.

Created in 1979 by Namco employee Toru Iwatani, the original idea was to try and come up with a game that might appeal to female players. To that end Iwatani eschewed **violence** in favour of a character who just wanted to eat. Based on a pizza with one slice removed, the iconic design of the eponymous character was nailed reasonably quickly, and Iwatani and his nine-man team turned instead on devising suitably non-threatening looking adversaries for Pac-Man to face.

At first glance the four ghosts (Blinky, Pinky, Inky, and Clyde) were the more appealing characters and in turn there seemed something strangely remorseless about Pac-Man's grim determination to eat everything in his path. However, any residual affection for the phantasms would be discarded as soon as you started playing the game.

Originally titled 'Puck-Man' it is said that the name changed when it was realised that vandals would probably alter the *p* to an *f* to create an altogether more offensive moniker for the little chap. With that adjustment made, the game was ready to hit the arcades. Although recognising its qualities, Namco didn't expect it to become a significant hit. Indeed they favoured the similarly maze-bound *Rally-X*. This preference was reinforced by initial industry comments also favouring the other title. However, once released, it became apparent almost straight away that everybody had underestimated the little yellow guy.

Yellow fever was immediate and widespread, an unprecedented 100,000 *Pac-Man* arcade machines were sold, *Pac-Man* made it on to the cover of *Time* magazine and was licensed to appear on over four hundred separate products. Home versions began with the crummy *Pac-Man* on the **Atari** 2600 in 1981 and a cartoon series sprung up too. Then, suddenly every new videogame was maze-based.

In 1982 *Pac-Man* got a family in the shape of *Baby Pac-Man Pinball* and *Ms Pac-Man* (which is the biggest selling arcade machine of all time). *Ms Pac-Man* (who looked just like *Pac-Man* but with a bow tie, lipstick and mole) didn't have that much to do with the original *Pac-Man* developers. Instead, she was put together by a team of college students, looking for ways to modify the original *Pac-Man* machine.

Over the years, *Pac-Man* has appeared on almost every conceivable electronic machine, and a multitude of official and unofficial sequels have flooded the market. Some of these have attempted simply to freshen up an old game, whilst others have tried to take *Pac-Man* into entirely new realms (including **3-D**). However, in truth there isn't a whole lot that can be done with the character: he exists to eat and that's it.

The greatest testament to the game occurred in 1999. Billy Mitchell, a *Pac-Man* super-fan, finally achieved the first ever perfect score (3,333,360). It took him six hours and required that he played all 256 levels, ate every dot, fruit and ghost; and did it all without losing a single life. Perhaps now he can stop playing it.

## Pole Position
### 1981

'*Pole Position*! Only their Uncle knows!'

Voted best arcade game in 1983, *Pole Position* represented a great leap forward for **driving games**, and was undoubtedly best played in motorway service stations, where the smell of petrol fumes and grease intensified the racing experience. Developed by Namco for **Atari**, it is almost pointless to describe it now, as its every element has gone on to become an arcade cliché, but suffice to say *Pole Position*'s realistic look and use of actual gears meant that those whose fancied themselves behind the wheel of a real car were of the opinion that they should be able to master this simple arcade machine.

Unlike later games, *Pole Position* had no bumps or hills to obscure your view, or even much in the way of scenery to admire, but that didn't matter; the speeds that you were able to reach meant that such things would have been a distraction anyway; and although its sequel would see the inclusion of additional tracks, *Pole Position*'s solitary Fuji Speedway was perfectly designed, starting and ending with a nice tyre-burning straight but with a seriously tricky 'S' bend to negotiate in the middle.

For sure, driving games such as **OutRun** and *Ridge Racer* have endured for longer, but neither would have existed had it not have been for *Pole Position*; and besides, how many other racing games can boast a spin-off cartoon that became one of the highlights of Saturday morning television?

'*Pole Position*! Sit back and watch them go!'

## R-Type
### 1987

*R-Type* is a king amongst **shoot 'em up**s – a shoot 'em up royale, perhaps. It oozes class from every pixel and in many respects is the last word in old skool blasters. Released into the arcades in 1987 by Irem, it single-handedly redefined the rules of the genre, combining innovative new ideas, fantastic graphics and a rock-hard gaming challenge.

The first things you noticed about *R-Type* though were the massive aliens and spaceships – some of which were bigger than the screen (a highly impressive sight in its day), not to mention the huge laser blasts that emitted from the front of your R-9 space ship. Everything about this game was big, bold, loud and chunky.

But below the surface there was a seriously difficult and well thought out game that required more from the player then simply hitting the fire button as rapidly as possible. From working out the best way to use your Force Orb (a cool add-on that you were able to utilise as either a shield or as an offensive weapon), to determining when it was best to launch a volley of small blasts versus holding down the shoot button for a few seconds to power up a super plasma blast, *R-Type* was all about decision-making. Similarly, the game required you to remember the best routes to avoid slamming into all-powerful giant enemies, and as such repeated play was essential to work out your best strategies.

A word too, for the obligatory end-of-level baddies – imaginatively designed and usually humungous in size, each one acted as a superb section finale, and with the exception of the level one boss (who was dead easy to kill) represented a fittingly arduous challenge, so that those who emerged from the **amusement arcade** victorious quickly became local legends.

## Shoot 'em ups
## 1961

The shoot 'em up (which is an abbreviation of the less exciting sounding 'shoot them up', and is itself often abbreviated as 'shmups') is the most ubiquitous gaming genre of them all. The first commonly recognised computer game, **Spacewar,** is a member of the shmups gang, as is the first ever video game to enter the national consciousness – **Space Invaders**. Indeed there are probably still people alive today who equate video games solely with shoot 'em ups.

There's no doubt that the Seventies and Eighties represented the glory years of the genre, with seminal titles released one after another. The pick of the crop were *Asteroids* (released by **Atari** in 1979) – a game that, even for its time, featured very rudimentary graphics but allowed the player to roam the screen at will; *Galaxian* (Namco, 1979) – the first colour shoot 'em up; *Defender* (William Electronics, 1980) – the first ever sideways-scrolling shoot 'em up and the first game to feature 'smart bombs' (devices that would kill everything on screen in one go) and *Tempest* (Atari, 1981) – which took the concept of *Space Invaders* and presented it from a first-person perspective.

After this initial flurry of activity, shoot 'em ups settled into a groove. In 1982, **Sega's Zaxxon** took the classic format and flipped it into an isometric perspective, but in the main, developers seemed to focus on refining what was obviously a winning format. This meant creating bigger and better bosses (fearsome behemoths waiting at the end of each level was an idea that first appeared in the 1981 Centuri title *Vanguard*), introducing more exciting weapons, and adding twists to the gaming experience such as co-operative two-player modes and levels that branched out, forcing the player to choose which way to go.

Although throughout the later years of the Eighties and on into the Nineties, masses of new shoot 'em up titles kept appearing in amusement arcades, the genre seemed to have passed its peak. This is not to decry the standards of the more recent titles, but with games such as **Doom** and *Quake* attaining massive popularity in the mid-Nineties, it was clear that those who had previously flocked to the likes of *Darius* and **Xenon** (two very decent old school blasters) were now too pre-occupied with kicking butt in **first-person shooters** such as *Hexen* or *Call of Duty* to care about was going on up there in space.

## Space Invaders
## 1978

Many people presume that Taito's *Space Invaders* was the first ever arcade game. This is not the case. However, it was the first arcade game that, for a lot of people, really meant anything.

In fact, it is probably not too much of an exaggeration to say that *Space Invaders* saved both the amusement arcade and home console markets from extinction, as prior to its release in 1978, video games were beginning to look like a passing fad. After a slow start, *Space Invaders* caught the public's imagination, first in Japan (where the game was so popular that it resulted in a national shortage of 100-yen coins), and then the rest of the world. For its time, *Space Invaders* was only marginally revolutionary: the animated characters were something of a novelty and the multi-colour graphics (achieved by sticking different coloured acetate overlays over various parts of the screen) looked quite nice. However, it was the gameplay pure and simple that kept the punters pumping in their small change.

'The player must strategically position' explained the game's promotional literature, 'then fire his laser missile launcher attempting to knock out the ever attacking invaders before they can drop missiles destroying the defender's protective bunkers and missile launcher'. Whilst it was certainly no 'avoid missing ball for high score', *Space Invaders* was not a complex game. But it did demand concentration and quick wits, and, crucially, its difficulty increased in accordance with the player's growing aptitude. Indeed, whilst many contemporaneous arcade games were restricted by a time limit, *Space Invaders* would allow you to continue ad infinitum. This meant that each game was destined to end with your demise. Again, the fact that *Space Invaders* wasn't actually winnable (all you were attempting to do was hold off the marauding aliens for as long as possible) was part of its appeal. This wasn't a game that you could ever master and so there was always a reason to go back for another go.

A massive worldwide success, many **amusement arcades** stocked up on *Space Invader* cabinets and lined them up one beside the other. When **Atari** attempted to enter the home console market, they immediately looked to secure *Space Invaders* as a **killer app** for their 2600 machine. The conversion was admirable and no one was in the least bit surprised when 2600s, complete with copies of the game, started to fly out of the shops. The 'arcade craze that was sweeping the nation' (copyright all news programmes everywhere) was all set to repeat its phenomenal success.

## Spy Hunter
### 1983

Midway's 1983 arcade game *Spy Hunter* was one of a very few titles that you knew you were going to enjoy playing even if it was rubbish. This was because it had a fantastic premise. Ostensibly a top-down **driving game** (with an added twist of having to shoot baddies that would regularly appear driving an assortment of vehicles), what made *Spy Hunter* stand out from the rest was its super cool secret agent trappings. Your car was equipped with missiles, oil slicks and smoke screens; but best of all should you turn off onto a side road, you could drive through a shed and turn your car into a boat, and continue your game on water.

Like you, the enemies also borrowed a trick or two from the world of *James Bond*, most notably driving cars equipped with tyre shredders and bullet proof shields (much like 007's famous Aston Martin DB5 from *Goldfinger*). Add to the mix the occasional appearances by enemy helicopters plus the odd friendly truck that you could drive into to replenish your arsenal, and you had a game that covered pretty much every car chase fantasy you could conceive (with the obvious exception of those dreamt up by JG Ballard).

When *Spy Hunter* was first in development, attempts were made by Midway to secure the James Bond theme for the in-game incidental music. However, when this proved impossible, they instead used Henry Mancini's iconic and bendy guitar riff, *Peter Gunn,* instead. This proved to be an excellent choice: the piece immediately evoked images of secret agents and covert activity in the mind of the player (even though they had probably never heard of the television series that the music had originally been written for).

The conversions to the popular home computer systems of the time weren't half bad either, and were certainly a lot more fun than Midway's own 1987 sequel *Spy Hunter II* (which introduced a two-player mode and presented the action from a **3-D** perspective, but somehow managed to be rubbish). It didn't take us long to realise we should stick to the original. Besides we still hadn't managed to shoot down one of those benevolent supply lorries that kept appearing. Perhaps we weren't meant to.

## Tron
1982

*Tron* was the computer film that had it all: hackers, evil programs and that bloke who would later appear in *Babylon Five*. Produced by Disney to cash in on the then burgeoning video game craze, it was the first film to extensively feature computer generated effects and it essayed a classy circuit board and neon aesthetic (that was actually achieved through traditional means rather than any computer jiggery pokery).

The story itself was rather secondary to the effects (as should be the case in a film about computers), and today most people struggle to remember precisely what the plot entailed (something to do with a programmer being sucked into a computer and having to locate the security program, Tron, in order to escape). However, sequences such as the Light Cycle dual live long in the memory, not least for the fact that it formed the basis of a level in the rather well-received *Tron* arcade game released in 1982 by Midway.

For all its storytelling shortcomings, *Tron* proved a popular film and somehow managed to encapsulate the excitement and optimism that surrounded the video game industry at that time. It also spoke a little of the growing unease that many felt about computers. For decades, science fiction writers had posited what might happen if a computer went mad, and with the increasing proliferation of arcade machines in our leisure centres, motorway cafes and not to mention **amusement arcades**, many felt that the invasion of the computers had already begun.

Whilst *Tron* has been derided for looking instantly dated, over the years it has taken on a kind of retro-chic that means today it looks strangely contemporary. Indeed in 2003, credible pop act The Strokes released a video '12:51' that was a direct homage to *Tron*. The movie, now over twenty-three years old, is currently enjoying something of an artistic renaissance amongst the trendy set. What chances an *Automan* revival?

## Yie Ar Kung-Fu
### 1985

Back in the mid-Eighties, when the **beat 'em up** was first finding its feet, Konami's *Yie Ar Kung-Fu* proved to be an important addition to the genre. Whilst the game's technical attributes only represented a modest advancement from Data East's

*Karate Champ* (released the previous year), elements of *Yie Ar Kung-Fu*'s gameplay would prove to be integral in the development of the beat 'em up format we know and love today.

Unlike earlier titles, *Yie Ar Kung-Fu* brought you face-to-face with a number of different opponents across multiple levels. There was Buchu, a big, fat, bald-headed chap who wore nothing but a pair of white tracksuit bottoms; Fan, an exotic looking Eastern beauty, who nonetheless proved to be a formidable fighter; and Tonfun, the notoriously difficult-to-beat Tonfa sporting bad guy. Each of these adversaries demanded a slightly different approach, ensuring that the game remained interesting, even after several plays.

*Yie Ar Kung-Fu*'s other great innovation was the introduction of an energy bar. Not only did this enable bouts to last longer than the two or three strikes required in previous titles, but it introduced the notion of the 'perfect' round, wherein a player would be rewarded with a simple verbal acknowledgement if they happened to beat their opponent without conceding any damage. The notion of a 'perfect' victory would later come to underpin several beat 'em up titles. But its real legacy lies with two-player bouts, in which each player, although desperate to win, knows only too well the ignominy of being on the receiving end of a 'perfect' victory.

## Zaxxon
### 1982

One of the oldest tricks in video games is to take a reasonably straightforward game, say for example a **shoot 'em up**, and then move the camera so that instead of looking at the action dead on, you are looking at it from an angle.

In essence this is all **Sega** did with their 1982 arcade game *Zaxxon*. However, that simple technique, although pretty dated now, resulted in what felt like a massive leap forward in video game technology. The objective in *Zaxxon* was nothing if not straightforward, you simply had to guide your way through each level, killing as many things as possible. However, the isometric viewpoint added a visual sheen, as well as an additional gaming element in the shape of altitude.

Though this could prove to be somewhat irritating when you found yourself smashing into the ground, it was also extremely exhilarating and even audacious when you got the opportunity to fly under something. However, it did take a little getting used to, particularly as the background, which in the past had played no bigger part in games than window dressing, was now something that needed to be negotiated – including some rather incongrously old-fashioned looking brick walls.

*Zaxxon* proved to be a big hit and appeared on a number of home systems, including a particularly good conversion for the ColecoVision. Less successful was MB's version, which took all the basic elements of the *Zaxxon* game (graphics and all) and threw them away in order to come up with, of all things, a *Zaxxon* board game. This bizarre conversion challenged you to take on a truly 'dangerous mission', and more than likely broke a few youngster's hearts in the process when crossed wires resulted in dad believing he had bought his kids the amazing game they had kept going on about, whilst the kids were waiting expectantly for their promised state-of-the-art arcade machine to arrive.

# Social Mores

In the late Seventies and early Eighties, there was nothing quite so much fun as watching your mum, dad or even favourite television presenter trying to get to grips with the computer age. They knew it was coming and knew it would be significant, but, beyond that, it seemed they were more or less lost as to what it all actually meant. Some seized on buzzwords such as 'silicon chip' and, much later, 'information superhighway', but mostly there was just a lot of head-scratching going on.

As computers shoe-horned their way into our everyday lives, a whole raft of other activities began to take off around them. Magazines sprung up that showed us how to program them, and clubs were formed to allow us to obsess over them. In the process, a rich sub-culture was formed, creating its own celebrities, social mores and controversies.

Perhaps the best way to understand how we have absorbed computers into our daily lives is to look at the ways they have been represented over the years on our television screens. Initially, it fell to all-purpose science programmes such as *Tomorrow's World* to file reports on the latest developments. This would usually consist of five minutes of whimsy as Michael Rodd, Judith Hann, Peter McCann or one of the many other avuncular presenters tried to dazzle us with a great new piece of technology made possible thanks to the 'silicon chip'. For the younger viewer there was also the odd item on the teatime news programme *John Craven's Newsround*. Here, the eponymous Craven would greet us every Monday to Thursday, ready to gush forth on the latest computer craze. However, with the odd one-off documentary excepted (such as the 1978 edition of *Horizon* 'Now the Chips are Down') that was it.

Things began to change as we entered the Eighties. First of

all, recognising the growing importance of the micro computer, the BBC broadcast *The Mighty Micro*, a six-part series that investigated the impact of the computer revolution. Then in 1981 came the groaningly titled *The Computer Programme*. Its educational, studio-bound magazine format was more in keeping with what would follow and featured Ian McNaught-Davis (a suitably friendly quasi-boffin) teaching a naïve looking Chris Serle how to carry out basic operations (such as **loading** a program from a tape) on the soon to be ubiquitous-on-the-telly **BBC Micro**.

After that, the BBC was up and running; *Making the Most of the Micro* featured McNaught-Davis once again, but added the excellent one-time *Play School* presenter Fred Harris. Then came *Micro Live*. Initially a four-hour, one-off programme broadcast on a Sunday morning in 1983, it started to crop up on a monthly basis, before eventually going weekly. As the title suggests it was broadcast live, which led to a number of tricky moments, such as the time one of McNaught-Davis' interviewees was almost sick on camera, or the occasion when **hackers** broke into the programme's **Prestel** account live on air.

Whilst the BBC seemed to have nailed the cosy magazine format, ITV's *Magic Micro Mission* (first broadcast in 1983) saw Adrian Hedley (who is best known for his mime antics on children's programmes such as *Jigsaw*) piloting a spaceship on the look out for celebrities willing to play a computer game. Meanwhile, Channel 4 adopted the BBC model for the mid-Eighties series *Me & My Micro* (even going so far as to nick a by now ill-advisedly bearded Fred Harris to present). Similarly their series *4 Computer Buffs* continued the tradition of pun-laden programme titles, but at least showed some attempts at innovation by featuring what *Sinclair User* magazine described as 'the first ever light transmission of sound, an interactive bulletin board for viewers, telesoftware via audio tones and telesoftware which can be downloaded from the TV using the new

4-Data adaptor manufactured by OEL'.

With the exception of *Magic Micro Mission* most of these programmes paid scant attention to computer games (unless it was showing you how to write one), and whilst explaining to viewers the best way to produce a club newsletter on your computer was very public spirited and all that, it only appealed to the hobbyists within the computing scene, who, by the mid- to late Eighties, made up a minority of the total number of computer users.

Meanwhile, computers were beginning to feature in more mainstream programmes. The early evening game show, *First Class,* consisted of fairly standard observation and general knowledge rounds, but also invited one member of each team to compete at *Paperboy* or the spring and vault and 110-metre hurdles in *Track and Field*. All the while, presenter Debbie Greenwood would provide commentary that never got much further than gushing in wonderment at the sophistication of the technology ('a rather complicated spring and vault' being a favourite term of hers).

In 1992 things changed forever as **Bad Influence** and **GamesMaster** shifted the focus of computer television programmes foursquare onto gaming. Sky One joined the fray in 1993 with *Games World* – a weekday programme that featured gaming contests and hints and tips. Today it is best remembered for its sardonic host Bob Mills, although it shouldn't be forgotten that it also gave early television exposure to *Little Britain's* very own David Walliams. In fact, some of the characters that Walliams paraded on *Games World* (such as DCI Mike Hatter, and the naked chap who was constantly asking for directions to Taunton) were excellent, and made all the more amusing because you knew that barely anyone else was watching.

Today's programmes about computer games seem to be far more at ease with themselves, and don't even bother expending any time bringing the uninitiated few up to speed. What this suggests is that we have at last accepted computers into our lives. No longer are they something that society as a whole needs to be fearful of, instead they are but one (albeit important) constituent part of modern day living.

But it has taken us a long time to get to this point – almost twenty years. This suggests that should something as truly revolutionary as time travel or teleportation ever become a reality, we will need the likes of Ian McNaught-Davis and Chris Serle to explain to us, very slowly and carefully, how to properly set the dials on our time machine, or program in the planned arrival location on our teleporter.

# Bad Influence
1992

Avast, ye slimy furtlers and welcome to the often excruciating-ly embarrassing spectacle that is kids' television trying to, well, get down with the kids.

The history of computer TV shows is neither extensive, nor in the most part distinguished, but *Bad Influence,* Yorkshire Television's early Nineties offering, was actually rather good; and if it is remembered today with some ambivalence then that's probably because lots of the people who watched it were surly teenagers at the time and not in fact the intended audience.

The main presenters, Andy Crane and Violet Berlin (who was replaced by Sonya Saul in the fourth and final series), came across as elder siblings attempting to relate to the audience in a way that 'grown ups' simply couldn't understand. This was punctuated each week with a studio backdrop of annoying chil-dren trying to create the impression of some kind of 'happen-ing'. The name of the programme was a further ironic wink to the kids amidst growing media concern over the effects of com-puter games; but for all that, the show's format was reasonably conventional, featuring investigations, gaming tips and reviews.

*Bad Influence's* main concession to innovation was probably the much-vaunted datablast that followed at the end of each pro-gramme. This consisted of lots of pages of texts being rapidly dis-played on screen that you recorded and then re-watched using your VCR's pause button. Other standing items included features from the USA presented by the ever cheery (in an uncool way) Z Wright, and most memorably, regular intrusions into the programme from a fictional pirate station run by Nam Rood, a bizarre character who would provide cheats and tips. Although his name was 'Door Man' backwards, the relevance of this was never made clear, nor why he needed to refer to us as 'slimy furtlers'. Anyway, he was dropped from the final series when research showed that girls didn't like him.

Of course boys didn't like Violet Berlin, but then there was nothing she could do about that, as the antipathy directed towards her was largely due to the fact that she wasn't a boy.

The gender divide also informed *Bad Influence*'s review section. Each week, the show's latest infestation of kids were split into boys' and girls' groups and invited to evaluate the latest software releases. This would culminate in summaries provided by Crane or Berlin informing us that whilst the boys might have thought that *Earthworm Jim* for the **Sega Megadrive** was 'hilarious and challenging', the girls though it was 'childish and boring'.

Sometimes naff, but always well meaning, if viewed today one imagines that the girls might conclude that *Bad Influence* is a lot better than most of the computer programmes that followed, whilst the boys would probably claim that, all in all, it was a pretty good show, if at times a little bit mumsy.

## Boys' bedrooms
### When you were 13

Let's face it, although there was no reason why your **NES** or **Sega Megadrive** shouldn't live permanently in the front room (after all that's where the big telly is), as soon as mum and dad's initial euphoria over buying the family's first **Atari** subsided, constant battles of **Mario** versus *Panorama* would ensure that the entire games system was moved lock, stock and barrel into your, or if you happened to be female then your brother's, bedroom.

Hitherto boys' bedrooms were a place where discarded Quicksilver Mazes nestled amongst half chewed Action Force figures and a pile of unread *Look and Learns* donated to you by a boring Aunt. Simply put, there was no reason for a community to be forged in there. However as soon as the computer or home console of your parent's choice (or rather your choice as confined by their budget) was rigged up (along with the black and white portable that had previously belonged to your sister), your house would become the meeting point for a group of like-minded, slightly scruffy and, usually academically gifted but not very popular boys; or in short – your friends.

Yes there was nothing like a bedroom with a computer in it to get people round your house, particularly if you had a game or system that was not yet widely available amongst your peer group (although this would result in your friends labelling you a 'rich kid' behind your back). As soon as the telly came on, boisterous, over-excited shouting would commence with each of the party forcibly making their case for why they should go first, why they should get another go, or how the computer kept cheating when they were playing. Often times these meet-ups would involve peripheral little scraps amongst those who were between goes, usually ending with someone getting forcibly restrained and farted on by someone else. However, as soon as the next turn came round, the restraining and pumping would cease.

One-player games would foster either a spirit of exploration (who can get the furthest) or competition (who can get the highest score) and each new milestone would be heralded by the achiever giving the bird whilst trying to shout cool one-liners in the style of Randy Savage the American wrestler. Multi-player games would create even more noise, with various participants arguing that they had been given the 'rubbish' **joystick**. These hard-fought victories were accompanied by malicious in-your-face victory celebrations that, if you were on the receiving end, made you want to punch someone really hard. However, nothing would stop you from picking up the joystick to have another go. Well, nothing that is until your mum and dad finally grew sick and tired of the 'incessant noise' and brought to an end a wonderful night of games playing. In so doing, they would usually remark on how badly your bedroom smelled.

## Chat Rooms
## 1973

Ah, the excitement of connecting to the Internet for the first time. The 'information superhighway' is spread out in front of you, and the world is your oyster. So what do you do? Well most likely you go to a search engine and type in the words 'chat room'.

It is generally agreed that the chat room was first born back in 1973 with the creation of the Planning Network (or PLANET as it was known). This program allowed users on the same network to exchange text messages in real time; however, it was primarily used by businessmen and the government. In fact, it wasn't until 1988, when Finnish IT administrator Jarkko Oikarinen came up with Internet Relay Chat (IRC) (a protocol for real-time text communication over the Internet), that online chatting really started to take off. Since then, chat rooms have evolved in all sorts of different ways. The introduction of graphical, on-screen locations has allowed the user to take their avatar for a stroll round a virtual bar, butt in on other people's conversations, or even try and entice an attractive looking graphic up on to the dance floor for a boogie. More recently, chat rooms have become ever more closely associated with instant messaging tools, meaning that instead of having to put up with a bunch of strangers it is now possible to get an online discussion going that consists solely of people you actually know and like.

For the chat room newbie though, the first port of call has to be an anonymous website. Having located somewhere where chat rooms seem to be, the Internet virgin then needs to negotiate the long and tedious process of working out how to join a particular room and setting up a profile to chat with, all of which dulls the initial excitement considerably. However, once chat has been embarked upon, the enthusiasm does regenerate a little.

Yet most will agree that any residual enthusiasm is short-lived. You see, chat rooms are actually rather boring, consisting primarily of bored people who are killing time whilst waiting for some file or other (usually porn) to download. The general rule of thumb is that the more generic the chat room is, the more banal the conversation will be. That said, it is surprising how little insight you can find in a 'Seventies Cheerleader Movies' chat room or how ill-informed those who frequent a *Silmarillion* message board can be. The 'party online' that your schoolmates keep on going on about seems to be full of idiots.

Undoubtedly the main objective of any chat room is to try and entice a fellow chatter into a private conversation. Indeed upon investigation it usually transpires that most of the real chat is taking place not in the public chatting space but in these whispering forums that most rooms provide. Actually getting someone to 'sidebar' with you is almost impossible as everyone else in the chat room already knows each other and your intrusion is about as welcome as a rugby player at a science fiction convention.

For those who frequent chat rooms on a regular basis, the concept of anonymity is often mentioned as being important. The theory goes that as you don't actually know the people you are speaking to it is a lot easier to be open and honest about yourself (you could call this the 'hairdresser' syndrome). However, there is a thin line that is easy to miss until you have crossed it. As your 'relationship' with your online buddy blossoms their position as someone outside of your day-to-day existence erodes, and soon, rather than being someone you can bitch to about how crap your life is, they become just another element of your crap life. Or to put it another way: it's only great to talk to the hairdresser about your terrible life up until the point they move in with you.

So what use are chat rooms? Undoubtedly most seasoned Internet users prefer other means of communication such as instant messaging or even good old-fashioned email. Whilst chat rooms still have some residual cachet as a potentially dangerous or spicy place to hang out (with stories regularly appearing in the media about unsavoury types using them as a stalking ground), the truth is that their usage has declined in recent years, presumably as the number of new Internet users has decreased. For those who are reduced to tears at the thought of having to read how Kandikitten's heart was broken when she found out her online lesbian lover Mistress Dark Angel was actually an obese one-legged man from Arkansas, then this is undoubtedly a good thing.

## Computer Club
### Ages 12 to 16

Whether or not your school actually had a formal computer club didn't really matter: the Computer Science class would all hang out in the Computer Room during lunch break and after school anyway. Generally speaking, this would either be a room out in the 'portakabin' (the curiously temporary, flat-pack style classrooms that would appear in the playground over the course of one summer holiday), or the small room in the English department that had previously doubled as a store-room-cum-bitching post for disgruntled teachers. Regardless of the location, these were always incredibly hot places, with the sun streaming in through the grey blinds and glaring off the computer monitors. Resultantly, there was usually a faint whiff of BO in the air, probably attributable to the bearded Computer Science teacher who had graciously agreed to administer proceedings.

Off-duty teachers were a little bit disturbing and always seemed a bit cross at having given up some of their free time. Now and again, for no obvious reason, they would make a joke at another teacher's expense and laugh manically in a way that suggested there was some kind of double meaning that you had failed to grasp.

Yet it was worth putting up with an unpredictable authority figure if it meant you could get a go on the school's Tandy TRS-80 or **BBC Micro.** However, even entry into the Computer Club did not permit you access to the enormous computers that used to sit in the corner of the room (like, for example, a RM 380Z), waiting for the occasional A Level student to power up their green-screen monitors and carry on inputting some completely impenetrable routine written in CESIL.

Whilst games were generally frowned upon, the odd title brought in from home would be permitted, particularly if it was *Elite* or some other game that the teacher was themselves stuck on. But for the most part, the Computer Club consisted of Computer Science O level pupils attempting to write crude **adventure games,** or applications that would generate a random insult whenever the user input their name (such as 'Michael Hughes is a pillock'). Occasionally such programs would spill out beyond the confines of the Computer Club to the general school populace. This would result in short term mass adoration for the programmer, followed by a reprimand from the head teacher along the lines of 'why don't you put your obvious computer **programming** talents to good use for a change?'

Computer Clubs enjoyed a brief upturn in membership during the early Eighties when *Grange Hill* ran a storyline in which one of the pupils developed a crush on 'Sexy Lexy' the Computer Science teacher. However, the only thing remotely connected with **sex** that you would find in a real Computer Club were the rather rude and crudely put together pornographic games that would invite you to 'waggle your **joystick**' at an image of a topless lady created purely from letters and numbers.

# Computer Magazines
## 1950

In 2005, there were somewhere in the region of seventy to eighty computer magazines available on newsstands in the United Kingdom, with around twenty or so alone dedicated to the **PC**. There were 'walk-throughs' and lavishly illustrated 'how to' guides popping up all over the place, not to mention publications that were little more than mouthpieces for specific home console manufacturers. However, the first generally recognised computer mag, *Computers and Automation* (first published in 1950 by Edmund Berkeley) was in almost every way unrecognisable in comparison to modern publications. Its articles were generally academic in tone and postulated such conundrums as: 'A Ball-Point Pencil...Is A Computer?' and 'The Coming Technological Society'. All in all, it took the subjects of computers and computing extremely seriously and should perhaps be considered more an academic journal than a high street magazine.

For a while, academia informed the dominant tone of computer publications and the American magazines of the early and mid-Seventies (such as the improbably named *Dr Dobbs Journal of Computer Calisthenics and Orthontia – Running Light Without Overbyte)* remained technical in focus. In the UK, things were much the same: *Practical Electronics* (which covered computers but wasn't wholly dedicated to them) told you how, with the aid of a soldering iron, you could construct your own, extremely basic computer that communicated via LEDs. In 1978 came *Personal Computer World*, perhaps the UK's first dedicated computer magazine and, at the time of writing, the longest-running. Amidst its pages you could find articles on understanding logic, the latest kit (which included computers such as the Research Machine 380Z) plus BASIC programs for you to try out for yourself.

By the end of the Seventies, Britain could proudly boast a handful of dedicated computer magazines (including *Practical Computing, Computing Today* and *Liverpool Software Gazette* as well as publications specific to particular models or manufacturers). In the early Eighties personal computers became more affordable and increasingly popular, and so the number of computer magazines grew. *Sinclair User* was a typical publication of the time. Started in April 1982, its early content included 'helpline' articles that appealed to the traditional hobbyist (the first ever edition included the following question: 'I am keen to understand how my **ZX-81** works but as a beginner I am perplexed by the manner in which addresses are stored in the system variables. I know, for example, that D-FILE is the beginning of the display file, but how is that information stored?'), and 'snappy reviews' (which meant extremely cursory with little detail) of the latest games as a sop to the more general user.

One of the most important British computer magazines began in November 1981. Editor Terry Pratt welcomed readers to the first issue *Computer & Video Games* (more commonly known as *C&VG*) with some particularly stern advice: 'don't just turn over pages that aren't featuring your particular machine's BASIC. Instead, look to see how other people have got round problems that may have baffled you and if a game interests you then try to convert it to your machine.'

It was this apparently superior attitude that spurred the following generation of computer journalists to pick up their pens. The arrival on the scene of *Crash!* magazine was of massive significance. Launched in February 1984, issue one boasted a futuristic alien on the front cover painted by the soon to be ubiquitous Oliver Frey. Its articles were pulled together by a small team working with the assistance of local school children. Between them, they crafted honest reviews of the latest games that actually resonated with the magazine's target audience. Whilst *Crash!* was dedicated to the **ZX Spectrum**, its approach soon spread, with *ZZAP! 64* providing similar coverage of the **Commodore 64** scene. The refreshing honesty and enthusiasm of such titles resulted in an obvious split on the newsstands. There were the magazines that you bought every month, read from cover to cover and pledged allegiance too, and then there were those that you also bought every month, but which remained unread stacked in a big pile next to your computer desk.

Indeed, the Eighties and early Nineties represents the apotheosis of the UK computer magazine market. The best writers and reviewers became micro-celebrities (helped in no small part by the magazines including little photographs of their troupe of writers, all of whom looked like they had once been members of Sigue Sigue Sputnik), and the computing magazine scene increasingly came to resemble its close cousin – the music press. Name journalists would send dispatches from the front lines, whilst indulging in a lifestyle that made us, the lowly reader, hugely jealous. It was no surprise then, to see computer magazines adopt the kind of torturous in-jokes that publications such as the *New Musical Express* and *Sounds* had been using for years. The net effect was to make readers in the know feel part of an exciting, but, more importantly, exclusive club.

The emergence of *Your Sinclair* magazine in 1986 took the predilection for in-jokes to even greater extremes, and made the double entendre a key part of its appeal (presumably a young Dominik Diamond was reading at the time). And whilst in July 1987, *Crash!* magazine gave away a free copy of the naughty kids' comic *Oink!*, in November *Your Sinclair* went one better by including a free copy of the adult humour magazine *Viz*.

The anarchic tone of the likes of *Your Sinclair* suited the magazine's production sensibilities; however, with the arrival in the early Nineties of desktop publishing, computer magazines began to look more professional (including proper screenshots from games instead of photographs taken of the telly screen). Consequently, their approach had to evolve a little too. The forerunner for this new generation was *ACE*. This multiformat magazine was launched in September 1987 and adopted a more restrained and mature tone. Whilst treating its readers as adults might have been its primary innovation, it's also remembered for its highly detailed game review scores and its 'Predicted Interest Curve' that through some arcane mathematical equation attempted to display on a graph how long each game would hold your interest for.

In 1993, Future Publishing launched *Edge* magazine and arguably the modern era of computer magazines began. Highbrow, weighty and stylised, *Edge* had superb production values and offered in-depth industry news as well as thought-provoking articles. Today, magazines such as **GamesMaster** (launched in January 1993 and, thanks to its associations with the television show of the same name, able to sell a staggering 200,000 copies of its first issue) try to keep the old spirit alive. But somehow slick layouts and logos with lens flare effects are just too professional for anarchy.

## Computer Shops
## 1979

The modern day computer shop comes in broadly three shapes and sizes: there are the large chain stores with over-bright lighting and shop assistants with cheap white shirts and patterned ties; there are the smaller independent shops run by some bloke who is always soldering something or other; and finally there are the stalls down the local market selling knocked off PS2 games that are copied as you wait and come in CD boxes with badly scanned covers printed on rubbish paper.

It was not always this way. Before the age of PC World, the average computer consumer would usually frequent their local Woolworths, John Menzies or WH Smith. These high street emporiums were the most exciting places to be of a Saturday morning, boasting a jaw dropping range of products. Whereas today your local WH Smith is a fine shop for books, magazines, pens and the like, back when computer games only cost £5.95, Smiths seemed to have a finger in every pie; it was a wool shop, travel agents and a record shop too. Menzies and Woolworth were similarly eclectic, with the latter even featuring a fish department in some outlets.

A visit to such a place was a step into a world of exotica. Although you might have come only to pick up some more C15 cassettes, the sight of every single Transformers toy ever produced, not to mention all of the Zoids range too was enough to ensure you slipped your parent's leash for a couple of hours for some hardcore browsing and time spent bugging the shop assistant with complicated questions about which version of Ocean's *Short Circuit* was best and why.

WH Smith's livery is worth recollecting; it embraced the full palette of the Seventies, meaning everything they sold came in a bag with a brown and orange logo. Meanwhile, John Menzies went for a distinctive white on blue look with a diagonal flash of colour that resembled a **ZX Spectrum**. Each was distinctively of its time, and today are somehow reassuring to recall.

Curiously, given how busy these shops seemed to be (particularly on Saturdays when they were crawling with kids), market forces dictated a move with the times. John Menzies' shops were bought over by WH Smith in 1998, and ever since there has been a marked reduction in eclecticism. Today's youth on a scouting mission for the latest **PlayStation** 2 title are, in comparison to us, impoverished shoppers; sure you can still buy *Railway Modeller*, a computer game and ten fags under one roof, but where's the love?

For those who were looking for something a little more niche, then there was nothing else for it except to brave your local Silicon Centre or Microdigital. Specialist computer shops started springing up in the late Seventies, with one of the very first being the aforementioned Microdigital which opened for business in Liverpool in 1979. Owned by future computing entrepreneur Bruce Everiss, the business expanded quickly in the early Eighties when music chain Laskey offered to set up a number of Microdigital outlets within their stores. For most other independent proprietors though, the best you could hope for was a nice little mail-order franchise through the advert pages of **computer magazines.**

Most, if not all, dedicated computer shops were run by computer fans, and so their emporiums would at some level reflect all of their computer prejudices, meaning that one could become subject to a sharp and disapproving intake of breath at any moment. Maybe you had expressed an interest in *Microsoft Excel* instead of *Lotus 1-2-3*, or maybe you had been eyeing up an *Interstate 31 Joystick Interface* rather than the Kempston variety. In truth many of these shops were just glorified **Computer Clubs**, and for any club to work it needs to have people who aren't members just as much as it needs to have those who are. Consequently, wandering in on a Saturday afternoon only to be greeted by a load of layabouts who were thumbing through books they hadn't actually bought whilst trying to determine through only the medium of furtive eye contact, which of them would serve you, was less than a welcoming experience.

Happily this kind of computer shop still lives on with most, if not all, of their eccentricities intact. Admittedly many have now broadened their range to encompass chipping mobile phones; however, it's nice to know that you can still find a place where you have to wait until the owner has finished his latest go of some bizarre Japanese game on the **Nintendo** Game Cube before he'll serve you.

## Conspiracy Theories
1981

Given that the type of person most drawn to a computer is like-ly to be inquisitive and possibly slightly anally retentive, it is of no surprise that conspiracy theories have found such a large and well-furnished home on the Internet. After all, what else do you need to start a good conspiracy theory other than an abili-ty to absorb lots of details and a propensity for asking annoying questions?

The ubiquity of half-baked theories on subjects as diverse as the assassination of John F Kennedy, and the real reason for bar codes (it's got something to do with Satan apparent-ly), has, in recent times, led to a conspiracy theory backlash as people have come to realise that the hundred or so differ-ent alternative explanations for the death of Princess Diana make, by the sheer volume alone, any one individual theory appear less plausible.

The computer industry itself is not immune to such theoriz-ing, and companies such as **Microsoft** are the subject of innu-merable hypotheses, some more plausible than others, but most featuring complex and Machiavellian motives at their heart. On a lighter note, some people still claim that NASA's original password to protect all of its computer data from **hackers** was 'spaceman'. For classic computer conspiracy the-ories though, the following 'unconfirmed rumour' that was submitted to American computer publication *Omni* magazine back in 1981 takes some beating; to whit: 'arcade games such as *Asteroids,* **Space Invaders** and *Tail Gunner* are programmed to record the initials of the highest scoring player. When you enter your initials, a photograph is secretly taken of you. The games are actually mechanisms for selecting, sorting and training slave labour for duty in **military** spacecraft and star bases. People who get good at these machines disappear under suspicious circumstances. You won't find my initials on one of those things no matter how good I get!'

## Dads
1980

Whilst the arrival into our lives of home computers has brought about many of the changes that the boffins and experts predicted (although we are still waiting for the holographic telly promised to us in the BBC play *The Flipside of Dominik Hide*), one of the most significant unforeseen developments has been how dads have receded from their once rightful position as family expert on technology.

Ever since dads were invented they have assumed mastery over all complex systems, be they patio doors or car phones. Indeed even home entertainment came under their governance, with the cabling up of the family record player to some ace amplifiers 'borrowed' from work one of their main functions. It was a dad too, who connected up your first ever video recorder, all the while muttering knowledgably about co-axial cables and the like. Even their den, office or garden shed was testament to their technical expertise with, at the very least, a Newton's cradle or some other frivolous office toy lying around.

As such, it was probably your dad who took responsibility for purchasing your family's first ever home computer – indeed he might have even bought it in kit form. However, after the reasonably straightforward business of connecting the thing up to the telly was over and the actual computer powered up, a strange thing started to happen. Somehow the internal logic of operating a computer wasn't as easy to grasp as, say, the combustion engine or a remote controlled model aeroplane. What's more, whilst dad struggled, the kids seemed to have an intuitive understanding of how to get a game to load and then, how to actually play it.

Initially your dad would try to reassume his once domi-nant position, and this would often take the form of inviting back friends from work to take a look at the new family acquisition. However, this led to the abjectly embarrassing situation of two dads fumbling around on a computer, neither able to get very far.

Today, it is a given that it is the kids who best understand computers. Somehow the complexities of window operated systems, icons and file types seem as much a part of their nat-ural world as gravity. For dads, their roles have fundamentally changed. No longer are they the family representative thumb-ing through the technology pages in the Sunday supplements, or taking a quick detour to the local electronics store whilst on a family shopping expedition. Still, at least it gives them more time to indulge in their favourite hobby: formulating offensive political and social views.

## The Domesday Project
## 1986

Back in the Eighties, it seemed that BBC employees were forev-er spending their time trying to dream up grand schemes and wheezes that involved computers. BBC TV producer Peter Armstrong masterminded the most audacious project off all. Realising that 1986 would mark the nine-hundredth anniver-sary of the original Domesday book, Armstrong decided that a new computerised version would make for an excellent BBC backed initiative.

The original book had constituted a comprehensive study of land and property carried out by William the Conqueror, and was commissioned for the purposes of determining how much extra tax he could squeeze out of his subjects. Happily for the peasants, old Will snuffed it before the project reached completion. Armstrong's intentions were far more hon-ourable, and what's more, would involve school kids doing a lot of the hard graft.

His plan involved dividing the United Kingdom into small rectangular areas of about twelve square kilometres in size. For each rectangle, a school within the designated area was assigned ownership and would gather together pertinent infor-mation relating to local events and everyday life. In total 14,000 schools were involved and the data recorded formed the basis of two laserdiscs (one focussing on the community and the other, titled National, dealing with issues such as leisure, work and society).

The end result looked suitably definitive and futuristic, but to actually acquire one you had to spend somewhere in the region of £4,000 for the Laser Disk player and BBC Master computer. This meant the Domesday Project was prohibitively expensive for a lot of schools and libraries. However, a few did pop up at events such as regional agricultural shows (where the BBC tent was often an oasis amidst a desert of farming machinery and demonstrations of olde style blacksmithery), and for those who managed to get to the front of the queue and grapple that trackball there were copious delights to be had.

The fact that the images weren't actually generated by the BBC Master (they came off the Laser disks) meant that the BBC could put together a really swish control interface. The com-munity disk, for example, opened up with a classy filmed sequence mixing from overhead shots of kids with clip boards to street maps and ultimately a shot of the whole United Kingdom. From here you could then click on any part of the map to access text, photos or more maps. The National Disc was even fancier, inviting you to select topics by taking a won-der round the 'Domesday Gallery'. From here you clicked onto an exhibit to open up a subject of your choice. This would often take you into pages of BBC Master text and even the occasional BBC Master generated graph, which was quite annoying, because all you really wanted to do was get to the bits where you could take a 'virtual' walk around a terraced house in Grimsby and take a look at a bedroom with classic Eighties diagonal striped wallpaper.

Although the Domesday Project was said to contain over 50,000 pictures and 25,000 maps, the prohibitive asking price meant that the project came to be considered a bit of a folly. However, recently there have been remnants of it turning up on the Internet, meaning that all the hard work put in to creating the project in the first place, perhaps some of it yours, has not gone to waste.

## Film and Television Tie-ins
### 1982

Computer game tie-ins have a long and largely undistinguished history. However, it all started off so promisingly. Midway's arcade version of **Tron** was the first game based on a movie license and it perfectly captured the film's look, right down to the circuit-lined cabinet and luminous **joystick**. The game itself consisted of four levels, the most memorable of which was Light Cycles. Playing it undeniably made you feel as if you were running around inside a computer with Jeff Bridges and Bruce Boxleitner, a senses-shattering experience if ever there was one.

Similarly **Atari**'s 1983 arcade version of Star Wars managed to successfully capture much of the spirit of the film, putting you right in the cockpit of a Tie-Fighter intent on blasting the Death Star into smithereens. Great **3-D** vector graphics, plus evocative snatches of speech from the film constituted a gaming experience that was far greater than the sum of its parts.

The trouble started when film spin-offs began appearing on home systems. Without the glitzy cabinets and really loud sound effects, not to mention half-decent graphics, the cinematic adrenalin rush that had translated so well to the amusement arcade was totally lost when played on a portable black and white telly with crappy speakers. In 1982, Atari rush-released a very poor version of *E.T.* for their 2600 system, and in many ways the die was cast: get the right licensing deal and forget about quality.

When the first computer game tie-ins started appearing on the UK market, back in the early Eighties, it was difficult not to feel a frisson of excitement that your latest hobby was becoming aligned with hit American television series such as *Blue Thunder*. However, we Brits took a more eccentric approach to computer tie-ins and programmes such as the quiz show *Blockbusters* were deemed worthy of a computer tie-in (released by Compusound for the **ZX Spectrum** in 1984 as the unlicensed *Blockbuster*).

Yet in the main, with Saturday night shows like the *The Fall Guy* and *Street Hawk* proving to be hits on our television screens, the mid-Eighties saw a concentration of games based on American action series. However, whether any of these were able to recreate the excitement of the source material is highly questionable. More successful was the Nifco version of *Hitchhiker's Guide to the Galaxy*, released in 1984. This text-based adventure worked so well because the appeal of the original version (which started out as a radio show before making the leap to television) was less reliant on stimulating visuals and more on comedic wordplay.

However, no lessons were learned by the computer games industry, and indeed they didn't need to be; film and television tie-ins proved consistently popular even though they were by and large rather ropey. Activision's *Ghostbusters* (also released in 1984) sold in excess of a quarter of a million copies, even though it involved little more than travelling around a maze trying to ensnare some ghosts. However, as with *Star Wars* before it, Activision put much stock in its inclusion of samples from the film. Unfortunately, whilst the speech in *Star Wars* had been perfectly decipherable, the samples in *Ghostbusters* on the ZX Spectrum sounded less like 'he slimed me', and more like a big dog barking.

Later titles carried on in this hit and miss vein, with some further bizarre tie-ins reaching our shelves such as DK'Tronics' *Minder* in 1985 (which featured a great photograph of Dennis Waterman and George Cole on the front cover each holding a drink aloft) and Tyne Soft's *SuperGran* in 1986 (based on the kids' television series of the same name).

In more recent years, film and television tie-ins have tended to focus on blockbusters. Given the huge costs involved in creating a computer game these days, this is inevitable. Besides, the sophistication of modern day gaming machines is such that the exploits of, say, *Spider-Man* can be created with the kind of fidelity that now makes parts of the game almost indistinguishable from the movie it is based on. Whilst this means that film tie-ins are at last beginning to realise their full potential, the downside is that the chances of software companies releasing idiosyncratic adaptations of less popular films or television programmes is increasingly remote, which is a shame as we would love to play a *Most Haunted* text-based **adventure game**, or frantically waggle our joystick in an attempt to stem a bleeding artery in *Holby City: You Are the Surgeon*.

## Film Versions of Computer Games 1993

If it is true that most computer games based on films have been pretty dire, then it should be noted that the traffic going the other way has been at least as bad, if not worse. Whilst the technical constraints of computer systems have often resulted in lacklustre and poorly realised computer versions of popular blockbusters, ironically it would seem that the ability to take a computer character and bring them to the big screen, fully realised and unconstrained by the meagre graphical capabilities of a **NES**, results in a product as equally flawed and unrepresentative of the source material.

The *Super Mario Brothers* film of 1993 is generally credited as the first live action Hollywood blockbuster based on a computer game. Featuring British actor Bob Hoskins in the title role, it attempts to take a number of the characters and scenarios from the *Super **Mario*** games and build a coherent plot around them. The problem is that that the likes of Yoshi and Princess Daisy were never designed to work within the framework of a proper narrative; they don't have any motivation or even emotions and so regardless of how authentic Bob Hoskins might look as the Italian plumber, the minute he starts emoting anger or frustration, the whole thing just jars. Besides we are used to Mario being someone under our control and not the filmmakers'.

It's not just the source material that handicaps such films, but a belief that if you can secure the right licence, the audience will come regardless of quality. Happily the relative commercial failure of feature films such as 1994's *Streetfighter* (which at least holds the distinction of being the only movie to feature the entirely odd combination of Jean-Claude Van Damme, Kylie Minogue and Simon Callow), 2001's *Final Fantasy: The Spirits Within* and 2005's *Alone in the Dark* demonstrates that the intended audience has the sense to stay at home and play the games themselves, rather than watch a professional actor turn in a far from convincing performance as Ken Masters.

## GamesMaster
### 1992

Undoubtedly the most successful TV show about computer games to date has been Channel 4's *GamesMaster*. Produced by

Hewland International, the programme was the brainchild of Jane Hewland, who recognised there was a gap in the market after becoming obsessed with her son's **NES** game *Duck Hunt*. Whilst it was initially a hard sell to persuade Channel 4 that there was an audience out there, when the series finally hit our screens it was an immediate ratings hit.

The format of the programme was reasonably straightforward, consisting of gameplaying challenges, reviews, the occasional feature and a regular tips item. Given that with the exception of ITV's *Bad Influence*, there was little else on our screens for computing fans to actually watch (at least until 1993 when Sky One began broadcasting *Games World*), then it might seem logical to conclude that *GamesMaster* succeeded almost by default. However, this is not the case. The series possessed a number of stylistic elements that particularly appealed to computer fans, including subversive humour inspired by television series such as *Blackadder* and *Red Dwarf*, and a pandering to computer gamers' seemingly limitless aesthetic obsession with post-apocalyptic landscapes. The inclusion of Patrick Moore as the titular GamesMaster gave the programme a suitably futuristic figurehead, and, more importantly, a mascot much in the mould of those found in the more irreverent computer mags.

Undoubtedly the highlights of each programme were the challenges. Here celebrities or, more often, members of the public, would attempt to collect fifty coins in two minutes on *Super Mario 3* on the **NES**, or get through stage one of level five on *Brat* for the **Amiga**. Initially, the contestants looked like they had just come from the Children's ITV **adventure game** show *Knightmare* stopping off to buy a biker jacket along the way. However, as the series progressed, *GamesMaster* was able to boast a more eclectic mix of contestants, including some that actually tried to be funny. For those who were successful at the various challenges the prize would be the 'GameMaster Golden Joystick', an ironic, if worthless, trophy that did little more then give host Dominik Diamond an opportunity for cheap double entendres.

Indeed Dominik was the lynchpin of the series, and consequently was much missed when after series two he decided to 'pursue other projects'. Although rumours circulated that Dominik had left in protest of *GamesMaster* signing up McDonalds as a sponsor, this may have been simply a story put about by computing fans, or indeed Dominik, to make him appear a bit hard. What isn't in question though, is that his temporary replacement Dexter Fletcher (previously best known to viewers as the insufferably smug Spike from the Children's ITV series *Press Gang*) wasn't at all suited to the programme. Aside from a moment at the beginning of series three in which Dexter held up Dominik's red jacket and made some comment about the previous fella not being able to take the heat anymore, Dexter was lumbered with an appalling script that made it apparent he knew absolutely nothing about computer games.

Dominik was lured back to present the remaining four series, but arguably by then *GamesMaster's* best years were behind it. In contrast to his series one and two persona, Dominik was a grumpy git and it seemed as if his return to the programme was an embarrassing admission that he couldn't 'make it' alone (rather like an *EastEnders'* actor forced to return to the soap when their hopes of a lead role in an ITV drama fails to materialize). Consequently, given that Dominik seemed to think the show was beneath him, it was very difficult for the viewer not to feel a bit like that too. Whilst we would still tune in, *GamesMaster* was no longer essential viewing, and by the time its final series aired in 1998, it was standard practice to complain about Dominik's endless 'type situation' one-liners. Still, given the programmes that have followed, you have to conclude that we didn't know when we had it so good.

## Hacking
### 1969

It's dark, all you can see is a glowing monitor screen and three kids furiously typing away. For a minute there are all manner of strange beeping noises and then the words 'initialising protocols' appear in big computery letters. The kid in the middle turns to his female colleague and gloats 'You see I knew they would have a back door. Now we're in!'

The above mini-scene typifies most people's preconception of what is commonly referred to as 'hacking'. However, the term doesn't actually mean what you think it does. 'Hacking' has its origins in model trains, whereby the process of altering the trains or tracks to make them perform better or differently was referred to as a 'hack'. Within the context of computing, a 'hacker' was someone who was highly proficient at **programming**, or able to adjust existing programs to make them perform functions that they weren't originally designed for.

The correct term for breaking into a computer system is apparently 'cracking' (and those who break into telephone exchanges are called 'phreaks'). However, for whatever reason, hacking has caught on as a general term to describe all of the above. The history of hacking and hackers stretches right back to the nineteenth century, when the first phreaks tampered with the nascent telephone system. The accepted origin of modern-day hacking took place in 1969, when students at the Massachusetts Institute of Technology began to adapt and improve on the source code of their multi-user operating systems.

Pretty soon, the opportunities for hacking into major public systems became apparent. One of the most bizarre examples occurred some time around 1972, when a chap called John Draper realised that a toy whistle he'd got out of a box of *Cap'n Crunch* breakfast cereal emitted a tone of 2,600 Hertz; precisely that which was required to switch his local phone system into service mode and thus allow him to make free calls.

Whilst Draper may or may not have taken advantage of his discovery, it is clear that in these early days hackers were largely a benign force who simply wanted to tweak existing programs or prove that they could find their way into supposedly impenetrable systems. Given that public access to computer networks was very limited during the Seventies, the main targets were generally telephone systems, with a number of American Yippies creating publications showing their colleagues ways to make free long-distance telephone calls.

Then in 1983 came the MGM/United Artists film **WarGames** and everything seemed to change. *WarGames* featured a well adjusted and likeable kid (played by Matthew Broderick) who inadvertently hacked into the Department of Defense's network and initiated a countdown to a thermonuclear strike. Given that at the time computers were just beginning to make major inroads into the domestic market, the film seemed remarkably well timed and, upon its release, summed up the hopes and fears of all computer users.

Crucially, it portrayed hacking as a glamorous occupation in which remote systems could be broken into simply by typing the words 'override password', whilst figures in authority watched helplessly, all the while harbouring a secret admiration for the mysterious and noble hacker.

Hacking was anything but easy; having to hook up an acoustic coupler to even get connected to the outside world was generally enough to deter all those except the most single-minded. However, the Eighties saw a massive upsurge, including the first real traces of hacking for financial or personal gain. Not long after the release of *WarGames*, it came to light that a group of hackers from Milwaukee broke into a cancer hospital's computer records and had inadvertently wiped a file whilst trying to hide their tracks.

By 1984, gangs of hackers had started to form, including the notorious Legion of Doom and their arch rivals the Masters of Deception. For a period in the Nineties these two gangs battled for supremacy by trying to pull off greater and greater telephone and computer hacks. Ultimately, it looked as if the Masters of Deception were victorious but it was to be a hollow victory as the defeated Legion of Doom simply grassed their adversaries in to the FBI.

This was all small fry though, compared to a computer heist that took place in 1988, which saw the National Bank of Chicago lose $70 million to hackers. This was followed in 1994 by a Russian hacker making off with $10 million of Citibank's money.

These days the image of the hacker has changed. No longer do we see them as bright and popular Matthew Broderick figures; instead they appear to be lonely teenagers, often based in Central or Eastern Europe. We don't think of them as inquisitive geniuses, but rather bitter obsessives, happy to wreak havoc just so they can prove their own existence. Thankfully, large organisations have learned some lessons, and whilst recent incursions into **Microsoft's** network have shown us that no system is ever wholly immune, we can safely assume that the old 'override password' command will no longer work on most modern-day servers.

## Interactive Movies
## 1983

There are certain ideas in the world of technology that seem to come around again and again, but never quite catch on. Executives analysing why their **virtual reality** games still aren't selling, conclude that the concept is ahead of its time. The same is true of interactive movies. Countless television items have come and gone postulating that in the near future all cinemas will be kitted out with keypads allowing the audience to influence the course of the on-screen story with the touch of a button, yet our multiplexes remain stubbornly keypad-less.

For some reason, interactive movies have become the Holy Grail of games creators and movie makers alike, even though we, the public, seem remarkably resistant to their charms.

In the Eighties, titles such as Cinematronics' **Dragon's Lair** and its follow up *Space Ace* (both released in 1983), paved the way for a new style of gaming that mixed computer and video images. However, it took ex-music journalist Tom Zito to marry actual filmed video footage (as opposed to animation) to computer games. Working in 1986 with ex-**Atari** head honcho Nolan Bushnell and toy company Hasbro, Zito and his team produced three trial titles, one of which was a four-minute interactive crime story that had taken three weeks to film at a reputed cost of $1.5 million. Bizarrely the footage was stored on specially modified VHS tapes that contained all of the data, (audio and video) required to run the game. All you needed to do was slot the tape into the custom-made games console (the Control-Vision) and you were away. The Control-Vision was supposed to be released in 1989, but spiralling production costs meant that Hasbro got cold feet and pulled out of the deal.

This was not the end of Zito's endeavour, and with footage for two complete games (*Sewer Shark* and **Night Trap**) in the can, he simply waited for the appropriate technology to come along. It would take only three years. **Sega** released an add-on for their hugely popular **Mega Drive** called the Mega CD. This basically achieved the same result as Hasbro's Control-Vision, but used CD-ROMs as the storage medium rather than VHS. Zito's games finally saw the light of day on this new system, but many concluded that they hadn't been worth the wait.

The insurmountable problem (as with *Space Ace* and *Dragon's Lair* before them) was that *Sewer Shark* and *Night Trap* were big on movies and short on interactivity. For example, *Sewer Shark* required you to do little more than shoot things and make the occasional decision as to which direction your craft should take.

Unfortunately, if you made a wrong turn there was no way back and you had to wait it out whilst your craft flew along the wrong tunnel for a bit before piling into a dead-end.

Zito's games were not the only entrants into the world of inter-active movies. Origin's science fiction based *Wing Commander* series has been praised and criticised in equal measure. Its 1994 release, *Wing Commander III: Heart of the Tiger*, marked the series' first dabble with interactive movie elements. It had a budget of $4 million and featured famous actors such as Malcolm McDowell and Mark Hamill; yet whilst many fans drooled over the prospect of flying out into space with the actor who had once played Luke Skywalker, the rest of us couldn't help find the acting and production values to be a little bit corny. Part of the issue is that whilst movie and television dramas consist of complex plots with multifaceted character motivation, a comput-er game provides you with straightforward objectives and absolutely nothing in terms of character development.

This incompatability between the two mediums has blighted most interactive movies, turning them into an unsatisfactory hybrid. For whatever reason we seem able to accept computer-generated characters dishing out exposition between levels, but whenever real people do it, it looks sort of silly.

# Piracy
## 1976

The point at which computer programs stopped being hard wired into the computers and started being stored externally (on tapes, cards etc) was also the point when computer piracy sprang into life. Given that most storage mediums were cheap to buy, all that was required to obtain the latest software release for free was to work out a way to access and copy the data from the original recording. When that storage medium happened to be a common or garden audio tape, this was no more difficult than sticking two cassettes into a half-way decent double tape deck. What could have been easier?

One of the first recorded cases of piracy occurred in the mid-Seventies when a young Bill Gates discovered that pirated copies of his MITS Altair BASIC were springing up hither and yon. This was small potatoes though; by the time tape **loading** computers of the early Eighties became commonplace, piracy was running rampant. Schoolyards in particular were a veritable marketplace with C90s containing the latest top ten games exchanging hands for a few quid. The twin gods of commerce and gaming were great levellers. The most unpopular kid in the class could become a much in-demand figure when it transpired that his dad had a number of connections to local retailers and – ergo – a ready-made supply of hooky games. Even the occasional teacher would sheepishly join the queue for a cheap, or free, version of *Chuckie Egg.*

For those who had no direct access to pirated games, there were obstacles to overcome if you wanted to become part of a chain. Given that many pirates weren't in the market for financial profit, but instead were seeking a reciprocal source of new games, the trick was to try and find two unconnected sources and trade one off against the other, all the while copying their copies for yourself. Unsurprisingly, vast and complex pirating rings sprung up in almost every school in the land.

The computer industry weren't altogether happy with their profits ending up in the pockets of some would-be junior racketeer, and attempted to take action. But software publishers were restricted in what they could do to make the process of copying the games harder. One of the main strategies was to introduce some kind of a password system so that when the game loaded the player would be prompted to type in a word that appeared on a certain page of the accompanying manual, or would have to align a sheet of coloured Perspex over the cassette inlay to be able to decipher a particular codeword printed in a bizarre colour.

But these were easy to overcome – manuals could be photocopied, or you could make a list of the first word that appeared in each paragraph, or if you had enough time on your hands you could simply load and re-load the original game until you had exhausted its selection of passwords (and had noted each one down of course). Upping the ante, software manufacturers then attempted to print manuals in blue ink. This was supposed to make them impossible to photocopy, but this was only partially successful. Indeed, using passwords derived from the manual came with its own perils for legitimate users. For example, the UK version of the manual might be slightly different from the USA one, meaning that when you were prompted to type in the first word of the fourth paragraph on page thirty-six, the word that you saw was different from the one the computer was expecting. Similarly, when games were released as part of a multi-title collection, all the manuals would be published in one book, so that when the computer asked you to look up a particular page number you could very well be staring at text that related to an entirely different game.

By the late Eighties, the predominant storage medium had changed from tape to floppy disk. On the surface this gave software manufacturers far more control. However, the hardened pirate didn't give up that easily. Legitimate software copying utilities such as *ACopy* for the **Atari ST** allowed you to copy games in discrete sections (referred to as 'tracks'). The pirates discovered that most games generally consisted of eighty or so tracks, with the bit of code that stopped the game copying successfully often contained on the last track. Therefore all you had to do was copy the first seventy-nine tracks, miss out the last one and you would end up with a fully functioning copy, minus that irritating anti-piracy protection. Nonetheless, the arrival of floppy disks saw the pirating scene move out of the schoolyard and down the road to the local Sunday market. Here makeshift stalls would be set up to sell hooky copies of the latest games, complete with badly photocopied covers (or if this was a professional pirating outlet then you would get badly photocopied *colour* covers). The pirates next innovation was to introduce a process called compressing which meant multiple games could be copied to one disk. These disks would boot up to a front screen proclaiming in loud letters 'hacked by the Happy Hacker' or some other moniker, and would present you with a menu of games. The chosen title would decompress before your very eyes (in a process that looked a lot like a **ZX Spectrum loading** sequence) before starting up.

Although such disks could be very tempting, there were negative repercussions to piracy, of which the most significant was that the games became much less fun to play. Given that you had to expend little in terms of financial outlay or effort to procure them, they rapidly lost much of their appeal (particularly when over time you acquired a massive backlog of titles, each of which would command your attention for just a few minutes before you moved on to the next).

## Role-playing
## 1972

At most schools in the Eighties and Nineties there would be a small gang of slightly smelly bookish boys that would huddle together conspiratorially in the playground, common room, or back of the Physics class. Their discussions seemed impregnable and potentially nonsensical with terms like 'a sixty-six critical fatality' and 'D10' bandied around. Every now and then a kindly girl with thoughts of trying to integrate these boys into the wider school society would ask them why they talked so much, only to be greeted with a response along the lines of 'you've only got one world to talk about, we've got several'; before the respondent deftly turned on his heels and re-entered an obviously heated debate about the relative skill sets of a level five wizard, versus a level seven ranger.

As computer and video gaming has grown in popularity over the years, it is inevitable that it would suck in the odd nearby sub-culture during its journey towards mass mainstream acceptance. Whilst the world at large was learning to let *Pong* into their lives, a group of American tabletop strategy gamers were devising a new form of entertainment that relied less on little model figures strewn across a dining table lightly decorated to resemble a Tolkein inspired battleground, and more on being able to create a gaming world that existed purely in your imagination, fed by a nominated rule keeper – the Dungeon Master.

For those who have never partaken in a spot of *Dungeons & Dragons* or one of the myriad role-playing games available on the market, it is extremely difficult to understand how a sensible game can be constructed simply out of a group of people sitting around a table listening to an account of a fictional storyline. Yet with the help of a few funny looking dice, a system of rules that govern imaginary actions within an imaginary world, plus the possession of a sheet of paper that outlines the attributes of each player's chosen character, it is actually possible to fashion a working game out of these less than inspiring constituent parts.

Without doubt, the success of a role-playing game is largely dependent on the Dungeon Master's ability to convey a decent sense of the world in which you are playing. Visual aids such as maps and diagrams can help conjure up a more tangible image of the inn your characters are supposed to be supping in, and so it is inevitable that, down the years, Dungeon Masters have increasingly turned to computer-generated images to aid their stories.

Many of the most significant writers of computer **adventure games** (such as Richard Garriott, author of the *Ultima* series) actually got into **programming** via a desire to recreate their role-playing experiences on the humble home computer. Unsurprisingly, there exists a whole load of games that explicitly utilise the mechanics of 'paper-based' role-playing (such as turn-based moves and numerically defined character attributes). However, even in the wider world of computer gaming it is possible to detect the values and principles of role-playing translated to the small screen. The **first-person shooter** genre, with its focus on exploration and enhancement of your playing character's abilities or arsenal, has simply dispensed with much of the artifice that was required to run a traditional role-playing game whilst retaining the same broad kind of gaming objectives.

So it is clear that we owe those strange adolescent, bespectacled schoolyard coteries a debt of gratitude, for it is they that (albeit sometimes indirectly) first galvanised the imaginations of the designers of some of our most favourite and fiendish computer games. But you still wouldn't want to stand to close to them, mind.

## Sex
1982

Sexual content might be a contentious issue in most entertainment mediums, but it is probably fair to say that when it rears its head in computer games it causes a particular storm, almost as if Dennis the Menace has just flopped his penis out in an edition of the *Beano*. This is, of course, because lots of people still consider computer games to be a medium solely for children and therefore a strictly no-go area when it comes to anything with even the vaguest of adult content.

Ironically, a lot of the early sexually explicit computer games seemed to appeal only to kids. Be it a game passed around the playground containing a crude version of a pair of breasts as visualised on the **Commodore 64,** or various untrue rumours regarding what kind of rumpo you could get up to in Sierra's

*Leisure Suit Larry* (released for the **PC** back in 1987). The major drawback that any supposedly 'sexy' game had to overcome in the early days was the extremely limited graphical prowess of the machines on which they were meant to run. Unsurprisingly, sexual content was therefore usually confined to a subsidiary role (such as in the 1982 Atari 2600 game *Custer's Revenge* wherein the eponymous character had to be guided through a volley of arrows before being 'awarded' with the opportunity to rape a native American girl tied to a pole). Really there was very little on the screen to get your rocks off to.

As computers became more powerful, this situation began to change, and every now and then some lad in computer class would boastfully proclaim that they had got hold of something hot. Usually this would be a rather weak version of *Strip Poker* in which a successful hand would result in the computer displaying a reasonable illustration of a women in varying stages of undress. Of course, when you eventually got to the point where you won enough hands to cause this fictional, pixellated lady to discard her final layer of clothing, the game would literally draw a discrete veil over the one image that had you had waded through the entire thing to see.

Indeed a number of games displayed similar levels of coyness. Infocom's 1986 *Leather Goddesses of Phobos* offered the player three levels of naughtiness: 'tame, suggestive and lewd', with the latter apparently including the 'seven words you can't say on television'. However, whether such games were explicit or merely tantalising, they were pretty much all to a man, extremely tedious or badly written and expected to sell purely on the back of their sexual content.

At least titles such as *MacPlaymate* (released for the **Apple Mac** in 1986 and featuring a lady lying prostrate that, via the mouse cursor, you were able to 'pleasure') didn't try and strap on a superfluous, poorly written game. Somehow it seemed more commendable when developers tried to create a computer sex game that at least attempted to focus the interactive element on the bit of the game that people actually wanted to get involved in.

Games are not the only place on a computer where you can find sexually explicit content. Aside from being flooded with good old-fashioned pornography, the Internet is also awash with **chat rooms** in which loveless or bored individuals can hook up and partake in 'dirty talk' with complete strangers. In the early Nineties, many speculated that in just a few short years the technology would exist to manufacture strap-on electronic sex toys that could be controlled by a remote user accessing your computer. This concept – known rather quaintly as 'teledildonics' – created much excitement amongst cybersex groups who were aroused at the prospect of being able to remotely rub up strangers whilst chatting to them over the Internet in a sexy way. Indeed one pundit went so far as to predict that there would be 'sanitary public sexual arcades games, resulting in winning orgasms, by the year 2000'. However, at the time of writing, the concept remains unrealised outside the realms of cheap science-fiction porno films.

## Social Acceptability
1994

Today it is acceptable to reminisce about hours spent bunking off school to play computer games all about bunking off school (*Skool Daze*). Similarly, if you tell your team leader that the reason you are late into work is that you and your mates 'got wasted and played **PlayStation** all night', then the poor underpaid fellow will probably give you a hearty slap on the back before cheerily telling you that 'seriously, try not to be late again, man, because the supervisor is giving me major evils about your timekeeping.'

Computers, and in particular home consoles, have today attained a level of popularity and social acceptability that they have never previously enjoyed. Although machines such as the

**ZX Spectrum** or **SNES** were widely played in the UK during the Eighties and Nineties, the common perception was that they were really for kids, and whilst playing on them was good for a laugh, it was also a bit sad.

Arguably this perception started to change in the early Nineties when **Sega** marketed their **Mega Drive** at teenagers. Through a combination of deliberately wacky, amusing and slightly dangerous ads, plus a machine that looked a little bit cool, the credibility barriers began to erode. The arrival on the scene in 1994 of Sony only served to break down these barriers further. Not only did they push their marketing even harder at this new older generation, but the PlayStation was sophisticated enough to be able to create on-screen sounds and visuals that closely reflected the interests of this new demographic. In particular, Psygnosis' 1995 release *wipEout* came with superb graphics, cool-as-you-like design and, most importantly, a kick-ass ultra-hip soundtrack (not to mention the self-consciously poseur lower case *w* and upper case *e* in the game's title). Indeed, for its time, *wipEout* was the least embarrassing computer game ever made.

Besides, the PlayStation came with one seriously cool 'get out of jail' card. If your hip mates started dissing you for owning a computer, then all you needed to do was to bung a CD into the machine and let it fire up its cool visualiser software (which translated sound into trippy on-screen visuals) and watch your street cred return.

## Typing-in programs
## 1960

The good – no – great news on Christmas day was that you were presented with a fantastic new home computer that you knew would obliterate boredom forever. The bad news was that rather than buy you some ace games to play on it, your parents instead handed you a thick, ring-bound (it was always ring-bound) book featuring an anonymous photograph of a bit of sky. If you were a Sinclair kid then more often than not the name Tim Hartnell would appear on the cover, but regardless of the author, the same feeling of dread would consume you: your parents were expecting you to type in your own games from this bloody great big book.

Typing-in programs was considered a popular pursuit in the early Eighties (indeed by 1985 the aforementioned Hartnell had published over fifty books on computing), but only by those who didn't have to do it. The basic drawbacks were legion; from a cursory flick through whatever book you had been lumbered with, it became apparent that the majority of the games were either extremely disappointing versions of popular arcade classics, or worse still, computerized versions of dull card games. **Adventure games** were also a big disappointment, as in the process of typing them in, all of the various elements of the game became apparent to you, and so any twists and turns in the plot were completely blown.

However, it was not just the quality of the program that one had to question, but the quality of the transcription of the program in the first place. Although program listings were a constant fixture of early Eighties **computer magazines**, so too were corrections published in the following issue. Indeed certain magazines went so far as to include programs that they knew wouldn't actually work. Of course, the frustration was further exacerbated by the fact that you had no **programming** knowledge of your own, and so had no idea where to start debugging, save for meticulously going back through line-by-line, desperately searching for typos.

On the odd occasion you were successfully able to transcribe the four pages of commands required to run a perfunctory version of the 'hit TV series' *Play Your Cards Right*, the initial euphoria at actually making the damn thing work had to fight hard against the inevitable feeling that the end result had been hardly worth the effort. Given it was almost tea-time you were going to have to turn the computer off anyway, thus wiping the last four hours hard work. God, it was depressing.

## Video Game Industry Crash 1982

One computer news story that received bemused and slightly amused TV coverage was the great video games crash of the mid-Eighties. As with most market crashes before and since (the 'dot-com bubble burst' springs to mind here), the crash itself was characterized by commentators knocking around phrases such as 'get rich quick scheme' with undisguised glee. America was hit far harder than the UK, and this only served to amuse British based observers even more.

Whilst the first real indications of a downturn did not become apparent until 1983 (during which the **amusement arcade** market in the USA fell by fifteen per cent), the seeds were sown the previous year when **Atari** ended up with a massive surplus of unsold *E.T.* and *Pac-Man* cartridges thanks to creating a rubbish game and too many cartridges of a moderately good one, respectively. Things got worse in December 1982, when Atari announced they were only expecting a fifteen per cent increase in sales for the last three months of the year as opposed to the fifty per cent they had previously reported.

It wasn't only Atari who was suffering. Other businesses had muscled in on the market, but in so doing had flooded the shops with far too many products. As a result, the smaller companies went out of business and their products became heavily discounted, meaning that those who remained now had to compete against lower price points. Companies such as Mattel (who had released the **IntelliVision** home console in 1980) abandoned the market entirely, even though 1983 saw their highest sales.

Over in the UK, the downturn wasn't without impact. Software publishers Imagine were 'hoist by their own petard' when forecasting mega sales in 1983, they decided to book the services of the software industry's biggest tape duplicating firm for the entire year. The idea was that not only would they be able to get loads of their games onto the shelves, but, more importantly (and certainly more cunningly), their competitors wouldn't. However, this ruse backfired spectacularly when sales proved sluggish, and Imagine were left with no option but to sell off their titles at cut prices.

Times remained hard for the industry for a couple of years, and it wasn't really until **Nintendo** came on the scene in 1985 that things began to turn around. Indeed, in the deepest darkest moments of the recession, industry commentators genuinely believed that computer games, like a passing fad, would soon be a thing of the past.

## Violence
### 1976

Computer games can be damn frustrating. Take Rockstar Games' 2004 title *Grand Theft Auto: San Andreas*; sometimes you are required to drive for miles to get to the right location, only for you to accidentally run someone over when you are almost there and attract the unwelcome attention of the police, leading ultimately to the failure of your mission. The aggravation of knowing you are going to have to start all over again is enough to make anyone blast a few caps into some innocent bystanders, or nick a car and see how many pedestrians you can run over before you get busted. Well isn't it?

The issue of violence in popular media in general is contentious, unresolved and ever present, but it is particularly thorny with regard to computer games. First of all, there is still a large section of the population who view computer games as a kids' medium, meaning that parents will blissfully purchase an '18' rated title for their little Johnny and then later baulk when they wander into his bedroom with a glass of pop and a plate of biscuits, only to witness some unspeakable act of carnage taking place on screen. Secondly, there is the wider question of whether the fact that computer games are an interactive medium means their influence is stronger than, say, television or comics. That the army uses computer simulations in order to get soldiers used to battle conditions, suggests that the **military**, at least, believes that violent computer games can desensitize your attitude towards real life violence.

In the early years of computer gaming, it took something pretty special to attract widespread public concern. Exidy Games' 1976 title **Death Race** managed to cause outrage because the game's objective was to run people over; however, titles such as **Space Invaders** or Namco's 1979 **shoot 'em up** *Galaxian*, were deemed to be perfectly acceptable even though the objective of both games was to annihilate as many of the enemy as possible.

The issue here was to do with representations of violence that could be equated with the real world. So although blasting the crap out of aliens was acceptable, particularly if they were in spaceships (and as such not even represented on-screen as living creatures), picking off 'real people' in a manner that could in some way be replicated was a no-no (although in the case of *Death Race* you would have to question how the impressionable youth would have been able to get behind the steering wheel of a real-life car in the first place, let alone know how to drive it sufficiently well to aim it at an innocent bystander).

Yet some games featuring human beings as cannon fodder (such as Muse's 1981 title *Castle Wolfenstein*), escaped criticism. This was because the graphics were so basic people felt a bit silly complaining about a game in which you ran around shooting yellow Lego men with swastikas on their chests. Clearly for a violent game to attract real controversy it had to look suitably realistic.

It was no surprise then, that in the early Nineties, games such as **Mortal Kombat** (which employed photo-realistic graphics) provoked far more hullaballoo than **Street Fighter II** – even though both were about duffing up your opponent. However, whilst the odd **beat 'em up** might have stirred a bit of moral panic, it is undoubtedly the **first-person shooter** genre (and its more recent third-person offshoots) that have provoked the most vociferous debates. This is presumably because not only do such games feature realistic graphics, but they put the player in a position where they are looking through the eyes of a marauding, gun toting killer. The concern regarding titles such as 3-D Realm's 1996 *Duke Nukem 3-D* is that not only do they make players more amenable towards violence but they actually provide training on how to kill. Indeed in 1997, American school child Michael Carneal opened fire on a school prayer group and managed to hit eight children with just eight shots (a formidable accuracy rate). When it was discovered that he was an avid player of first-person shooters, the conclusion was drawn that playing such games had honed his shooting skills far beyond those of any trained police officer.

Since 1994, the computer gaming industry has become increasingly self-regulating with bodies such as the Entertainment Software Ratings Board determining which titles should be on sale to kids. This hasn't stopped controversial games being released though. Indeed the inclusion of an 18 certificate has allowed publishers to sidestep some of the furore and release openly violent games safe in the knowledge that they will only be targeted at an adult market. One of the most violent games to date is Ripcord Games' *Postal*. Initially released for the **Apple Mac** in 1995, and then for the **PC** in 1997, the game cast you in the role of a deranged lunatic whose main objective is to kill as many police officers (and anybody else who happens to wander into the crossfire) as possible. It was immediately banned in ten countries and kicked up a massive storm of protest; however, for those who actually played it, the main problem was that it wasn't really all that good.

Whether violent computer games do actually inspire real life violence is ultimately unanswerable. However, the debate that rages seems to be based just as much on a natural suspicion of a new entertainment medium, as it does on empirical evidence demonstrating cause and effect. The big question is if someone is insane enough to go out and start killing people, isn't it just a matter of time before something (be it a violent computer game, a brutal scene in a movie or simply a spell of bad weather) triggers their destructive urge?

## WarGames
## 1983

Released the year after Disney's *Tron*, MGM/United Artists' WarGames trod similar ground insomuch as it featured a computer running amok (were there ever any films featuring computers in which that wasn't the case?) However, whereas the Disney film drew heavily upon the iconography of video games, WarGames' inspiration was drawn from the then hazy public perception of **hacking**.

The film featured a school kid's unintentional hacking of a war computer, the resultant accidental initiation of a nuclear strike, the obligatory race against time to stop it, and the compulsory final scene in which the computer controlled countdown is only halted by the imparting of a nugget of wisdom from man to machine (in this case that a nuclear war is unwinnable).

Although an entertaining and gripping film in its own right, many of the clichés and stereotypes that defined the mass media's perception of computing were either established in

*WarGames*, or at the very least, reinforced. In particular, the notion that all computers could be hacked into via a 'back door' code (in this case neatly explained away as a pass code set up by the developer to sidestep any additional security that might have been added once the computer had been set up) would serve espionage films of the future in good stead, allowing the most impenetrable computer security system to be breached in a way that sounded vaguely plausible to those ignorant of how such matters actually work in the real world.

Similarly archetypal was the scene in which the film's young hero David Lightman (played by Matthew Broderick) hacked into the school's computer and changed his grades. Other things we learned from *WarGames* were that everyone's top secret password is the name of a (preferably deceased) loved one, and that should you come across a top secret computer you are given an infinite number of attempts to break in. Whilst nitpicking, one might also make mention of the film's super computer – WOPR (War Operation Planned Response) which looked suitably large and impressive (cue loads of superfluous LEDs), and furthermore recognised the first dramatic principle of computers in films: namely that they must fuse and catch fire whenever attempting to resolve an illogical command.

Still, it was a freewheeling, roller coaster of a film, and one that glamorised the hitherto secretive world of the hacker. You could also contend that its anti-nuclear message influenced the eventual demise of the cold war; after all if the Joshua program could understand that when it came to a nuclear strike 'the only winning move is not to play', then surely we could too. Now, how about a nice game of chess?

# The Machines

It would seem that many historical figures jostle for the title of Inventor of the Computer. Not only are there lots of names in the frame, but there is also no real consensus on what a computer actually is. Some suggest that a machine that is able to carry out a calculation is a computer, but others would contest (quite reasonably, you would think) that it isn't – it's just a calculator. A popular definition would have it that a computer is a device that stores a program in the same form as the data it produces when the program is run. Some also say that a computer is a device that can be used to solve a variety of logic problems. Therefore machines that can only be used to solve one type of problem are not 'real' computers either. Are you keeping up with this?

If you follow this line of reasoning, then the works of such famous thinkers as Pascal and Babbage (whose greatest legacy isn't that the big computer on TV's *Family Fortunes* was named after him) are to be disregarded, and we are left trying to sift through a glut of mechanical and electronic devices created during, and after, the Second World War.

Whilst he might never have had a game show computer named after him, mathematician and ace code-breaker Alan Turing is undoubtedly a significant figure in the development of the computer. His 1936 paper 'On Computable Numbers with an Application to the *Entscheidungsproblem*' addressed theoretically how a computing machine might be able to solve an array of logical problems simply by having the ability to change the data in the program that it was being fed. During the war, Turing's huge intelligence was focussed on constructing machines that could decipher intercepted coded German messages. As the complexity of the German codes grew, Turing and his colleagues were required to develop increasingly sophisticated code-breaking machines, leading ultimately to the creation of a huge 1,500 valve machine called Colossus. Whilst this could read up to 5,000 characters per second, later refinements boosted this to in excess of 25,000; and although Colossus proved remarkably effective at breaking German ciphers, it was also shown to be able to tackle other types of arithmetical and logical problems, providing they could be expressed using Boolean logic (an algebraic form in which values are defined as either true or false and then manipulated using certain statements).

Moving on a few years, and arguably the first commercially available computer was J Presper Eckert and John Mauchly's UNIVAC I (Universal Automatic Computer). Weighing in at an immodest thirteen tonnes, the original model was acquired by the United States Census Bureau in 1951. UNIVAC I's greatest hour came the following year when US TV station CBS used it to correctly predict Eisenhower would win the upcoming presidential election, even though most political pundits thought otherwise. Although a few UNIVAC I computers were sold, it was clear that the immense size and cost meant it was prohibitively expensive to all but the largest of organisations. The invention in 1958 of the integrated circuit (or silicon chip as we know it) paved the way for a new company called Intel to release the first commercially available microprocessor in 1971.

Measuring just a few centimetres, this little device had as much computational power as the computers of 3,000 cubic foot in size constructed just twenty-five years earlier. Intel's 4004 microprocessor was followed by the 8008. This microprocessor is of particular significance as it was used in what many regard as the first ever real personal computer.

Just as there is fierce debate surrounding the identity of the inventor of the computer, many machines jostle for the title of the first ever personal computer. Although some would claim that this should be bestowed upon Edmund C Berkley's Simon (for which the plans on how to build were published in the American journal *Radio Electronics* during the course of 1950 and 1951), most would agree that the first personal computer in the modern sense of the word was the MITS Altair. This chunky bit of hardware (that looked rather like a modern day computer server) was released in 1976 and named after a planet from an episode of *Star Trek*. It could be purchased ready-made for just $498, but didn't come with a keyboard or a mouse; users programmed it by simply flipping switches on the front panel and watching the LEDs light up in response to the commands. Primitive though this sounds, it appealed to future **Microsoft** founder Bill Gates, who, along with colleague Paul Allen, created the computer language BASIC 2.0 on the Altair – the first ever Microsoft product.

The home computer age had begun.

## Acorn Archimedes
1987

There were certain home computers that – although we might have been aware of their existence – seemed beyond the reach of you or me, not because they were particularly expensive, but because they were somehow too mature to be part of a computer owning lineage that included a **Binatone** and a **Commodore 64**. The Acorn Archimedes was just such a computer.

Unlike your **ZX Spectrum**s or **Amiga**s, you never saw an Archimedes in your local WH Smith bundled up with an enticing twelve game Starter Pack. If you wanted to check one out then you had to track down a proper, dedicated **computer shop** run by people who looked like they still played with their Lego Technic sets. As a result, the Acorn Archimedes attained an aura of exclusivity and superiority over the standard high-street offerings.

Perhaps it was the Archimedes' affiliation with the BBC that marked it out for 'specialist computer shops only' (that funny little BBC owl logo had, by the late Eighties, pretty much become a watermark for spod products). Either that or the Welcome Disc which consisted of a painting program, a font designer, a floating point emulator and absolutely nothing of any fun. Everything about the Archimedes seemed to be telling the casual home computer owner to bugger off and only come back once you had, 'boned up on podules'.

Well, not quite everything. There must have been something about the 'Archie' (every home computer required a friendly nickname and this was the best Acorn could come up with) that made it stick in the memory, and like so many home computers before (and after), the Archimedes' saving grace was a **killer app**. This was Superior Software's 1987 title *Zarch*, written by David Braben, one half of the computing powerhouse behind *Elite* – the spidery looking, massively popular space trading game.

Although *Zarch* consisted of little more than flying a triangular space ship over an undulating patchwork quilt landscape, it was a minor sensation, principally because it was one of the first home computer games to feature what many people referred to as 'solid **3-D**' graphics. Previously, objects in 3-D games were wire frame only. This meant that when TIE fighters appeared in the *Star Wars* arcade game all you actually saw were their skeletons – the upside to this was that regardless of how many came at you they were never able to spoil your view of the beautiful starry night behind them; the downside, of course, was that whilst you were busy admiring the various constellations the TIE fighters were busy killing you.

*Zarch*'s smooth graphics and realistic gravitational physics did look and feel fantastic, and the icing on the cake was the inclusion of a shadow cast by the ship over the rolling land-scape, which at the time seemed like a particularly audacious innovation. All this was enough to earn *Zarch* universal plaudits (with *ACE* magazine awarding it the then all-time, and very pre-cise, record score of 979 out of 1000). The title went on to become the Archimedes' biggest seller.

But what of the Archimedes? Well, whilst the system was undoubtedly more powerful than the **Atari ST** or Amiga, it found little mainstream appeal and was largely confined to the classroom. Sadly, it was all but blasted into extinction when teachers across the land began to hanker after **Apple Macs** (peculiarly popular in Scottish schools in the early Nineties) and those new-fangled **PCs** that boasted the term 'multimedia' and came complete with that Windows program.

## Amiga 500
### 1987

The genesis of the Amiga 500 is a little convoluted. Amiga actu-ally started out as a small and struggling microcomputer man-ufacturer based in California. In 1983 it is believed that **Atari,** who were keen on Amiga's research into a new computer nick-named 'Lorraine', almost bought the company outright. However, the following year, Commodore stepped in and snapped it up, in the process repaying a $500,000 loan that Atari had made to keep Amiga afloat.

Second to market after the **Atari ST**, just like the **C64** before it, Commodore made life hard for themselves by being both a little off the pace and more expensive than the opposition. They had also initially focused the Amiga 1000 (the immediate predecessor of the 500) at the business end of the market even though just a few years earlier, the phenomenal success of the Commodore 64 had shown them that the home market was ripe for the picking.

The launch of the Amiga 500 was as a direct result of the beating that the Amiga 1000 was receiving at the hands of the aforementioned Atari ST. Whilst the A1000 was technically superior to the ST, many of the games that ran on it were Atari ports, and given that it cost £1,500, compared to the ST's £600, it was no surprise that the public were choosing the Atari option. In addition, the A1000, with its separate keyboard and base unit was far bulkier than the all-in-one ST. The Amiga 500 solved all of these problems, and with a confident and well-planned launch it began to claim a substantial portion of the 16-bit market, forcing Atari to offer thirty-game bundle deals with the ST. In fact, things got so fierce that in August 1989 the formerly peaceable *ST Amiga Format* magazine announced a split to allow devoted Amiga and ST fans to focus on their respective machines without having to endure any mention of their deadly rival.

The Amiga 500, with its superior capabilities went on to sell a million units in the UK, making great play of its versatility as both a games machine and a serious business tool. Sold with its own **software bundles** (such as the package launched in 1992 featuring *Deluxe Paint 3*, **Lemmings**, *The Simpsons* and *Captain*

*Planet*), long-term success for both the Amiga and Commodore looked assured. However, in 1990, Commodore tried to break into the consumer device market with the launch of the CDTV. Promoted as a next generation video recorder rather than a computer, the CDTV confused everyone and marked a down-turn in Commodore's fortunes that by 1994, with the help of 1993's equally doomed CD32, would prove to be terminal.

## Amstrad CPC-464
## 1984

The prime directive that drove Amstrad's entrée into the world of home computing was to construct a computer that looked 'proper' (as opposed to the petit and rather slim line **ZX Spectrum** which somehow never looked completely legit). As a result the Amstrad CPC-464 certainly looked the part: it had a chunky keyboard that contained a built in tape deck, something that neither of the 'big two' (i.e. the Spectrum and **Commodore 64**) could boast, and its own proper monitor, again an innova-tion compared to its rivals. Actually, there was a choice of mon-itors: the expensive one that gave you full colour images, and a cheaper monochrome version that was the shade of green you previously only found on serious, grown-up computers.

Yet for all its aesthetic legitimacy, the Amstrad CPC-464 did carry with it something of a stigma. Due to having been released a whole two years after the 'big two', ownership of a CPC-464 was an obvious admission of being a late entrant into the com-puter scene, and as anyone will tell you, getting into a scene after it has become popular is one of the most heinous crimes of all. As such, kids who were (un)lucky enough to own one would often keep quiet about the fact. However, for those who dared enter the protracted and often rather vicious playground **system rivalry** skirmishes, beyond the obvious advantages of the CPC-464's all-in-one design, it was difficult to construct a clear-cut case as to why your rather pricier machine was any better than the big two. The most convincing argument that you could make in favour of the CPC-464 was that its graphics were more colourful than the Spectrum's and less blocky than the Commodore 64's. On the minus side, it was very easy to take umbrage at a computer that required you to shell out extra for its own custom telly screen. Indeed for some people the fact that the CPC-464 wouldn't work on your television was reason enough to dismiss it out of hand.

Unsurprisingly, the CPC-464 failed to break the mass market and would forever play second fiddle. Tellingly, the year after it was launched, the next generation of computers, the much vaunted '16-bit machines', were starting to hit the shops. For those who had invested in a home computer in the early years of the Eighties there was no reason to purchase the CPC-464 when it was obvious that in a couple of years time there would be far more desirable computers available. However, that was just in the UK – in the rest of Europe it was a different story and Amstrad shifted thousands of both the CPC-464 and its successor the CPC-664 (which was just like the CPC-464 except with a floppy disk drive).

## Apple
1976

For our purposes, Apple plays a largely peripheral role. You sort of knew the company existed and that they made computers but largely they did their things and you did yours. Founded in 1976 by Steve Jobs and Steve Wozniak, they first came to prominence thanks to the 1984 Ridley Scott directed advert (featuring a female athlete chucking a hammer at a big Orwellian screen). This campaign launched Apple's most important range of computers – the **Macintosh**. The '**Apple Mac**' was to become synonymous with computer savvy folks of an artistic disposition (particularly designers) and would provoke the longest running **system rivalry** spat in the history of computing as Apple Mac owners took the 'Betamax' position (i.e. better technology but less popular) to the **PC**'s 'VHS'. Apple (or at least its supporters) still affect a haughty demeanour, but these days an Applephile is more likely to be heard banging on about how the shuffle mode on their iPod has literally changed their lives.

## Apple Mac
## 1984

If your GP tapped you on the knee with an Apple Mac you would likely spontaneously yell 'DTP' before kicking him in the head. Yes, over the years, the Mac has become synonymous with desktop publishing (it was Apple chief Paul Brainerd who first coined the term back in 1985). Yet from a historical perspective the Apple Macintosh is almost without parallel in terms of its influence on the modern day home computer. It is very strange now to think that in the same month **Apple** were unveiling their newest bit of kit (named after a type of apple, apparently), Clive Sinclair was launching the now long-forgotten Sinclair **QL**.

Heralded with a fanfare of publicity including the historic Ridley Scott commercial (shown once during the Superbowl and then not again officially for twenty years), the Apple Mac (as it is universally referred to) was, all told, a bit of a raging success, and whilst its influence on the **ZX Spectrum** and **Nintendo** loving masses might not have been immediately apparent, it was responsible for introducing a number of **peripherals** and computing concepts that we come face-to-face with every time we sit in front of a **PC** to forlornly check our Friends Reunited account.

The Apple Mac's chief evolutionary contribution was the inclusion of what is known in the business as a GUIOS (Graphical User Interface Operating System). To you and me this is basically the stuff we see, the desktop, when we first boot up our PC. Although the Mac wasn't the first computer to have a GUIOS (indeed the Apple Lisa, released in 1983, was the first business computer to have a GUIOS and a mouse, and also introduced the world to the trashcan as a handy means of disposing of unwanted files) it was the first *affordable* computer to have one.

If this wasn't enough to retrospectively earmark the Mac for posterity, it was also blessed with arrow keys and a numeric keypad (or at least the Macs produced from 1986 onwards were), function keys (1987 onwards) and the ability to run more than one program at a time (again from 1987 onwards).

Unfortunately the Mac wasn't so good when it came to games (apparently Apple deemed it a 'serious' machine) and as a consequence, it didn't really register for quite some time on the average British computer user who was too busy expending energy on being hugely disappointed with the aforementioned Sinclair QL to notice anyway.

## Atari
### 1972

Computer pundits often say things like 'if you say the words 'computers' or 'arcade games' to the average man in the street they instantly think of **Nintendo** or **PlayStation**'. However, this is simply not true. Assuming the average man you meet is 25 year of age or older (which sounds like a good age for an average man), then somewhere buried deep in his heart he knows that all of the interactive digital entertainment medium can be summed up in one word – Atari. Admittedly these days, that famous Atari logo is more often spotted on T-shirts being worn by nostalgists than actual games systems, but once Atari stood as mighty an empire as the Romans themselves.

Founded in America in 1972 by Nolan Bushnell, for a while it was going to be called 'Syzygy' (which means the straight line configuration of three celestial bodies), before Bushnell decided to opt for a Japanese word for 'checkmate' instead. In many respects, Atari invented the coin-operated arcade video with early titles such as *Pong* spreading like wildfire. Although in the States the growth and success of Atari was palpable and measurable, over here it felt somehow like an attack on our subconscious; we weren't quite sure what it was or how it had got into our brains. It was as if Atari had somehow entered our drinking water. Like Scalectrix, Hoover, or Transformers it transcended being simply a brand name, and became a synonym for arcade games and computers, such that your dad would ask you whether you were going upstairs to 'play on your Atari' even though he knew it was a **Binatone** (or at least he should have as it was him who bought it for you in the first place).

And whilst now it is reasonable to expect the average man in the street to know that *Sonic The Hedgehog* is the creation of **Sega** and *Mario* is the property of Nintendo, virtually all the earliest arcade sensations seem somehow attributed or linked to Atari. For example, was *Pac-Man* an Atari invention? How about *Space Invaders*? For us excited Brits, the Atari revolution was largely mediated via the likes of *Nationwide* and *Tomorrow's World,* and quibbling over which one was Namco and which one was Taito seemed irrelevant.

So, the arrival in the UK in the late Seventies of the Atari VCS games console was literally earth-shattering news, with one television commercial in 1980 proclaiming in a suitably computerish voice that '*Space Invaders* have landed at Selfridges. The game Earth people have been waiting for is now on sale for the first time'. The commercial also helpfully went on to add that there were '112 ways to stop the invaders landing' although we only needed one, blasting the little buggers out of the sky. The console itself was a thing of beauty, consisting of six flick switches (including one to specify the level of difficulty) and a lovely woodgrain finish designed to coordinate with your television.

Predictably the Atari VCS (later re-named the 2600) went on to sell by the truckload. However, as the Eighties progressed, Atari seemed unable to capitalize on their early monopoly. Perhaps their name was so interchangeable that buyers assumed that an **IntelliVision** or an Odyssey2 was simply a make of Atari. Meanwhile the Atari 5200 (released in 1982) was pricey and annoying to play thanks to a **joystick** that refused to co-operate (it wouldn't centre itself properly). Things got even worse in May 1982 when Atari manufactured twelve million copies of *Pac-Man* for the 2600 even though only ten million 2600 consoles had actually been sold.

All the while, Atari were attempting to nail the home computer market. The Atari 400 and 800 were both released in 1979 and although the 800 was hugely popular in America, it proved too expensive for us Brits who stuck with our **VIC-20**s and **BBC Micro**s. For the mainstream computer gamer, Atari disappeared from view as the likes of Sinclair and Commodore started to muscle in on the UK market. So it proved a surprise when Atari scored a mainstream hit in the late Eighties with the **Atari ST**. However, inevitably, having made in-roads, Atari conspired to balls up again. The handheld unit – Lynx – was no match for Nintendo's fearsome **Game Boy** and Atari's last hurrah (certainly as far as game systems are concerned), the Jaguar, looked cheap and nasty and was soon swallowed up by Sony's PlayStation and Sega's Saturn.

But without Atari, the world would be mighty different; and besides, who knows if Scalectrix, Hoover, or Transformers are still in business today?

## Atari ST
1986

There is a sub-section of the computing community who go all dewy eyed and proclaim that computer games stopped being any good the moment the **Amiga** and Atari ST arrived on the scene, for it was they that marked the next phase in the evolution of the home computer; the '16-bit era'. Quite what '16-bit' actually means is difficult to fathom (although it has something to do with the processing power of the computer); suffice to say if 8-bit was good (and it seemed to have been, given that most of the machines up until then had been 8-bit) then 16-bit was better. And for the many who had dipped out of the computing scene in the mid- to late Eighties, the arrival of home computers that actually had the power to display photo images (albeit in a low resolution) was something of a sensation.

To most of us Atari was synonymous with simple games machines and so the impact of going round to your mate's house to check out his spendthrift parents' latest acquisition was immeasurable. For those of us not in the know, the Atari ST came out of nowhere, yet here it was, living and breathing and running a demo of a proper film (albeit rendered in 16 colours) of a flying bird of prey. Next up was an even greater thrill as Rainbird's *Starglider* (released in 1986), a vector graphics **shoot 'em up**, was slotted into the 3.5 inch disk drive. This was particularly exciting as when you got to the game's title screen you were greeted with a burst of 'real' music (although it cut off after just a few seconds). That a home computer could look and sound a bit like stuff you would see on the telly (albeit in 16 colours and for just a few seconds) was earth-shattering and represented a giant leap forward in, at the very least, our understanding of what could be achieved on a home computer.

However, the ST was never without competition, and in the **system rivalry** stakes it was drawn against the aforementioned Amiga. On paper, Commodore's kit was certainly superior; however, given that most competitive computer owners would use the quality of the latest games as a barometer, generally it was honours-even between the two (primarily because lots of games were ported by developers from the ST to the Amiga or vice versa, meaning that the code was essentially the same on both machines). As was the way of classic computer rivalry, even the tangible differences pretty much evened themselves out. The Amiga might have had a far superior colour palette, but musicians favoured the ST because of its ability to be used as a sequencer.

But what of those computer purists we mentioned earlier? Whilst computer games in the 16-bit era might have often lacked the elegant simplicity, or to put it another way, the crap sound and graphics, of their more primitive predecessors, the Atari ST was awash with great games, some of which unashamedly emphasized the new computer's technical abilities at the expense of the gameplay. Not that it mattered one jot; just to own something as splendid looking as Cinemaware's 1987 classic *Defender of the Crown* was happiness enough and the game's joust sequence (which was constructed from real images) was something that was surely meant to be looked upon with awe and wonder as opposed to actually played. For those who did want something that resolutely focussed on gameplay though, then what better than Atari's very own *Midi Maze* (also release in 1987) – a three dimensional *Pac-Man* and one of the very first entrants into the genre that would become known as the **first person shooter**? Although bumming around the various mazes on your lonesome was entertaining in itself, the real purpose of the game (and hence its name) was to link up several Atari STs via the computer's MIDI ports and get stuck in to some multi-player sessions. This sounded great fun but outside of **Computer Club,** who did you know who owned two Atari STs?

Perhaps though those gaming curmudgeons that we keep coming back to were thinking of games such as *Xenon II*. Whilst in itself a fine shoot 'em up in the mould of arcade classic *R-Type*, the inclusion of music by Bomb The Bass suggested a new direction in gaming that would surely seal its ultimate destruction, namely being cool. Previously computer programmer's attempts at being hip had never got further than whacking a picture of a Harley Davidson on a **loading** screen and accompanying it with some squealing, anonymous soft rock guitar riffs as essayed through the computer's patently not-up-for-it sound chip. Arguably with the patronage of a credible music act, computer games were heading up a rocky road that would lead them out of smelly **boys' bedrooms** and into the sanctified arena of the mainstream, where they would eventually take their place as another 'lifestyle choice'.

## BBC Micro
## 1981

In 1979, BBC television broadcast a six-part series called *The Mighty Micro* in which computer scientist Christopher Riche Evans speculated on the future of microcomputers. The series was deemed to be significant enough to merit a BBC campaign, the government-backed Computer Literacy Project. In support of this initiative the Beeb reasoned that they needed a computer of their own as a focus for their activities. A list of requirements was compiled and sent to the likes of Sinclair Research and Dragon; however, the BBC ultimately settled on a prototype computer demonstrated to them by Acorn Computers. Thus was born the home computer that would go on to secure more television airtime in the early Eighties than Noel Edmonds.

Being the subject of a government-backed initiative it was evident that the BBC Micro (which came in two versions: Model A contained only 16KB Ram whereas Model B had 32KB) would have to be a reasonably serious machine, and its cream and black finish, orange function keys and petite BBC owl logo suggested that this was no computer for the frivolous. Games too were reasonably conspicuous by their absence, and those that were produced and prospered on the machine (such as *Elite* and *Sentinel*) tended to be cerebral in nature. As a side note, it is surprising that a whole suite of games based on BBC series weren't considered. There were a couple of attempts at *Doctor Who* games (1983's *Doctor Who: The First Adventure* and 1985's *Doctor Who and the Mines of Terror*) but you can't help but conclude that a number of great gaming opportunities were missed (imagine a *Juliet Bravo* text adventure or a madcap **platformer** only loosely based on Johnny Ball's *Think of a Number*).

Upon its launch in December 1981, the Beeb put the full force of the corporation behind the BBC Micro and the machine featured on programmes such as *Beat the Teacher, Tomorrow's World, The Adventure Game* and *Doctor Who*. Appearances on the latter programme were particularly ingenious with the BBC Micro's beep being used as the sound of an unlikely desk intercom in one episode in 1983. However even more incredibly, the Doctor's TARDIS, or at the very least its graphics engine, was, in the same episode, shown to be powered by a BBC Micro. In addition, there were a few actual TV programmes all about computers that featured the Micro heavily, usually accentuating the machine's educational and **programming** abilities.

By the mid-Eighties, seven out of ten schools that owned computers owned BBC Micros. Sadly, they never seemed to do much with them, and they could generally be found languishing in the English department being subjected to wistful gazes from students who would much rather be having a go of *Suburban Fox* then hand writing an essay about characterisation in *The Haunting of Chas McGill*. Those that were pressed into action were often used in nascent Computing classes, allowing bored thirteen-year-old kids who thought they'd signed up to build a robot or infiltrate US military supercomputers, to get to grips with programming using BBC Basic.

By 1985, the BBC Micro was starting to get a little old, and teachers in the know were eyeing up more exciting computers such as **Apple Macs.** Acorn released the BBC Master range; however, although technically far superior to the old BBC Micro, they were far more expensive than equivalent computers on the market such as the **Atari ST.** The BBC's last hurrah in the computer market was its association with 1986's **Domesday Project**, an exercise of enormous historical value, if for no other reason than it documented the fact that in the Eighties, orange juice was a legitimate starter dish in local restaurants.

## Binatone
## 1976

The rampant success of **Atari's** *Home Pong* in 1974 opened the floodgates for manufacturers large and small to muscle in on the home console market and carve out a piece of the action for themselves. Consoles such as the Videomaster Home TV Game and the Lasonic 2000 TV Game offered European video gamers an opportunity to play electronic tennis, squash or football, (all of which were, essentially, much like *Pong*). For many of us in the UK though, our first console came courtesy of Binatone.

A British based company, Binatone certainly made hay whilst the silicon sun shone. They released loads of consoles in the mid- to late Seventies, with their first being the TV Game Unit in 1976. For under £25 you got a nice cream coloured machine with funny little knobs and a spinning number dial that you had to manually adjust to keep score. So far so good; however, the downside was that the TV Game Unit could only play the Binatone version of *Pong*. Indeed none of the Binatone consoles supported any form of game cartridges, and as a consequence players were stuck with whatever came hard coded in the system.

Later Binatones offered more variety with the TV Master 4 Plus 2 featuring not just the obligatory tennis, but squash and football too. Even more exciting though were two shooting games that could be played with a light gun rather than the customary **joysticks** (or paddles as they were called). Meanwhile, the TV Master MK 10 was a veritable console Olympics, adding ice hockey and gridball to the mix. However, as repetitive play would make all too apparent, all of these games were simply a variation on a theme. As if to compensate for this, the consoles proudly boasted of 'on-screen' scoring and larger size bats for rubbish players.

Although Binatone consoles came in many shapes and sizes, the livery remained largely consistent, with most sporting the little Binatone three-pronged crown logo and a fine black and orange colour design (indeed the exact shade of orange used can only be described as 'Seventies'). This made for a range that somehow reflected their inherent Britishness, meaning that for those who owned one there was always an undeniable sense that you were getting the console equivalent of supermarkets' own brand cornflakes – something serviceable that did the job intended but without any of the glamour of a proper brand name. Certainly you could sense that they lacked the indefinable, but at the time impossibly exciting, aura of being in some way or another associated with the USA.

## Commodore 64
### 1982

It may be the world's biggest selling 8-bit computer (some reckon Commodore shifted 16 million units), but the Commodore 64 is only the second most-loved home computer in the UK. Yes, much about the C64 (as it was generally referred too), is defined by its opposition to its fierce rival on these shores; the **ZX Spectrum**. You were either a 'Commodore kid', or a

'Spectrum kid' and only rarely would any one person own both. For Speccy fans there was much to be jealous of, there was no horrible bleeding of one colour into another when your character passed in front of another moving object and none of the awful beeping that passed for music on the Sinclair computer either. The Commodore 64 looked more the part too, with a proper keyboard and everything. What's more, it had greater memory (hence the titular '64').

The Commodore 64 owes much of its existence to the great **video game industry crash** of the early Eighties. Having already released the **VIC-20** in 1981, Commodore had turned its attentions to developing new sound and graphics chips for a proposed arcade machine. But when it transpired that the arcade market was disappearing at a rate of knots and that the VIC-20 was actually doing rather well, Commodore redirected the development into the construction of a new home computer. The initial plan was to focus the Commodore 64 on the business community, whilst releasing a cut-price version called the Commodore MAX for the home market. At £400, the Commodore 64 was competitive in the business market (where computers such as the **Apple** IIe would set you back somewhere in the region of £2,000); however, it became apparent that the machine's actual competitors were the home computers such as the Spectrum (which was about half the price). Initially owners of the C64 were viewed as rich kids, and it wasn't until the price was slashed in 1984 to just £200 that this situation was reversed. But by that time Sinclair had already established a massive lead in the UK market.

That is not to deny the Commodore 64's place at the top table of home computers. Whilst Speccy fans might have happily gloated about the Spectrum's isometric graphics (as masterfully essayed in titles such as **_Knight Lore_** and _Batman_), the Commodore kid was able to hit back with examples of truly impressive and authentic soundtracks in games such as Ocean's

1986 title *Short Circuit* and, even more remarkably, actual (albeit fuzzy sounding) digitised speech in Activision's 1984 release *Ghostbusters*. The Commodore 64 was also able to handle colours far more effectively than the Spectrum. This was particularly important when it came to conversions of coin-op games (which by their nature tended to be graphically very colourful).

In addition, for many Commodore kids, the C64, along with an acoustic coupler modem, provided them with their first tentative steps onto the Internet, although when your parent's saw the resultant phone bill such early online exploration often proved to be short-lived.

### Crashes
#### About sixty seconds before the end of the game

Can there be anything as frustrating in any leisure pursuit as a crashing computer? Be it three stupid bombs appearing on the screen or the message '? Syntax Error OK', it is clear that whoever it is that designs these crash messages either has an unlimited capacity for understatement or is a contrary bugger. Simply put, a computer crash is not deserving of anything so facile or mild as an 'OK'. What we want to see is something like 'Oh my god I am so sorry. I am a crappy computer and unfortunately I am going to crash now and wipe all the work you've been doing for the last three hours – can you ever find it in your heart to forgive me?'

Given its external RAM pack, the **ZX81** was particularly prone to crashing, usually as a result of the mildest nudge, but practically all computers were susceptible to an inexplicable loss of power if they were moved even slightly at a critical point. Of course, an overheating computer would flake out too, and this was especially galling as the only reason it would overheat in the first place would be because you'd had it on for ages whilst working your way to the last screen of *Arcadia* or *Hunchback II*. The process of then having to restart your computer, reload your game and take it from the top was too much for any of us to bear.

You would have thought that with such massive advancements in technology, crashing would have become a thing of the past, but it is an issue that is still with us today. Rather like the common cold, our advanced scientific knowledge hasn't been able to combat this terrible ailment. Whilst today's computers offer autosave and autorecovery features, the IT technician's famous diagnosis 'what you've got there is the blue screen of death' still chills our bones and means that the fiercely complex formula we had just finished setting up in *Microsoft Excel* has been lost forever.

## Deep Blue
### 1989

Another hardy perennial of the 'whimsical news story and *Tomorrow's World*' circuit, the development of computer chess, that deadly earnest enterprise that pits man's intellectual and intuitive brilliance against mind-bogglingly powerful computers, has somehow never been taken completely seriously by the media. Yet, the construction of a man-beating chess machine has engaged some of the foremost minds of our time. Alan Turing, for example, the chap who pretty much invented the computer, was sufficiently interested to write one of the earliest known chess programs back in 1950 (it is claimed that the first ever chess program was written by Konrad Zuse in 1946). However, it would take another eight years for a computer to actually beat a human, and for that feat the computer required an opponent who had only been taught how to play the game one hour earlier.

Throughout the Seventies and Eighties, various computer

boffins would wheel out their latest all-powerful chess machine, and each would be routinely laughed at as a human opponent took it apart. Things hit fever pitch in 1989 when IBM began working on Deep Blue, and one sensed that these folks were grimly determined to emerge victorious. And victorious they finally were. Although it took another eight years, in 1997 Deep Blue vanquished chess world champion Garry Kasparov, heralding the first time a machine had ever beaten a chess playing world number one. Since then you sense that all concerned have, understandably, lost interest a bit and even the occasional media sniggering that usually accompanied such events is notable by its absence. Having beaten the best that humans can offer there seems to be nothing left for Deep Blue to achieve.

## Dragon 32
### 1982

How many computers can boast a Welsh heritage? Well the properly Welsh sounding Dragon 32 can. In fact, it was manufactured on the Port Talbot industrial estate on the premises of a company called Dragon Data (a division of the toy company Mettoy). First produced in 1982, the Dragon 32 proudly boasted of the robustness of its keyboard and casing. Indeed Dragon Data went so far as to promise that the keyboard was good 'for twenty million depressions'. This was a number so dizzyingly high that you could be assured that nobody would attempt to disprove the theory, but all the same it sounded good.

Whereas the likes of **Commodore** and **Sinclair** had WH Smith and John Menzies all sewn up, chains such as Boots, Comet and Dixons stocked the Dragon 32. Retailing at £199, it was a competitive machine with a number of factors in its favour. First of all, it came with Microsoft Extended BASIC, a robust programming language that is well remembered today by those who used it to generate impressive spinning hoop graphics. It could also handle nine colours (crucially one more than the **ZX Spectrum**) and could rely on the support of local government (which strongly backed the Welsh based company). On the deficit side, the Dragon 32's video display wasn't full screen and **loading** programs from tape was a notoriously unreliable business.

Whilst a decent enough machine (with a 64KB model released in 1984), the Dragon 32 suffered from the wider downturn in the computer industry. Being a reasonably small company, there was little Dragon Data could do to protect themselves, and as the cold wind of the computer recession began to bite, bankruptcy became a sad inevitability with the company going under in June 1984 – Port Talbot's foray into the computing industry was over.

Loading...
1980

In the Eighties, an important part of the growing up process was to have one special game that every week (usually Sunday lunchtime after *Thunderbirds* had been on) you would attempt to try and load. This ritual would involve adjusting the volume control on your tape recorder by the smallest of increments, and trying as many different combination of mic to ear connections as you could come up with. As the loading process began, the computer screen border turned first red and blue, then yellow and black. From this you would try to divine the likelihood of the game loading by determining how narrow each of the stripes were, or how quickly they darted up and down the screen. What you certainly didn't want to see was a metronomic flicker from one colour to the next. Although you knew little about the correlation between the success of the loading process and the movement of these crucial stripes, you knew enough to realise if the stripes didn't move in time with the loading noise, then something was seriously awry.

Some weeks you would be rewarded with the sight of a loading screen starting to appear, and others you would get nothing at all; but crucially, the game should never ever actually properly load. Of course the person who copied it for you (these were usually pirated games) would insist that their version worked perfectly, but for reasons unknown, it would remain beyond the capabilities of your computer and trusty cassette recorder; and would even refuse to load when you were feeling a bit unwell and so, by rights, should work.

The worst moment of all was that very rare occasion when the actual loading process would seem to complete. The tape would fall silent and there would be a never ending pause during which you held your breath as the loading image remained on the screen for a couple of seconds. One false move, one hair out of place and you knew all would be lost. Regardless of how still you managed to remain, just seconds later three poorly realised bomb icons would appear and your computer would reset, sending you into the type of rage that mothers would insensitively chastise you for.

## Magnavox Odyssey
### 1972

The very first home console came not from **Atari** or indeed any other games manufacturer that you are likely to have heard of but from a company with an exotic sounding name who did a nice line in tellys. The Magnavox Odyssey was an idea that had been kicking around for a few years before it reached the shops, nevertheless it was still pretty quick off the mark given that the first ever arcade game, *Computer Space* only appeared the year before.

Billed as the 'electronic game of the future', Magnavox leaked stories to the electronics press of an exciting mystery product weeks before its official launch. When it was finally unveiled in March 1972, the subterfuge and rumour mongering proved to have been worthwhile, as effusive press coverage ensured the Odyssey got off to a flying start.

The console itself is a curious mixture of sensibilities. To those well accustomed to such things, the Odyssey's mock wood finish, cool computery logo and games stored on cards are all very familiar. In fact the inclusion of games cards is one of the most significant elements of the whole machine, and one that would inform all major games machines that have since followed.

The Odyssey was entering a world in which home gaming still meant board games, and cards, so Magnavox wisely packed it with a myriad of items familiar to the more traditional gamer (such as pretend money, stickers and poker chips). Given the rudimentary nature of the machine's graphics, each of the sixteen titles also came with acetate overlays that you would attach to your screen, so that your game of *Haunted House* actually took place within something that resembled a ghostified mansion. In fact, if truth be told, a few of the games scarcely required the actual Odyssey at all, and relied more or less on traditional devices.

Originally retailing for $100, Odyssey made a great noise in the market place, but once the initial brouhaha subsided, it only achieved modest sales and was finally discontinued in 1975. However, for being the first console to take games out of the amusement arcades, off the dining room table and on to our television screens, it has rightfully earned its place in the halls of computing history (albeit near the front entrance).

## Master System
1985

The first thing you notice about **Sega**'s Master System (or Mark III as it was referred to in Japan) is its rather natty logo that adorns both the top of the unit and the controllers. The second thing you notice is that compared to **Nintendo**'s **NES** (which sort of looks a bit like a fax machine), the Master System is a snug, albeit somewhat angular construction. But underneath the bonnet, the Master System was far superior to the Nintendo machine, boasting twice the memory of the NES and able to generate more colours on-screen.

In addition, the Master System was able to run games off cartridges (which is what Nintendo used) and smaller, thinner cards as well. This latter medium supported less expensive software titles, but they were more simplistic too and were soon phased out (the redesigned Master System omitted the card slot altogether). Much like Nintendo, Sega had a wealth of successful arcade games ripe for home conversion, and the Master System was bundled with a version of Sega's popular arcade motorcycle game *Hang On*.

Taking on Nintendo was always going to be a tough task, Sega's arch rivals had already secured a massive NES user base and in addition had been savvy enough to sign developers up to contracts that prevented them from working on rival systems. As such, Sega had no real hope of overturning Nintendo's domination, but they were able to make inroads into a number of territories. In particular, Europe and the UK were a successful hunting ground (the Master System was launched in the UK in 1987). Due to poor marketing, the NES had never really developed the strangle-hold in Europe it had enjoyed elsewhere. In addition, whilst the NES retailed for £140, the Master System would set you back only £99.99, a price that compared favourably not only with Nintendo's machine but also the most significant challengers to Nintendo and Sega on this side of the pond – the **Amiga** and **Atari ST**.

Although creating new titles for the Master System proved to be a bit of a struggle, Sega were able to produce a number of very decent games, of which arguably the best was the 1986

release *Wonder Boy III* (a **Mario**-esque **platformer**). Less successful though were the Master System's **peripherals**. These
included a **joystick** add-on for the controller pad, a tracker ball
supposedly designed with **sports games** in mind, and a pair of
**3-D** glasses that via a process of opening and closing shutters
in each lens actually did produce a passable 3-D effect.

Sega introduced a redesigned version of the Master System
in 1991 that abandoned the angular look of the original in
favour of a friendlier, compact and curvy design. Named the
'Master System II' it retailed for only £59.99; however, by this
time Sega were focussing their attentions elsewhere and the
Master System was gradually phased out.

Although not an earth-shattering console by any stretch of
the imagination, the Master System did at least soften the UK
market's disposition towards game consoles. With the success
of first the **ZX Spectrum** and **Commodore 64**, followed by the
aforementioned Amiga and Atari ST, it had seemed at one time
that we Brits had turned our back on simple games machines
for good. This was to prove to be very far from the truth.

## Mattel IntelliVision
## 1980

The early Eighties saw **Atari,** and in particular their 2600 games
console, at the very peak of its powers. In fact it looked like
they had got the video game market entirely sewn up. However
other companies caught a glimpse of Atari's sales figures and
decided there was some serious money to be made. Amongst
the first wave of contenders was Mattel. Having already entered
the **handheld gaming** market with a series of extremely basic
machines, Mattel set to work on a home gaming system
designed specifically to blow Atari out of the water.

The end result – the Mattel IntelliVision – seemed to have the
2600 beat hands down. It was more powerful than the Atari

machine, had more detailed graphics (159 x 56 pixels to be exact), a superior control device (a little disc that could be pushed in one of sixteen different directions, twice as many as the 2600), a nattier looking mock wood finish and there was even talk of a keyboard peripheral that would change the IntelliVision into a proper computer. Mattel's software and marketing strategy looked far superior too; their analysis showed that **sports games** were the most popular amongst the home market, and so they licensed pretty much every mainstream sport under the sun. For their advertising, they shelled out $6 million in 1981 alone, most of it spent on highlighting the 2600's inadequacies in comparison to their machine.

The campaign worked. Even though at $299 the IntelliVision was $100 more expensive than the 2600, 175,000 were sold in 1980 alone. Then in 1982, Mattel released the IntelliVision II and after that the IntelliVision III. Not only did these abandon the woodgrain look for a light grey finish, but they retailed at a far more competitive $150 and could even play Atari 2600 cartridges. Consequently, in 1983, Mattel sold a whopping 3.5 million consoles.

1983 was also the year of the **video game industry crash**, with hardware and software manufacturers undercutting each other out of business. Mattel also had to contend with the US government imposing punitive measures on them for failing to release their keyboard as previously promised. Being fined $10,000 for each month that went by with no keyboard was a drain on cash that Mattel could have well done without.

In early 1984, a group of investors, including Mattel's Senior Vice President of Marketing and Sales, bought the rights to the IntelliVision from Mattel and set up their own company to continue manufacturing further versions of the console, as well as new games. They managed to keep the IntelliVision going reasonably successfully until 1990. Meanwhile, Mattel closed down their computing subsidiary, Mattel Electronics, in 1984, after having botched an attempt to release a mainstream home computer (the Mattel Aquarius) the previous year.

Supporters of the IntelliVision would cite its ten-year tenure as proof of the console's success, and they would be right. You suspect Mattel must quietly wonder what the future for their IntelliVision range might have been had the market not experienced such tumult.

## Mega Drive
## 1989

Of all the **system rivalries** down the years, the greatest (even surpassing **ZX Spectrum** versus **Commodore 64**) has been the **Sega** Mega Drive versus the **SNES**. In the creamy grey corner there was **Nintendo**'s powerful 16-bit machine, a little late to market, but building on a massive bedrock of existing support. In the sleek black corner there was the Mega Drive – the young upstart that had been making a lot of noise around town (including seeing off the SNES' little brother, the **NES**). In the early Nineties, these two mighty titans battled it out for ultimate supremacy and in the process completely reinvigorated a home console market that had previously been in the doldrums.

Whilst Sega's **Master System** had allowed the company to make inroads into the console market, by the late Eighties it was clear that Sega would need to bring out something revolutionary if they wanted to eat into Nintendo's user base (which then constituted around 90% of the market). Accordingly, development began on a brand new games machine that would blow the NES out of the water.

In every respect the Mega Drive was superior to the NES. *Altered Beast* (the first game to be bundled with the machine) featured huge graphics, much like the original arcade version, and it was clear to even the most casual observer that here was something that was far in advance of Nintendo's humble, and by then rather aging machine.

Released in America in 1989 under the name 'Genesis', the Mega Drive was backed with a smart campaign that not only focused on a slightly older age group than Nintendo but also drew explicit comparisons between the rival machines with the memorable strap line – 'Genesis does what Nintendon't'.

Aesthetically too, Sega hoped to put some distance between themselves and the competition. Nintendo's consoles were rounded and decked out in an inoffensive creamy grey; the Mega Drive – much like its predecessor the Master System – was black, angular and sleek. In short Nintendo offered family entertainment, but Sega offered something altogether cooler.

In the two years before Nintendo was able to get the SNES on to the market, the Mega Drive made up a lot of ground, such that by the end of the SNES' first year on sale Sega had occupied fifty-five per cent of the market, undoubtedly in part due to their canny marketing. Sega also worked hard to secure a number of licensing deals for their sports titles (it was thought that **sports games** appealed to the older player), and crucially stuck up a fruitful partnership with the influential software company Electronic Arts.

Over time, Nintendo were able to claw back some of Sega's advantage and the SNES and Mega Drive were well matched adversaries in terms of technical specifications and market performance. Things started to go wrong for Sega in the mid-Nineties when they attempted to elongate the lifespan of the Mega Drive by releasing the Mega CD and 32X add-ons. Neither gained much support from game developers, and furthermore, for a console that previously looked so sleek, they both made the Mega Drive look clunky and resolutely unhip.

Nonetheless, during its ascendant years, the Mega Drive and SNES were the last word in game consoles; no one else got a look in. More importantly they created a paradigm shift in the computer industry, and paved the way for the consoles of today.

Microsoft
1975

To many, Microsoft is the evil Empire of the computing world, and Bill Gates its very own Darth Vader. However, the company has its origins in the far more benign world of the computer hobbyist. Microsoft head honcho Bill Gates originally started the company with his childhood friend Paul Allen after the two of them created a version of the BASIC **programming** language to run on the MITS Altair computer. Although the two joined MITS in 1975 (and licensed their version of BASIC at the same time), they formed a partnership that they called 'Micro-Soft' and the following year registered the revised version, 'Microsoft', as a trademark. By 1977 they'd wrested back control of BASIC from MITS and began to license it to the likes of Commodore and **Apple**.

Microsoft really took off in 1980, when Gates and Allen landed a contract to provide IBM with a computer language and an operating system for their new **PC** computer. The end result of the deal was the arrival of the Microsoft-Disc Operating System (MS-DOS). Although other companies came up with the own versions of DOS, a number of **killer apps** were developed (such as the spreadsheet application *Lotus 1-2-3*) that relied on MS-DOS to run. As such, customers wanted to buy the computer which ran the operating system that made *Lotus 1-2-3* work, and that meant buying Microsoft's product. For those talented companies that were able to come up with a *Lotus 1-2-3* compatible version of DOS, Microsoft simply made things even more difficult by introducing **Windows** 3.1, a graphical user interface that would only run on MS-DOS (if your computer used a non Microsoft version of DOS, Windows would report an error and fail to start).

Such aggressive tactics were used to similar effect to gain dominance in the web browser market too. Although Microsoft

Internet Explorer was arguably no better than the most popular competitor of the time (Netscape), Microsoft bundled it in free with their hugely successful operating system Windows 95. This meant that those users who wanted to run Windows 95 on their computers had no real reason to use any other Internet browser than Microsoft Internet Explorer.

Today Microsoft has what has been declared by the US Department of Justice as a monopoly in the PC market. Whilst a number of computing purists refuse to use Microsoft products for what they describe as ethical reasons, or simply because they think they are not as good as some of the other products out there, most of us are disinclined to swim against the tide. The obvious issue this creates is that without significant competition there is very little to compel Microsoft to create products that are as good as they can be. That's not to say though, that Microsoft aren't releasing the best possible products, just that the market conditions don't require it of them, and that is not an ideal situation.

## Neo-Geo
## 1991

Whilst you might get an occasional glimpse of one of these on something like *GameMaster* or *Games World*, SNK's killer home system, the Neo-Geo, was definitely the Rolls Royce of the home console world. First released in 1991, the Neo-Geo Advanced Entertainment System (to give it its Sunday name) offered home users an opportunity to play pixel perfect home versions of arcade classics – but at a price. The Neo-Geo came out of SNK's development into arcade cabinets able to store multiple games. These cabinets (first released in 1989 under the moniker of the 'Neo-Geo MVS') proved popular with **amusement arcade** proprietors who found that with a simple change of the cabinet livery and the swapping of one game cartridge for another they had a completely new arcade game for a fraction of the cost of procuring a new machine.

The concept obviously had viability outside the arcade scene but given the prohibitive cost of manufacturing the machines and game cartridges, SNK initially targeted the rental and hotel businesses. However, the reaction to the Neo-Geo was so positive that SNK began to focus on the home market. Although the thought of having a title such as *King of the Fighters* (SNK's 1991 answer to Capcom's **Street Fighter II**) running on a home system in perfect arcade quality was enormously tantalising, the Neo-Geo retailed for a whopping £440 making it far more expensive then any of its competitors; and even worse – you could expect to pay up to £160 for a single game.

Still, as well as performing fantastically, the Neo-Geo looked the business too. Compared to other consoles it was massive; the cartridges alone were two or three times the size of a **Mega Drive** cart, and it was equipped with possibly the biggest **joystick** controller ever seen on a home system. These aesthetics were an important reassurance to consumers and further differentiated the console from others on the market. SNK's boastful advertising sought to accentuate even further the differences between their machine and the rest. In one campaign, SNK proclaimed 'if you are still playing **Sega**, NEC or **Nintendo** you're nothing but a weenie! If you are playing the incredibly powered Neo-Geo system you're a real hot dog!' A later campaign would simply depict a frothing pit bull with huge fangs straining at the lead with the strap line 'bigger, badder, better'.

Given SNK's previous pedigree in the **beat 'em up** arena it was unsurprising that such games prospered on the Neo-Geo. However, the specific type of beat 'em ups that worked best were two dimensional and sprite based in design. In general this was a limitation of the system as a whole, and one that was sorely exposed in 1994 with the arrival of the Sega Saturn and Sony **PlayStation**. These machines were better equipped to handle **3-D** polygon based games; which, sadly for SNK, were becoming overwhelmingly popular by the middle years of the Nineties.

SNK tried to keep up with the pace by releasing the Neo-Geo CD in 1994. Although this helped resolve the issue of prohibitively expensive games (without the cost of manufacturing cartridges SNK could retail games round the £30 mark), the technology was no longer cutting edge, and there was simply no compelling reason to buy one, when for the same amount of cash you could land yourself a PlayStation.

The Neo-Geo remains much loved and titles are still being released for it to this day. Mind you, given the initial outlay, it is little surprise that those lucky few who were able to afford one at the time are still looking to extract as much value for money out of it as possible.

## Nintendo
1889

Truly one of the behemoths of the video game market, Nintendo's dominance has been on the wane for the last decade or so; however, it still retains an important foothold in the industry and culturally, it is still Nintendo, more than any other organisation, that informs the West's opinion of the moral and aesthetic preferences of Japanese computer culture.

Nintendo actually started out in 1889 as a manufacturer of playing cards, but by the late Sixties they were looking for other business opportunities and branched out into all manner of weird and wonderful products, including an extending arm contraption and, in 1973, the world's first Laser Clay Range (a kind of electronic shooting range).

In 1975, Nintendo president Hiroshi Yamauchi grew increasingly interested in the success of the nascent American video games industry, and so struck a deal with games company Magnavox to license and manufacture the **Magnavox Odyssey** home console in Japan. By 1977, Nintendo had entered the video games industry themselves with the release of their Color TV Game 6. This system offered the player six different versions of *Pong* and sold over a million copies. It was followed one year later by the similarly million-selling Color TV Game 15. At around the same time Nintendo began producing arcade machines, such as 1978's *Block Fever* and *Computer Othello*.

Always one to keep an eye on developing markets, in 1980 Nintendo moved into the **handheld gaming** arena with the first of their long-running and soon to become hugely successful **Game and Watch** series. Up until this point Nintendo was simply just another video game company. Their games were often derivative and pretty anonymous; there was definitely nothing about the likes of *Space Fever* (a 1979 Nintendo arcade machine) that made it stand out from the rest of the fast flooding market.

All of this was to change with the arrival of Nintendo's first big hit, **Donkey Kong,** in 1981. Apart from offering the gaming community something reasonably novel, *Donkey Kong* also possessed bags of character and loads of imagination. To Nintendo's enormous credit, they recognised a good thing when they saw it and began to major on these traits with their next arcade and Game and Watch releases.

In May 1983, Nintendo released a new games console onto the Japanese market. Named the Famicom (short for 'Family Computer'), it sold 500,000 units in just two months. In part this was because there was little in the way of significant competition in the Japanese market, but also due to the fact that the machine retailed at a reasonably low price (Nintendo's strategy was to sell hardware cheap and make the money back on the software).

The Famicom was renamed the **NES** for the Western market, but its launch in the USA didn't go quite as smoothly. By that time Nintendo had struck a deal with Coleco, allowing that company to make a version of *Donkey Kong* for their Adam computer. With its strongest asset already available on another home system there seemed little reason to buy a NES. A period of tense negotiation managed to put the kibosh on the Adam version before it was released, but by then Nintendo had got caught up in a botched licensing deal for the NES with **Atari**, and found themselves in a tight knot that would take until 1986, and the arrival of *Super **Mario** Bros,* to undo.

Their next console, the **SNES**, was released in 1991. This time Nintendo made no mistakes. Designed to compete with **Sega**'s **Mega Drive**, the SNES (or 'Super Famicom' as it was known in Japan) sold well over a million units in the first three months. The machine's fortunes were boosted by the release of the hugely popular *Super Mario World*, and the SNES would go on to rule the home console market (along with its eternal enemy the Mega Drive) for the next five or so years, turning over as much revenue as all of the American film studios combined.

It is a little harsh to use terms such as 'downfall' in relation to Nintendo's recent fortunes, but clearly its subsequent consoles such as the Nintendo 64 and Game Cube (not to mention the **Virtual Boy**) have failed to capture the market in the way their predecessors did. Still, Sega have long since exited the home console market and **Game Boy** remains the best-selling games machine the world has ever known. The likes of Sony still have some way to go to match the Big N's contribution to computer gaming and popular culture.

## NES
### 1983

In the UK it is undoubtedly the **SNES** that endures in the heart of most **Nintendo** fans; yet in all the most important ways it was its predecessor, the Nintendo Entertainment System (NES) that set Nintendo on a course that would end in global dominance. Although immediately popular in its homeland of Japan (sold under the name of 'Famicom'), it took the NES around three years to make it into the European shops. The original USA bundle retailed for around $250 and came with a light gun and a little plastic robot called ROB (Robotic Operation Buddy) that interacted (albeit somewhat slowly and with limited movement) with two specially designed games, *Gyromite* and *Stack-Up*. ROB's appeal was definitely limited, and although he demonstrated that the NES was more than just a simple games console, actually all people really wanted *was* a simple games console. Never one to take their time to cotton on to public option, Nintendo quickly scrapped ROB in favour of a cheaper bundle that offered users nothing but games.

Looking at the NES today, it is clear that it embodied a number of Nintendo's guiding principles; whilst its competitors were trying to produce gaming machines that looked dangerous, futuristic or credible, the NES adopted an altogether more charming aesthetic. Its unfussy construction, pale colour scheme and lack of superfluous detail somehow hinted at a wholesome kind of family entertainment. Its controllers were wonderfully simple, and the inclusion of a *start* button resulted in the popularisation of the in-game pause mode.

In the UK, it's probably fair to say that the NES never quite achieved the mainstream acceptance of, say, a **Commodore 64** or **ZX Spectrum** (even though it managed to sell 60 million units worldwide). Perhaps at the time people felt that games machines were artefacts from the **Binatone** age, and that the future lay with full-blooded computers. Well if that's the case, they were both right…and wrong.

# PC

## 1981

Although PC is an acronym for 'personal computer', which sounds like a generic term to describe any computer that happened to belong to you, over the years it has come to mean something more specific, something that is inexorably tied up with three companies: IBM, Intel and **Microsoft**.

The first IBM PC was released on 12th August 1981. Named the IBM 5150 Personal Computer, it came about due to IBM's concerns regarding the burgeoning home computer industry and the effect it was having on their mainframe business. In creating the 5150, IBM collaborated with Intel (who produced the 8088 processor that drove the machine) and Microsoft (who supplied the operating system – DOS). But IBM retained ownership for the part of the computer that initiates the operating system, the BIOS (Basic Input-Output System. This ensured they retained complete control over the final product and forced any other companies wanting to create their own versions of the PC to license the BIOS directly from them.

These plans were scuppered in 1982, when rival firm Compaq successfully created their own non-copyright infringing version of IBM's BIOS. In order to achieve this, Compaq had to set up two teams, one to examine IBM's code and work out exactly what it did, and another to take those findings and construct a new code that possessed all the functionality required to successfully operate. Given that Compaq could then demonstrate that their second team hadn't examined or copied the IBM BIOS code, IBM had no grounds for prosecution. This was pretty bad news for IBM, made worse by the fact that the Microsoft and Intel contracts weren't sufficient to prevent those two companies from offering their wares to the competition. In 1982 the Compaq Portable Computer – the first non-IBM PC – hit the market and IBM were a bit miffed.

Nevertheless, they followed up with the PC XT in 1983 (which was one of the first ever computers to contain a hard drive) and the PC AT in 1984. Recognising a good thing when they saw it, other companies soon began to abandon their proprietary computer systems and start making IBM PC clones. This led to a confusing evolutionary process in which companies mixed and matched the best element of each other's designs to produce ever more complex machines. As a result, today's PC market can be very confusing for the uninitiated. Expansion slots, drivers, operating systems, applications – it all seems very bitty and off-putting. Certainly in comparison to the pure-bred **Apple Mac** the PC is a bit of a mongrel, but then again it's also the most popular computer in the world.

## PlayStation
## 1994

The Sony PlayStation marks the point when computer gaming finally breaks free of its hobbyist shackles and comes kicking and screaming into the mainstream. Computer games are just one of a number of leisure pursuits now, and somewhere along the way a little bit of the geeky magic died.

Still, fair play to Sony, given that the PlayStation was their first entrée into the home console market, they did a superb job and in the process shifted 50 million units. Their phenomenal success can be attributed to a number of factors. First of all, the PlayStation's timing coincided with the point at which home systems were able to create graphics that could rival those seen in the **amusement arcades**. The games looked credible, and more importantly, were capable of supporting stylish design. Suddenly games could look like they'd been created by the Prodigy.

Secondly, recognising that most **Commodore 64** owners were now in their 20s and had cash to burn, Sony designed their promotional campaign to appeal to a generation of clubbers who had fallen out of love with computers but still retained fond memories of *Manic Miner*. Given the core computing audience were likely to buy the PlayStation anyway, this served only to widen the demographics of the user base.

Finally, using their corporate clout, Sony lined up a stack of developers for the machine and ensured that there were suitably impressive titles available from the launch date. As such, whilst **Sega** was betting the farm on their Sega Saturn (technically a superior machine to the PlayStation, but comparatively poorly supported both in terms of marketing and software releases) and **Nintendo** procrastinated on where to go next, Sony slipped in between them both and attained premiership of the home console market. From here on, gamers had to put up with endless references to all-night *FIFA* sessions by studiously trendy stand-up comedians, and watch as previously geeky computer commentators attempted to reposition themselves as hip correspondents issuing dispatches from the heart of the *zeitgeist*. The PlayStation may well be a beautiful machine, but by god doesn't it know it.

## Programming
1976

Ever since the glory days of flicking switches on the MITS Altair, the ability to actually write a working computer program has been seen as a pinnacle of technological achievement.

Within small computing circles, those who could program were treated like wizards, endowed with a potentially unlimited ability to create fun. But in reality, most self-styled programmers couldn't do much more than tweak a few lines in an already existing bit of code, or change the text descriptions in someone else's game. Not that this was without merit. It required inventive tinkering to take something like the 1981 **Dragon 32 adventure game** *Calixto Island* and transform it into 'Brixton Island' complete with 'bikers' instead of 'dwarves' and 'greasy chippies' in place of 'dark towers'.

For most of us though, programming meant little more than half-completed rambling text adventures that relied on countless 'GOTO' instructions to build up a computer world of choice and consequence. By the time we had completed pulling together a momentous odyssey and then realised that we still had to go back and write something suitably gripping to occur if the player chose to go 'west' at the beginning of the game rather than 'east', it was clear that this programming malarkey was just too much like hard work.

Similarly, changing the sprites in someone else's game initially looked like a cheap way to create an exciting new title, but attempting to take the main character in Tynesoft's 1986 **Atari ST platformer** *Mouse Trap* and turn him into Superman took an absolute age and resulted in a game that still played exactly the same, but now looked a bit more rubbish.

Of course, the elite of the casual programmers quickly mastered BASIC and moved on to the likes of machine code (officially the hardest thing in the world when you were thirteen), PASCAL, C++ and all manner of incomprehensible languages that required you mastered horrible things like algorithms. Whilst initially it looked like we could all be programmers, the rapid progress of those who really understood what they were doing as opposed to the rest of us, revealed that most playground programming wizards were in actual fact no more magical than the local animal balloon magician, and about as likely to come up with something entertaining.

## QL
### 1984

Undoubtedly, the QL (which stood for 'Quantum Leap') is the best looking computer that Sinclair ever produced. Decked out all in black, it was very rectangular and ordered, and came with something approaching a proper keypad. In comparison to the **ZX Spectrum**, the QL looked like a proper, serious home computer.

And indeed it was. Unlike their earlier computers, Sinclair were keen to establish a significant business user base, and to that end the QL's sober aesthetic was incredibly important. First released in January 1984, the computer press were expecting great things. Technically speaking, the QL didn't let them down. The hardware far exceeded anything else on the market at an equivalent price (the QL retailed at just £400), and it was able to handle multitasking almost ten years before the **PC**. Similarly, the early software for the machine, although of not much interest to the average home user, made for a pretty decent suite of applications for business use.

So all was looking good for the QL. Television commercials featuring Sinclair head honcho Sir Clive rather ungainly leapfrogging over competitors' computers were all well and good in terms of illustrating the superiority of his brainchild; however, some fundamental issues scuppered the QL from day one. Perhaps the most serious problem of all was that the machine wasn't even complete when it was first marketed. This meant that although Sinclair started taking orders in January 1984, some users had to wait until June before receiving their QL. Even then they had to put up with a little dongle stuck on the back (this unwelcome add-on had proved necessary when it was realised that the initial batch of manufactured machines hadn't been properly completed).

But even with dongle attached, lots of users still found their QLs to be defective and had to send them back. All the while, IBM, Intel and **Microsoft** were carving out a substantial slice of the market for themselves and their standardised **PC**. For Sinclair, the timing couldn't have been worse, and to add to their misery, the ill-fated **C5** was about to become a national laughing stock

Sinclair were only able to shift about 100,000 QLs before the machine was dropped in 1986. At a stroke, Sinclair, once the pre-eminent computer developer in the UK, was viewed as a failure, and whilst the QL wasn't their last computer, it did mark the end of the company – and of Sir Clive – as a major force in British home computing.

## Sega
## 1952

Often spoken of in terms of its rivalry with **Nintendo**, most people assume that Sega, like the aforementioned 'Big N', has its roots in the Far East, and that the word 'Sega' is Japanese. Well actually neither is really the case. For a start, Sega is simply a contraction of 'Service Games', and the company, although created and headquartered in Japan, was founded by Americans.

For the early years of its existence, Sega traded in slot machines for the Japanese market. However, in 1966 the company released *Periscope,* one of its first ever own coin-op machines, which although expensive was popular in Japan, and later in the USA. From that point on, Sega's focus changed from importing games machines to creating their own, and between 1967 and 1979 the company produced a staggering 140 mechanical coin-ops. However, in the late Seventies, Sega moved into the video games business and were involved in the production and distribution of a number of seminal titles including *Frogger* in 1981 and *Zaxxon* in 1982. However, the company was canny enough to recognise that the video games industry was about to take a down-turn and began to diversify into the home market.

The SG-1000 was released in Japan in 1983 and was Sega's first attempt at a home console. Although it fared reasonably well at home, it never really made it to US shores (although a cloned version released by Telegames did) and was soon snuffed out in Japan by Nintendo's then all-conquering Famicom. The Mark II version of the SG-1000 suffered a similar fate, but by 1985, Sega were in a position to outflank Nintendo (at least in regards to technical specification); and so their Mark III machine received a global launch (albeit appearing under the name of the Sega **Master System** in the West).

Although an entertaining marketing battle ensued between

Nintendo and Sega (with each one predictably claiming that they had the better system), Nintendo's NES user-base was just too great for Sega to overcome. However, Sega had made inroads and in the process had raised its profile and learned a few lessons, of which the most important was to ensure that next time they released a new console they didn't give the 'enemy' a head start.

Thus, in 1989, Sega launched their brand new 16-bit machine the **Mega Drive** and so stole a march on Nintendo who had yet to launch their own 16-bit console. Although there were other 16-bit machines out there (most notably NEC's PC Engine), Sega had a full two year start on Nintendo and from this point on, the battle lines were truly drawn as computer gamers started having to make some stark decisions as to whose side they were on.

Between them, Nintendo and Sega would dominate the console market for the next six or seven years. However, by the mid-Nineties, Sega seemed to lose their touch. First of all they released some add-ons for the Mega Drive that proved to be both unpopular and poorly supported. Then they somehow managed to bungle the release of their 'Next Generation' console – the Sega Saturn (released in Japan in 1994) – by bundling it with an unimpressive home conversion of their successful coin-op title *Virtua Fighters* and retailing it at around about $100 more than Sony's **PlayStation**.

By 2001, losses accrued from poor sales of the Saturn and its successor the Dreamcast (launched in the UK in 2000), meant that Sega could no longer afford to stay in the hardware business. Today they produce decent software for a number of consoles (including Nintendo's Gamecube), and the Sega brand is still respected by purveyors of quality arcade games. It is a shame that they have left the console business, but Sega can at least look back with some pride to a time when they part-ruled the video game world.

# SNES
## 1991

The yin to the **Mega Drive**'s yang, the SNES (short for Super Nintendo) remains one of the best-loved games consoles of all time, signifying a time when **Nintendo** was at the peak of its powers and all was well in the video gaming world.

First released in Japan in late 1990 under the moniker 'Super Famicom', much about the SNES is defined by its comparatively late release. Given the success of the **NES**, Nintendo were understandably reticent to release a system that would supersede it, particularly when they realised it would be impractical to create a new console that was backwardly compatible. However, whilst the NES had been able to see off all the competition, the emergence of the Mega Drive had changed the balance of power, making a riposte from Nintendo very necessary.

The SNES was designed to be technically superior to anything else then on the market, and its specifications were impressive, including a 16-bit processor, and the ability to display up to 32,000 colours on screen (compared to the Mega Drive's 512). In addition, the SNES made great use of its Mode 7 graphics capability, enabling programmers to create games that contained backgrounds that scrolled horizontally in a realistic looking way (as seen in games such as **Super Mario Kart**).

Whilst the spec might have been good, Nintendo were well aware that it was the quality of games that would determine the success of their console, and so a lot of time was invested in ensuring their early **Mario** title *Super Mario World* was up to scratch. Another big factor was, of course, cost, and although the Super Famicom was a hit in Japan (with somewhere in the region of 1.5 million pre-orders being placed), its retail price of $200 in the USA compared unfavourably with the $150 that **Sega** were charging for the Mega Drive, and so the system didn't initially sell as well as had been anticipated.

Nonetheless, Nintendo were in it for the long haul, and had a few tricks up their sleeve to boot. First of all came the 'FX' chip. Announced in 1992, the chip featured in a number of special games (most memorably the 1993 title *Starwing*) and greatly improved the console's ability to handle **3-D** graphics. Then in 1994 came **Donkey Kong Country**. Developed by Rare, it featured revolutionary graphics (most people who saw it assumed it was running on what was then referred to as a 'next generation' console) and went on to sell over nine million units, making it the biggest selling game since *Super Mario Bros 3* some four years earlier and the fastest selling title in twenty years.

So by the time the SNES and Mega Drive were breathing their last, Sega's initial lead had been eroded and even surpassed. Whilst the Mega Drive was undoubtedly a fine machine with some excellent games, Nintendo's tight quality control meant that there were far less dud games available for their machine. Today, many of the SNES titles still remain unsurpassed in terms of sheer playability, and although the console was never very hip, the charm and appeal of such titles as *Super Mario Kart*, *Pilotwings* (released in 1990 by Nintendo) and *Legend of Zelda: A Link to the Past* (Nintendo, 1991) endures.

## System Rivalry
1982

During our school years, one of the most important lessons we learn outside the classroom is that we are defined by whose side we are on. In the process we are taught to defend our affiliations with arguments that prevail, not through their inherent good sense and reason, but by their steadfast refusal to concede any ground to an opposing view, regardless of its merit.

All the best rivalries (such as Duran Duran versus Spandau Ballet or My Little Pony versus Care Bears) work because the two opposing forces are actually pretty similar (or maybe even identical), meaning that any affiliation to one or the other must have been forged under arbitrary circumstances (such as your mum happening to buy you a My Little Pony instead of a Care Bear in the first place).

Whilst rivalries might have been common currency in school playgrounds, it is fair to say that there was a specific breed of school child that was particularly keen to debate the merits of *Whizzer and Chips* or DC Comics versus Marvel. Happily, in the Eighties those kinds of kids were also the type to embrace the burgeoning home computer scene, meaning that fierce debates regarding which computer was the best were almost an inevitability as soon as the likes of the **ZX80** or **VIC-20** started appearing in people's homes.

Undoubtedly the most prominent system rivalry in Britain in the early Eighties was between '**ZX Spectrum** kids' and '**Commodore 64** kids'. Whilst the former group had their machine's ubiquity and groundbreaking software to fall back on, the latter knew that they were supporting the world's biggest selling computer. Generally speaking it was the Commodore 64 kids who had the upper hand: their system boasted more colourful graphics and far better sound and, besides, they could show empirically that their computer had more memory than the Spectrum. However, the arrival of games such as ***Knight Lore*** in 1984 and Ocean's 1987 title *Head Over Heels*, gave the Spectrum a definite edge in terms of **3-D** graphics – and boy didn't the Spectrum kids let their opposite numbers know it.

Of course, the Spectrum versus Commodore 64 war was just the start of a long-running campaign that remains active to this day. The most memorable system rivalry of all took place between **Mega Drive** and **SNES** owners; however, the **Atari ST** and **Amiga** hostilities were just as fierce, and there has been nothing to match the nastiness of the on-going **Apple**

**Macintosh** versus **PC** feud. What makes all of these debates so endlessly entertaining are the often spurious arguments used, or rubbish insults bandied around (such as **Nintendo** fans referring to the **PlayStation** as the 'Grey Station').

Adding fuel to the fire, **computer magazines** have a long history of, not only dissing rival systems, but having a go at rival publications too. This even extends to encouraging readers to send in poorly drawn pictures (usually done on lined paper obviously ripped out of a school exercise book), depicting a tableau of **Sonic The Hedgehog** wiping his arse on **Mario** themed toilet paper, Sonic being annihilated in a volley of machine gun fire, or, for those particularly lacking in imagination, a PC being used as a door stop (oh the dry wit).

Indeed it is this apparent irrationality and need for puerile name calling that underpins much system rivalry. After all, if you base an argument on empirical fact alone you can't really sustain it for very long, or – more importantly – get very passionate about it, can you?

## VIC-20
### 1981

Latterly referred to in derogatory terms by mathematics teachers trying to be hip; to wit 'Come on Simpkins I've got VIC-20s that could work out the answer to that equation quicker than you', the Commodore VIC-20 was actually quite a formidable machine for its time. Built on the foundations of Commodore's earlier PET range (a reasonably basic computer that according to rumour could be made to erupt into flames simply by writing one of those looping 'GOTO 10' type routines which repeatedly instructed the PET to turn its tape motor on and off again), the VIC-20 was, for many home users, their first experience of a colour computer.

The press advertising campaign hailed it as 'the wonder

computer of the Eighties' and featured William Shatner in homely sweater and open neck shirt enquiring 'why buy just a video game?' Other ads in the series depicted Shatner in a smart suit pointing lovingly at the VIC-20 whilst the copy implored: 'Why get just another game that could end up in the closet? Get an honest-to-goodness computer'.

Compared with its UK contemporaries of the time (such as the **ZX 81**), the VIC-20 was an accomplished looking machine. Not only did it come with a proper looking keyboard, but the aforementioned colour graphics (the first on a sub $300 computer) couldn't help but look impressive. Resultantly, in its four-year lifespan the VIC-20 became the first home computer to sell over one million units. Indeed one wonders how many more Commodore could have sold had they not decided to launch the vastly superior **Commodore 64** just a year or so later.

Incidentally, the VIC-20 was marketed as the 'friendly computer' and this sense of bonhomie even applied to the '20' in the VIC-20's moniker, which apparently was chosen simply because the numbers sounded somehow welcoming.

## ZX81
### 1981

This modest little black number with a raised 'Sinclair' logo, touch-sensitive keypad and ugly looking plug in RAM pack is undoubtedly one of the most important machines in the history of British home computing. Indeed the phenomenal success of the ZX81 (350,000 units were sold in its first year, and by the end of year two that figure had risen to over one million) signified the point where home computers began to emerge from their academic background, and become something that could conceivably play a part in every household in the land. It also pretty much sounded the death knell in this country for the previously popular home consoles manufactured by the likes of

**Atari** and Mattel, and moved Britain away from viewing computers as merely games machines.

But before the ZX81 came the ZX80. Who gave a stuff about RAM and ROM when here was a computer with touch sensitive keys? A bit like escalators or electric toothbrushes, the ZX80, with its membrane keyboard, seemed for at least three seconds to be the very stuff of tomorrow: an affordable (only £99.99) computer that you could actually buy in the shops (albeit specialist **computer shops**), take home, plug in and start using.

The ZX80 was by no means universally praised, and in fact was often ridiculed for looking like a bit of cheese and featuring a clunky computer language that many found completely impenetrable. It was no computing powerhouse either; whenever you typed on the keyboard, the screen image would momentarily disappear (the ZX80 didn't have the necessary computational power to process what you were typing and display it on the screen at the same time). Yet these subtle nuances mattered little when you stacked it up against the fact that you could proclaim 'I've got a computer...in my house!'

The ZX80 sold only a modest number of units – around about 100,000, but it set the stage for what was to follow. Named after the year of its release, the ZX81 represented a significant improvement on its predecessor in terms of memory and capability (the ZX81 could handle equations involving non-integer numbers, something that was beyond the ZX80's capabilities). Indeed promotional material proclaimed that the ZX81 was powerful enough to run a power station (which is probably true, albeit very, very slowly). However, no one should run away with the idea that it was anything other than a rudimentary piece of kit, particularly in regards to gameplaying. Computer fans would have to wait a little bit longer for a Sinclair machine that could handle colour, or even sound; and what's more the ZX81 couldn't even calculate square roots (an omission that caused great embarrassment to its creator Sir

Clive Sinclair).

Instrumental in the ZX81's success was the deal that Sinclair cut with high street retailers WH Smith, meaning that for the first time you were able to purchase a home computer directly from a major high street retailer. Employing new manufacturing techniques also meant that the ZX81 could be constructed from just four chips, allowing Sinclair to retail the finished machine for as little as £69.95 (more than £30 cheaper than the ZX80).

The massive success of the ZX81 seemed to kick off a whole industry. Not only did other manufacturers (such as Dragon) sit up, take notice and start producing their own machines, but the number of **computer magazines** on the market also began to increase. Similarly, the ZX81's success injected new life into the low-quality cassette player market. These small, rather basic machines had found themselves supplanted by shiny new affordable hi-fis; however, computer consumers discovered that cheaply made portable models were perfectly suited to the job of **loading** programs from cassettes.

Another first for the ZX81 was arguably the arrival of commercially released games that would in any way stand the test of time. In this respect, the machine was well served with loads of titles including a pretty decent version of chess released by Artic in 1982 and a passable conversion of *Galaxians* (also released by Artic in 1982). Undoubtedly the best remembered game on the ZX81 was JK Greye's *3-D Monster Maze* (released in 1981), which was a revolutionary first-person perspective **adventure game**, featuring (for its time) some excellent graphics. The object of the game was to navigate your way out of a maze, all the while attempting to avoid a marauding tyrannosaurus rex.

The ZX81 gave its owners many happy hours of tinkering, **programming** and playing. In fact the machine's only major drawback was its aforementioned RAM pack. Although designed to plug into the back of the machine, this connection was never properly secure, meaning that halfway through typing in a particularly long program you would press down on a key just a little bit too hard, slightly dislodge the RAM pack and thus crash the computer. There seemed to be no universally satisfying solution to this predicament, although a piece of Blu-Tack wedged in nice and tight usually did the trick for a while.

## ZX Spectrum
### 1982

Most people think kindly of the ZX Spectrum (despite its irritating colour clashes and crappy sound). Certainly Sir Clive Sinclair does (it earned him a knighthood). Released in 1982, it built magnificently on the groundwork of Sinclair's two previous 'ZX' computers, busting a yet greater hole into the high street market, and pushing home computers even further towards the mainstream. Computers came and computers went, but for six long years the ZX Spectrum dominated the British home scene.

But what was so great about the 'Speccy' (its rather familiar sounding nickname)? Well to start with the obvious, it was Sinclair's first colour computer (although only a few people had ever heard of 'cyan' or 'magenta' before) and the first to feature something that at least resembled a proper keyboard. Indeed in terms of looks, the Spectrum was a departure from its two predecessors. The raised, slightly futuristic 'Sinclair' logo remained but the computer itself was more compact, with greater space dedicated to the keyboard. Of course, one of the most striking design elements of the ZX Spectrum was its shock of multi-coloured lines running diagonally up across the bottom right hand corner. The metallic casing that covered the keyboard is today well remembered for it reassuring looseness, meaning that prying hands could prise it away from the rest of the computer and amass crumbs in the gaps between keys that would over time cause them to become unusable.

Whilst some described the Spectrum's keys as feeling a little like dead flesh, the way the computer heated up after prolonged exposure actually made those keys feel, if anything, almost alive. Yes, if there was any computer ripe for anthropomorphising then it was the good old Speccy.

As with Sinclair's previous releases, price points were essential to the Spectrum's success. The 16K version originally retailed at just £125, and the 48K for £175. However, within just a few months the price of the 16K Spectrum was slashed to the psychologically important sub-£100 figure of £99.95, more or less the same price that the ZX80 had retailed for back in 1980. But, although highly competitive on the market, the Spectrum's greatest selling point wasn't its price, but the abundance of affordable games on offer.

Almost every conceivable genre was catered for, and a vast number of all-time classic titles released. Definitely one of the most important elements in sustaining the Spectrum's success over the years was games developers' ability to push the machine harder and harder to produce results that were well beyond its original capabilities. In fact, if you compare a Spectrum game from its early days (such as Vortex Software's 1983 release *Android 1: The Reactor Run*) with one released a little later (for example, Ocean's 1987 classic *Head Over Heels*), it is very difficult to believe that both were created for the same computer. What the latter game has over the former is its realisation of a **3-D** gaming environment that instantly makes everything look far more sophisticated.

Over the years a number of upgraded versions of the ZX Spectrum were released. The first came in 1984, when Sinclair released the Spectrum+. Although its actual capabilities were identical to a standard Spectrum, it came with a smart looking, 'proper' keyboard (very similar to that which would later accompany Sinclair's next computer – the **QL**). In 1986 there came the

Spectrum 128, which as the name suggests had additional memory. It looked much like the Spectrum+, but in addition replaced the rather inferior sound chip of the original Speccy with something a little more substantial. Given this release resolved the Spectrum's keyboard and sound problems (two perennial criticisms directed at the computer), you might have thought that the Spectrum 128 would have sold well. However, with Sinclair caught up in their unfolding **C5** and **QL** debacles, the machine was inadequately marketed and not helped by the fact that some earlier Spectrum software wouldn't work on it.

Once Amstrad bought Sinclair in 1986, three other versions of the Spectrum were released, none of which came anywhere close to matching the success of the original. Given the arrival of far superior machines such as the **Atari ST** and **Amiga**, it was clear that trying to prolong the Spectrum's life was a hopeless cause. However, by the time the curtain was finally pulled, five million units had been sold, and somewhere in the region of 12,000 different games produced; all in all, the single most successful (as well as best loved) British computer ever made.

# The Paraphernalia

Back in 1982, a company called William Stuart Systems Ltd released a speech recognition system for the **ZX Spectrum**. Named *Big Ears*, it would set you back £49, and for that you got a microphone, and a box labelled 'Speech Recognition system interface SR'. Once you'd hooked the thing up you were able to train it to recognise up to six words spoken into the microphone. The system was fraught with drawbacks, the most significant of which was how easily it was confused by similar sounding words. But, with some careful enunciation it could be made to more or less work and, for a while, this was very exciting. Computers that understood verbal inputs seemed the stuff of dreams, yet here it was in all its glory in your front room. Once the initial euphoria died down though, it became apparent that there was very little you could actually do with it given the aforementioned six-word limitation.

But William Stuart Systems Ltd weren't finished yet. At around the same time as *Big Ears* hit the market, they also released *Chatterbox*, a nifty piece of hardware that made your ZX Spectrum speak. Again, it wasn't particularly straightforward (it relied on the user stringing together phonemes to create a final sound that slightly resembled a word), but nonetheless, the prospect of owning a computer that could actually talk was thrillingly futuristic.

Neither *Big Ears* nor *Chatterbox* set the computing world alight, but they were representative of the scores of companies who were working away to come up with a whole range of add-ons and accessories that would transform your ordinary computer into something far more exciting and futuristic. Generally, such devices (and let's not forget the various lightpens, drum machines and teletext page savers that were all released for the ZX Spectrum in the Eighties) struggled to function properly, and most were ideas that probably should have waited until the technology had grown sufficiently sophisticated to properly support them. But that's what made them so brilliant. We knew that they wouldn't really work, but they allowed us to believe, even for just a moment, that our computer was capable of doing things that you had previously only ever seen in the movies.

Electronic pocket devices were great too. Walking around with a little bit of computer on your wrist was a mighty fine feeling back in the Seventies and Eighties, even if it was just a digital watch. After all, what could be more futuristic than a liquid crystal display (LCD) and a button that allowed you to switch from time to date, and back again? **Pocket calculators and digital watches** were portable proof that we were becoming as tooled up as the best on-screen Secret Agents.

It didn't take manufacturers long to realise that the promise of a little bit of the future was a tantalising prospect, and in the late Seventies and early Eighties all manner of toys and games appeared on the shelves that contained either silicon chips, or (as was the case with MB's 1977 *Electronic Battleships)* some flashing lights which gave the impression of advanced technology.

As we moved into the late Eighties and early Nineties, it was no longer enough for toy companies to simply add some light emitting diodes (LED) to their latest release. Manufacturers instead turned their attentions to enhancing the computer gameplaying experience. This led to a slew of **peripherals**, encompassing light guns, steering wheels and all manner of exotic looking add-ons. Sadly, in recent years the appetite for bizarre computer paraphernalia appears to be on the wane in favour of multimedia add-ons such as DVD drives, MP3 players and other excellent, albeit rather sensible, devices.

All of which is sadly a mile away from the days when bundling every **NES** with a superfluous robot seemed like a viable marketing strategy.

Barcode Battler
1991

Best remembered as the subject of innumerable torturous 'whatever will they think of next' type news stories; during 1992, the Barcode Battler was for a tiny moment all the rage with Trevor MacDonald and Alastair Stewart, but never quite managed to set the gaming world alight. So what warranted the visible loosening of the tie and wry smile from Sir Trevor?

The Barcode Battler was a **handheld gaming** device that featured a couple of one-player games as well as a two-player combat option. The games themselves were hard-coded into the machine and were relatively derivative (the one-player game consisted of a quest to locate some keys and fight some baddies). Barcode Battler's hook though was that the attributes of your on-screen character were defined by, of all things, barcodes. Basically by scanning the barcode from a can of soup or bottle of fizzy pop you were uploading data to the machine that would dictate the strength and skills of your character. The fun of it was that you wouldn't know in advance which barcodes would prove most powerful, and so players would scour supermarket shelves in search of the codes that would bestow upon them the greatest abilities.

For a brief spell, the Barcode Battler entered into our shared lexicon of subjects to make jokes about (alongside Mr Blobby and David Mellor's tryst with Antonia de Sanchez) and world weary commentators took great delight in exploring the allegorical connections between our consumerist society and the Battler's function. Meanwhile broadsheet columnists would obtain cheap copy from endlessly going on about how the device would put an end once and for all to the Pepsi vs. Coke debate. The press attention probably reached its apotheosis when rumours began to circulate that the Holy Grail of barcodes was printed on the side of a Pot Noodle. This was too

convenient, given that the Pot Noodle was at that time the chosen 'amusing' food item of Fleet Street wags.

With limited scope and game-play, the Barcode Battler
quickly became yesterday's news; however, the notion of introducing an additional factor from outside the confines of the
actual gaming machine has endured, and remains to this day an
appealing concept that has not yet been fully exploited.

## Big Trak
## 1979

In 1979 **Space Invaders** and, as a consequence, all things related to video games, were on the lips of every child and parent
in the land. It didn't take long for analysts to boil down the success of this phenomenon into a single phrase that thereafter
could be applied to any other piece of merchandise that
required a sales boost. The phrase was 'silicon chip', and once
you had got passed the obvious and unamusing potato references, it was clear that these little things had an almost unlimited number of potential applications, many of which could be
used for making toys more interesting.

A flurry of products soon hit the market, and amidst this slew
came MB Electronic's Big Trak. This decent sized six-wheeled
vehicle resembled something out of an episode of
*Thunderbirds*. It came with exciting stickers and a 'photon cannon' that was actually a tiny light bulb plus some sound effects.

However, not content with just looking the business, MB's promotional material for the toy boasted that it was fully programmable. This was indeed the case, with the user able to punch in up to
sixteen different commands, each one consisting of a direction and
duration. The Big Trak would then be free to carry out your orders,
be they a kamikaze mission to the top of the stairs and beyond (a
particular favourite if it wasn't actually yours) or a sortie into the
kitchen to harass mum whilst she was cooking. All of this sophisti-

cated play was thanks to the toy's TMS1000 Microcontroller that was able to perform its function very adequately.

Of course, the problem with **programming** in commands is that it is not very exciting and loses some of the immediacy of just rattling around with a toy truck. In truth, Big Trak didn't really need any computerized gimmicks as it looked brilliant. However, whether it would have gone on to become such a popular toy without the lustre of technology is very doubtful.

## C5

1985

If you play a game of free association with the letter *c* and the number *5* then it is likely that you will end up with the phrase 'bad stand up comedy' or, more simply, 'Jasper Carrott'. Quite how a Brummie comedian with no chin and a pair of beady eyes came to be our barometer of acceptability in the Eighties is a mystery, but undeniably, if Carrott decided that Ladas or *Sun* readers were worthy of derision, then derided they became. Sadly for C5 inventor Sir Clive Sinclair, his innocuous little electronic vehicle (released in 1985) soon joined the Hall of Naff.

However, a number of factors advantageous to the creation of the C5 fell into place in the early Eighties. For a start, the notion of electronic transportation had grown increasingly attractive to political parties aware that the ecology was becoming a vote-winning topic and to that end, on 26th March 1980, the Government abolished motor tax for electronic vehicles. This was followed up three years later with further electrically-assisted pedal cycle legislation. In the meantime, Sinclair' own fortunes had taken a significant upturn. The release of the **ZX81** computer had set the UK home computing market alight, and there seemed no reason to suspect that its successor, the **ZX Spectrum**, would do anything other than sell by the truck load. Thus, to Sir Clive the timing seemed to be right to once again explore his electronic dream.

Given that the concept had been gestating in Sir Clive's mind for a few decades, the actual design of the C5 itself was, for want of a better word, eccentric. It looked a little like a car seat secured to a sledge secured to a flattened tricycle, and it became difficult to imagine who (save children mucking around) would want to ride in one. Apart from the fact it was necessarily slow (the top speed was limited to fifteen miles per hour), it didn't really look very credible. In addition, initial road testing threw up other concerns such as the battery power being partially dependent on the weather, meaning that on a cold day you could end up running out of juice before you made it back home.

Regardless, Sinclair pressed on and decided to commit a healthy sum of cash to launching and promoting his brainchild. Whilst the lavish brochures made a decent fist of extolling the C5's virtues, the press launch in January 1985 was a different matter, with journalists invited to test drive what turned out to be defective models. It then became apparent that both ex-employees of DeLorean (at that time an infamous car manufacturer) and Hoover (manufacturers of vacuum cleaners) were involved in the construction process, and all of a sudden you could see journalists rubbing their hands in glee at the sheer incredulity of it all.

Whilst all kinds of anti-C5 jokes were bandied around the media a real and significant concern came to the fore, namely safety. Commentators began to question whether consumers would feel comfortable taking a C5 for a spin in the rush-hour traffic and if lorry drivers would be able to spot them given that they were so close to the ground. These reservations would ultimately lead to the introduction of a 'hi-vis-mast' that would allow the C5 to be spotted from afar; however, the mental image of being stuck behind a juggernaut blasting exhaust fumes in your face was totally unpalatable.

It became pretty clear, pretty quickly, that the C5 was commercially speaking a 'dead duck'. Shops began to slash prices in an attempt to flog them and to make matters worse, in April 1985 the Advertising Standards Authority upheld complaints that the C5's promotional material had contained unsubstantiated claims. By August, Hoover ceased production and by November, TPD (the company that Sinclair had formed to create the vehicle) went into voluntary liquidation. Only around 4500 C5s had been sold.

Given that the same year had also marked the suspension of production of Sinclair's ill-fated **QL**, it was clear that for Sir Clive, 1985 was far from an excellent vintage.

## Choose Your Own Adventure Books 1979

In terms of technical evolution it would seem logical to conclude that *Choose Your Own Adventure* books came before computer **adventure games**; after all, what are such books if not nascent and rather crude attempts at **programming**? However, the first *Choose Your Own Adventure* title was published in 1979, by which time computer adventure games had been around for a good seven years or so.

The basic premise of *Choose Your Own Adventure* (and the other similar ranges such as *Fighting Fantasy*) is that you, the reader, are able to participate in the unfolding plot. The mechanism by which this works is pretty crude, and consists of you reading a few paragraphs of a story and then being asked to a make a decision such as signing or not signing a piece of paper, or turning back to 'explore the town' instead of 'pressing on towards the castle'. Once you have made your decision you are then directed to the appropriate page or paragraph in the book, where you adventure picks up again.

Some adventures added further complexity by asking the reader to roll a die at various points in order to determine whether or not they were successful at a particular task (usually fighting a troll), but in essence, all of these titles offered you the same thing – a tree structured story that you would follow until you arrived at a precarious narrative twig that resulted in your usually rather abrupt demise.

The correlation between such books and computer gaming is obvious: the limitations inherent in a *Choose Your Own Adventure* are just the same as those you find within a computer game; namely you can't really go anywhere that the writer/programmer hasn't already created, or do anything that they haven't permitted you to do. However, the books did serve as some kind of compensatory service for kids who didn't have their own home computers.

Given such structural similarities it was little surprise that in the mid-Eighties a number of *Fighting Fantasy* titles were turned into games for the **ZX Spectrum**, **Commodore 64** and other popular home computers of the day.

These titles evolved in other ways too, most notably the introduction of adventures that could be played over the telephone. The best remembered is Fantasy Interactive Scenarios by Telephone (FIST), which was a typical dungeon-based adventure. In truth, the gaming mechanics were no more advanced than those found in the books, but at least here there were sound effects to be enjoyed. Unsurprisingly, these services proved to be a thorn in the side of parents who not only had to contend with being unable to use their telephone, but also had to foot the bill.

## Cover Mounted software
## 1983

As a comics reader it was a pretty sure bet that about the best free gift you could hope to receive from your chosen publication was a packet of strange synthetic sweets that popped on your tongue, or maybe a paper 'whiz-bang' that you only knew was fun because the comic told you so. One of the fringe benefits of getting in to computers then was that not only were you able to upgrade your copy of *Whizzer and Chips* to something more substantial like *BBC*

*Micro User* magazine, but you stood a good chance of getting some free cover mounted software with each edition too.

Although it is difficult to pinpoint the first UK **computer magazine** to affix a tape to their front cover, *BBC Micro User* must have been amongst the pioneers, given that issue one (published way back in March 1983) came with a tape that helpfully included all of the interminable program listings featured in that edition. The highlight of this collection of twenty-five programs was undoubtedly *Deathwatch* a 'superb arcade game that challenges you to use your skill to fight off enemy battleships, tanks and helicopters'.

By the mid-Eighties free tapes with computer magazines were becoming increasingly commonplace. *Your Sinclair* issue one (published in 1986) featured a demo of the computer game *Rasputin*, and by issue 22 the mag was giving away titles such as Elite's *Batty*. Even stodgy old *Sinclair User* submitted to peer pressure and offered readers in March 1988 what it billed as 'the best tape ever' with **shoot 'em up**s and **pokes and cheats** galore.

But such actions had consequences, and as free tapes grew increasingly commonplace it became evident that the term 'free' wasn't strictly accurate. Newsfield Publication's *Crash* magazine gave away a tape with each issue from June 1989 onwards; however, such generosity was accompanied by a twenty-five pence increase in cover price.

There was another hidden cost too, namely sustained damage to the cover of your magazine. Always a perennial cause for complaint in the letter pages, publishers adopted one of two strategies: either they would affix the cassette to the front of the magazine via a strip of sticky tape that, when you attempted to prize the cassette free, was guaranteed to take part of the cover off; or they would use a bizarre form of glue that closely resembled snot (to the extent that it often found itself stuck up some waggish reader's nostril). In truth, neither method was wholly satisfactory and it is an issue that has dogged the magazine industry to this day.

Over the years there have been some truly great freebies (such as the magazine that gave away an audio tape of the arcade soundtrack to **After Burner**). Though as we moved from the 8-bit to the 16-bit age it became clear that free software could also pack a nasty punch. November 1990 was a turning point, when *Atari ST User* gave away what appeared to be a very serviceable free disk that contained a number of programs including a sprite designer and something called *Chronicles of Omega*. However, unbeknownst to most readers it also contained a rather nasty virus that would copy itself onto any non write protected disks that you would happen to slot into your **Atari ST** after having looked at the free disk. Unsurprisingly, rival publication *ST Format* made much of the boob, and *Atari ST User* offered readers a free two-game special disk by way of an apology a little while later. From then on, it became commonplace for computer magazines to periodically include on their cover disks the latest versions of public domain virus killers, as well as some small print to the effect that the publishers could not be held responsible for any viruses that they might give you.

Game and Watch
1980

Just when you thought you had attained your rightful hierarchical place at the top of school society, someone (usually with richer parents than you) turned up with a Game and Watch. These pesky handheld games systems were easily one up on your ruler calculator, and as soon as the first one made it onto school grounds they became the talk of the lunch break.

They were strange things though; produced by **Nintendo**, these little handheld devices didn't actually seem to have any proper graphics at all, rather pre-printed cells that could be strung together in some basic form of animation during the course of a game. Indeed they owed their existence to the breakthrough in LCD technology pioneered by **pocket calculator and digital watch** manufacturers in the Seventies.

The first Game and Watch hit the streets in 1980. This was *Ball*, a rather boring juggling game in which all you had to do was move the juggler's arms left and right to catch the balls. Games continued in this rather simple, if esoteric, vein for some time with other earlier titles such as *Judge* (also released in 1980) featuring two characters holding hammers, with random numbers appearing above their head to signify which fellow was able to hit the other. Things started looking up in 1981 with *Parachute*. In this game you simply had to try and catch all the people parachuting from the overhead helicopter. Yet it was somehow more entertaining than the games that had preceded it and was one of the first titles to become commonplace in the playground.

Of course, the really cool Game and Watches were those with multiple screens. The **Donkey Kong** one (released in 1982) was particularly memorable. It came in a garish orange plastic case and opened up to reveal two screens, one above the other, over which the sprawling *Donkey Kong* platform was depicted. Many British gamers got their first glimpse of *Donkey Kong* and Jump Man not in the amusement arcade at all, but up by the goalposts on the school sports field.

Shrewdly recognising that parents might not wish to buy their child a device that was designed solely for gaming, Nintendo added a clock element to their Game and Watches so that they could be seen to possess a practical use too. However, this was purely a Trojan Horse to allow Nintendo to get their ware to the kids.

Nintendo released their last Game and Watch title, *Mario The Juggler*, in 1991. Rather appositely, the objective of the game was very similar to that set in *Ball* some eleven years earlier. Single game handheld machines do still exist and can for some reason principally be found in seaside tourist shops selling for a few quid. However, as a playground currency, they became devalued almost as soon as Nintendo released the **Game Boy** in 1989.

## Game Boy
## 1989

The veritable jewel in **Nintendo**'s hardware crown, the Game Boy, was the first major handheld system on the market in ten years to allow users to play multiple games. It was also at first glance the least interesting and most technically unaccomplished of the various handheld systems released in the late Eighties and early Nineties. The **Atari** Lynx was back lit, the Game Boy was not, the **Sega** Game Gear was full colour, the Game Boy was limited to just four shades of grey, and the **PC** Engine GT came with a television tuner, whereas the Game Boy simply didn't.

It was Nintendo's machine that won a place in our hearts. Its pleasingly unfussy design (a little *plus* sign controller, *A* and *B* buttons and *Start* and *Select* keys) and robust casing signified the Game Boy as a 'take anywhere' kind of machine. There was no reverence for cutting edge technology on display here; the Game Boy was friendliness personified, it wasn't snooty or snobby, it was your best mate and you could even knock it around a bit if you wanted.

Although other systems might have looked and sounded better, Nintendo appreciated that what you wanted for that long car journey to grandma's was a portable gaming system that wouldn't conk out on you halfway there (the Game Boy could run for ten hours on four batteries, whereas most of its competitors would run out of juice in just three or four hours). A handheld system shouldn't be about technical specifications, it should be about fun.

As if to emphasize the point, the Game Boy came with a free copy of *Tetris,* the one game above all others that best personifies the pursuit of fun over graphical or sonic excellence. Predictably a **Mario** game turned up for the system not long after its launch (*Super Mario Land* was released for the Game Boy in 1989) and in three years Nintendo shifted a whopping 32 million Game Boys (later rising to over 120 million).

Over the years, there have been further iterations of the basic model including the Game Boy Pocket in 1996 and the Game Boy Light in 1998. In 2004, Nintendo released their latest handheld system – the DS. Whilst its dual screen is an echo back to the glory of Nintendo's **Game and Watch** series, you can bet it is the Game Boy's illustrious and record-breaking footsteps that it is hoping to follow in.

## Game Genie
## 1990

As long as there have been computer games, there have been computer game cheats. Several **computer magazines** have a longstanding tradition of regularly publishing '**pokes and codes**' that allow players to obtain infinite lives or unlimited ammo. The Game Genie was a device that took this approach one step further. Marketed by Lewis Galoob Toys in 1990, the user simply inserted their game cartridge into the Game Genie which was in turn inserted into the cartridge slot of the appropriate console (Game Genies were made for the **NES, SNES** and **Sega Megadrive**). When you turned the console on you would be presented with a menu screen that allowed you to type in up to four codes which would provide you with extra lives, unlimited cash or whatever souped-up attribute was required to make the game in question easier to play.

But what were these codes, and how did you go about finding them out? Well, when you purchased your Game Genie it would usually come with a booklet listing out the codes for the various games for your machine. In addition, it was possible to sign up to a quarterly newsletter that would provide you with codes for the latest titles. In respect to how this all worked, most gamers didn't really care to know; however, the enterprising few were able to suss out that the Game Genie operated by intercepting requests made by the console to the cartridge for information relating to specific gaming attributes. Instead of allowing the data on the cartridge to be fed back to the machine, the Game Genie would send a modified value of its own (as defined by the code numbers input by the user). There was an occasional unfortunate by-product of this though, that sometimes meant the Game Genie would misunderstand the type of requests being made of it, leading to some weird, but usually minor, corruptions appearing in the game itself.

Although companies such as **Sega** were quite content to endorse the Game Genie, **Nintendo** were rather less happy about it and in 1991 took Lewis Galoob Toys to court claiming that the Game Genie infringed copyrighted work of others by changing elements of games that Lewis Galoob Toys had not themselves created. However, the Judge deemed this to be an unconvincing argument and furthermore pointed out that Nintendo couldn't demonstrate that the existence of the Game Genie was having any kind of detrimental affect on sales. Given that Nintendo had been able to secure a pre-trial injunction to prevent Lewis Galoob Toys from selling any further Game Genies until the matter had been contested in court, Nintendo were forced to pay the toy manufacturers $15 million by way of recompense.

## Handheld gaming
### 1976

Although **Nintendo** have come to dominate the scene, handheld games have always proved to be extremely popular; which is pretty unsurprising, given that when you first clapped eyes on one, you felt as if you were looking at the tool that would result in the total and utter elimination of boredom. Just the thought of being able to carry a computer game with you at all times seemed to suggest that you had at hand an ever-present weapon to combat the tedium of a day out at a local area of interest, or the drive to visit your grandparents.

The first ever handheld electronic game was Mattel Toys' *Auto Race*, manufactured in 1976. This very simplistic piece of kit used light emitting diodes (LEDs) to represent both your car and the obstacles that you had to dodge. However, the problem with LEDs and, by extension, *Auto* Race was that they didn't really look like anything other than what they were. So, whilst the game might have depicted speeding racing cars on the packaging, you could never really get away from the fact that you were controlling a little light trying to avoid other little lights.

Clearly, handheld games benefited tremendously from the introduction of both liquid crystal displays (LCD) and vacuum fluorescent displays (VFD) in the late Seventies and early Eighties. These technologies meant that instead of having to use little lights to signify characters or vehicles, it was now possible to create recognisable images on screen, and with less battery consumption than a LED game too. In fact, VFD games generated their own light so you could even play them under the duvet cover – brilliant!

Over the early Eighties, a number of manufacturers got involved in creating handheld games including, MB, Parker Brothers, Tomy, Bandai and Popy (who produced the unforgettably named *Dr. Slump Ncha Bycha*). However, some games were definitely more memorable than others. For example Tomy's 1983 *Stereo Skyfighters* looked impossibly futuristic and exciting (indeed it resembled a ViewMaster), although kids who owned it would never let anyone else have a go. Similarly, Coleco's range of mini-arcade machines were impressive, sporting all the flash livery of the real coin-ops in a size that would fit into one giant hand, or more usually, one ordinary sized tabletop. Of particular note was Coleco's version of the seminal **3-D** shoot 'em up *Zaxxon*. Although far too big to hold in your hand, its clever use of a dual VFD display, plus two-way mirror produced something that looked truly awesome back in 1982.

For most of us, handheld games usually meant cheapo models such as Grandstand's *Thunderbird* series released in 1991 (well after the glory years of the original handheld games) or Casio's competent but uninspiring range featuring gems like 1983's *Fire Panic*. Whilst MB's *Microvision* (released in 1979) came with little cartridges (meaning that you could play more than one type of game), the rise in popularity of home consoles meant that before long, your handheld game ended up forgotten and covered in black ink, dumped in a school bag with a broken pen.

The second generation of handheld games were altogether different, with the likes of **Nintendo, Sega** and **Atari** wading in with proper gaming systems that were in every way analogous to the home consoles of the time. Whilst indisputably successful, these later devices lost almost all of the idiosyncratic charm of their one-game forerunners, wherein each system was uniquely designed to extol the virtue of its solitary title, and so might feature bright pink livery or even a protective cover for the gaming screen that came in the shape of a giant eye.

## Joysticks
## 1977

To the uninitiated, joysticks are a crucial part of any computer gaming set-up, yet with the exception of **flight simulator** games, the traditional joystick has long since fallen into disrepute in favour of the control pad (or joypad as it is often referred too).

This is a great shame for computing purists but for the rest of us it's a simple matter of ergonomics. Since the arrival of the first computer joystick (for the **Atari** 2600 in 1977), the essential problem has always been that for a joystick to function properly you need to be able to rest it on something.

Atari actually borrowed the design and function of the joystick from those devices that pilots have used in aeroplanes since the early years of the twentieth century. Indeed the name is thought to derive, not from some euphemistic moniker coined by a bunch of cheeky aviators, but rather as an allusion to the term 'joyride'. Computer joysticks broadly come in two varieties, digital and analogue. The former recognises only up, down, left and right movements, whereas the latter can detect more subtle directional controls. Atari's 2600 joystick stuck rigidly to the more simplistic digital controls, but its follow-up for the Atari 5200 was designed to allow full 360 degree movement. Although revolutionary for its time, it was also completely unplayable. Not only did the joystick not self-centre but it made playing **platformers** (where precise movements were required) almost impossible. In fact, so bad was the 5200's joystick that is probably fair to say it was a significant contributory factor to the console's relative commercial failure.

By the early Eighties, it was becoming increasingly clear that the traditional joystick, whilst working well on bolted down arcade machines, was not really appropriate for the home market. Taking inspiration from their own **Game and Watch** series, **Nintendo** developed a control pad which relied on a simple, risen '+' shape that the user could rock in the appropriate direction. The new style controller made its debut on the **NES** and from that point on, the traditional joystick's days were numbered.

## Killer Apps
### 1979

As any computer or console manufacturer will tell you, the 'killer app' (the 'app' being short for application) is an essential element. Whilst the marketing collateral can speak of processor power, graphics cards or memory sizes, such jargon will only capture the interest of the hardcore user. What is required is a piece of software that provides a palpable demonstration of the unique and essential attributes of your great new machine. Without a killer app your brand new system has little chance of selling even if it has the most fantastic technical specifications.

The first ever 'killer app' was *VisiCalc* for the Apple II. This application (which came in a natty brown vinyl folder) was the first-ever computerized spreadsheet, and also the first piece of software that was of real use to the business community. Although those who saw it in action were initially non-plussed (as is often the case with groundbreaking technology), *VisiCalc* soon became a compelling reason to fork out the required cash for an Apple II. Similarly, in 1985 Aldus' *PageMaker* drew would-be desktop publishers to the **Apple Mac** in droves.

Within the gaming community, killer apps usually mean games. Generally speaking these are titles that provide something new and exciting in terms of graphics or gameplay; or a decent home conversion of an already established arcade hit. *Space Invaders* for the **Atari** 2600 was the most successful gaming killer app in history, driving sales of the 2600 through the roof, as customers bought the console simply to get at those aliens. Atari tried the same trick again in 1994 when they released a completely faithful version of the hit arcade game *Tempest* under the moniker *Tempest 2000* for the Jaguar. On this occasion, whilst the conversion might have been first rate, it wasn't enough to change the fortune of what very quickly came to be known as the 'ill-fated' Atari Jaguar.

During the same year, Sony proved that it wasn't just Atari who could plunder the arcade back catalogue in order to boost system sales. Namco's *Ridge Racer* was one of the launch titles for the **PlayStation**, and although it could be argued that **Tomb Raider** also helped to shift a few units, it was *Ridge Racer* that showed the suspicious computer gaming fraternity that console new boys Sony actually knew what they were doing.

Thanks to the sheer speed and graphical brilliance, **Sonic The**

*Hedgehog* is one of the few original games to have established itself as a killer app (this time for the **Sega Mega Drive**). Similarly, Cinemaware's lush *Defender of the Crown* (released for the **Atari ST** and **Amiga** in 1987) was a compelling enough reason for any **Commodore 64** or **Amstrad CPC-464** owner to turn in their aging 8-bit computer in preference for these 16-bit wonder machines. Indeed, common to all successful home computers or consoles has been the release of one or more essential titles that have literally compelled customers to go out and buy both machine and game. Be it the superlative *Super Mario 64* for the Nintendo 64 (released in 1996), or JK Greye's *3-D Monster Maze* released for the **ZX81**), coming to market with a new system without something special up your sleeve is a foolhardy business.

## Mindlink
## 1984

Whilst the evolution of technology has taken us to some unexpected places (such as EyeToy), there are certain technological goals that seem to be shared by all developers. **3-D** television for one, 'smell-a-vision' another, and the ability to control your computer via the power of your mind yet another. However, whilst boffins are still working on a practicable version of 3-D telly that doesn't rely on donning silly glasses, and the breakthrough in telly you can smell seems to be as far away as ever, it will probably shock you to learn that **Atari** nailed the old mind control over twenty years ago.

'An entirely new and exciting way to use Atari game systems and computers' proclaimed the advertising copy for the Mindlink. Compatible with the 2600, 7200 and Home Computer range, the idea was that you strapped on a special headband that detected activity in the muscles on your forehead and translated them into movements on screen, or as Atari put it in their brochure: 'It relies upon special software designed to interact with every individual's unique EMG readings. It encourages you to concentrate and relax, and is both fun and challenging to master'. Packaged with a **Breakout** style game called *Bionic Breakthrough*, Atari believed they were onto a winner, something that would have appeal across the board.

But prolonged testing of the system revealed that it was little more than a glorified eyebrow waggling control device that ultimately gave you a sore head. Consequently the Mindlink was never released. Still, it did sound like a great idea at the time.

## Packaging and marketing
## 1972

Today computer games occupy an extremely well-defined corner of the consumer market. Advertising campaigns push not only the merits of the game itself, but its intangible assets like, for example, street-cred. In short, the acquisition of a particular software title for a particular machine is in some way a statement of affiliation to some kind of ethos or sensibility in much the same way as purchasing a CD or DVD is. Today we predominantly seem to buy things that we think are cool.

But for much of its lifespan the computer game has been marketed in completely amateurish and unsophisticated ways. In the late Seventies and early Eighties it wasn't uncommon for games to be sold as cassettes in plastic bags with little sticky labels on them. Those that did come with some kind of cover art, often featured a second-rate pen and ink job drawn by the game's author, which had then been photocopied onto sheets of A4 before being cut by hand to the requisite cassette size. Admittedly the end result wasn't altogether eye-catching, but then it didn't need to be; at that time computer games weren't competing against LPs or VHS cassettes, they just needed to compete against each other – and in that respect it didn't really matter very much what the packaging looked like.

As computers gained more widespread appeal in the Eighties, games began to appear in mainstream high street stores and so had to smarten up their act. One of the first software companies to recognise the need for decent packaging was Electronic Arts. They produced covers that were comparable to the LPs sitting on the opposite shelf of the shop, and it wasn't long before other companies started to pick up on the fact that a nice picture could actually shift games.

In the middle years of the Eighties a curious half-way house philosophy of computer game marketing seemed to prevail. British companies such as Ocean and Ultimate: Play the Game released impressive looking promotional material and even employed traditional marketing strategies such as teasers published in the press. Many of these campaigns took great stock in a presumed company loyalty amongst the computing fraternity. Whilst this might have worked well on those who actually played the games, a mother popping into Woolworths in 1985 wouldn't know the difference between another Ultimate: Play the Game masterpiece and a cheapy Mastertronic game.

Up to this point television advertising had been largely restricted to stores such as Selfridges announcing the arrival of **Space Invaders** on the Atari 2600. However, by the late Eighties, companies like Commodore began promoting their wares on television. In fact a television commercial for the **Amiga** provoked a number of complaints, due to it featuring graphics that were obviously well beyond the capability of the machine it was advertising.

Whilst companies such as **Sega** attempted, through promotional material, to re-position computer games as a credible mainstream activity, it was undoubtedly Sony, and their mid-Nineties campaign for the **PlayStation**, that finally unleashed the full force of mainstream marketing on computer games, in the process changing forever the way computers were viewed by mainstream audiences.

Peripherals
1989

Consoles have been subjected to many bizarre developments over the years, but it is probably in the arena of peripherals (i.e. those things that come with the machine but aren't actually part of it) that the most curious concepts have taken shape. For example in 1989 Mattel produced the PowerGlove (for the **NES**). Apparently this device (which looked like a prop from the TV series *Battlestar Galactica*) tracked your hand motions and translated them into on-screen movements – or at least that was the theory; somehow in practice it never seemed quite that simple. Other ideas that have failed to catch on include force feedback vests and Amiga's 1983 innovation, the Joyboard (a **joystick** that you controlled by standing on it and shifting your weight from one side to another).

But probably the stand out peripheral (almost) came from the UK. In 1989, British company Konix were putting together the finishing touches to what looked to be the most ambitious console ever made. Aside from its impressive technical specifications, the Konix Multi-System came with a multi-purpose controller that could be contorted into a steering wheel, a flight sim yoke or motorcycle handlebars. Even more impressively, Konix were proposing to market the Multi-System with a full-size hydraulic chair. Sadly manufacturing delays allowed those upstarts **Nintendo** and **Sega** to flood the UK market with their new 16-bit machines and the Multi-System bit the dust, taking with it the most audacious peripheral of all-time.

It is only in recent years that novelty gaming peripherals have established any kind of secure footing in the marketplace. Konami's *Dance Dance Revolution* series (which began in 1998) has made a successful transition from the amusement arcades to the home scene, bringing into our front rooms large mats that we jump around on when playing the game. Similarly,

EyeToy (a little camera that sits on top of your television and effectively turns you into the game's controller) amassed sales on two million in the UK alone during 2003.

These devices look as silly as their forebears, but crucially they have added an additional social element to computer gaming that has enabled them to crash through the embarrassment barrier in a way that the PowerGlove was never quite able to manage.

## Pinball
### 1931

Regardless of cool American Jocks obsessing over it in Brat Pack films, pinball is an inherently boring game, enlivened only by superfluous flashing lights and scrolling marquee messages.

Nevertheless, it did clear a lot of the way for the far more exciting **amusement arcade** games that were to come, and for that reason (and probably that reason alone) we should be grateful. Just as arcade games have their origins in the flipper and bumpers of pinball, so pinball owes its existence to an earlier iteration of amusements. Indeed the genesis of pinball can be traced back to Bagatelle – a popular game played in the nineteenth century that was a bit like billiards and a bit like a strange sort of table golf game.

The first proper pay-to-play pinball machine appeared in 1931 (although the term 'pinball' didn't come about until 1936). Called *Baffle Ball* it was incredibly basic compared to later models but it was an excellent proof of concept for pinball as a viable money spinner. Later enhancements such as tilt mechanisms (1932), battery operated machines (1933) and flippers (1947) introduced more complexity and control over the game; however, another innovation – adding 'pay-outs' to pinball machines proved to be less successful, not because it put players off, but because it attracted the attention of the authorities, who, in New York City, adjudged that playing pinball was tantamount to gambling and so in 1942 outlawed it. Incredibly, this ban was to last until 1976, and whilst pinball machines may have continued to flourish elsewhere, there was now a sense that they were a slightly unwholesome pursuit which has arguably been passed down to video gaming.

Surprisingly, pinball machines still hold their own today, and have successfully transitioned from the grimy old arcade halls into pubs and clubs in a way that the good old electronic coin-op has yet to emulate.

## Pocket calculators and Digital Watches 1970

Before the home computer age there was the 'talking about the soon-to-be home computer age' age. This consisted of presenters of popular science television programmes going on at great lengths about how the 'silicon chip' was going to revolutionize our lives, and informing us that by the year 2000 we would all own personal robots that could run down to the shops and buy us a packet of Pacers. This talk created such an enormous sense of expectation that we were desperate to get our hands on anything with flashing lights regardless of it is use, just so we could proclaim that the home computer age had finally started.

For a long time pocket calculators seemed like the nearest we were ever going to get. Being able to carry round a device in your shirt pocket that actually possessed some computational power was a thrilling and futuristic experience. However, electronic calculators have actually been around for a very long time (since 1961 in fact), and even its smaller sibling, the pocket calculator, first arrived on the scene as far back as 1970 (although with Canon's Pocketronic measuring in at over twenty centimetres tall, the term 'pocket' was admittedly applied rather loosely).

In 1972, Hewlett Packard released the first handheld scientific calculator (which meant it was now possible to do sums involving logarithms and trigonometry), and although not the most scintillating functionality you could ask for, the word 'scientific' did carry with it a cache far beyond that of an ordinary calculator. During that same year, future creator of the **ZX81**, Clive Sinclair, entered the market with his slim line Sinclair Executive calculator. He immediately laid claim to having produced the first 'proper' pocket calculator (the Executive was only fourteen centimetres tall), but there was a downside to the Sinclair machine: namely if you left it on for a prolonged period of time it was liable to overheat and explode. This didn't stop them selling by the truckload though.

Up until this point, pocket calculators had favoured LED displays; however, in 1976 liquid crystal (of the type you might find on digital watches) became more commonplace. This was then followed two years later by the introduction of solar powered calculators. For a while these were the source of tremendous, albeit very short-lived entertainment as owners experimented with varying degrees of light in order to ascertain at what point the calculator batteries would die (with early models all it seemed to require was a single cloud passing in front of the sun).

After this it seemed that we had arrived at the calculator's highest evolutionary state. Further refinements could be made (generally in the field of miniaturisation), but with the introduction of the calculator watch excepted, there was nowhere else for the poor old electronic adding machine to go. As such it was left to us, the consumers, to think of ever more inventive tasks. Typically this meant trying to come up with words and phrases that you could type using upside down numbers. We only got as far as 'HELLO', 'BOOBLESS', 'SHELLOIL' and a very poorly realised 'SHIT' before we realised there wasn't an awful lot more you could make a calculator say, and turned instead to looking up rude words in the dictionary.

The evolution of the digital watch follows very similar lines. The liquid crystal technology on which it was founded had been around since the 1880s (when scientists Friedrich Reinitzer and Otto Lehmann became the first to notice what happens if you jam some liquid crystals between two bits of glass and apply voltage to them). But it would take almost another hundred years for the technology to be applied to a wristwatch. In the meantime, a company called Hamilton released their breakthrough LED watch in 1972. This 18-carat gold number cost in excess of $2,000 and would display the time using tiny little red LEDs only when a button was pressed. Thankfully, during the same year, work began on the production of the first LCD digital watches. These had an enormous advantage over LED watches in that their power consumption was low enough to allow the time to be displayed at all times.

In 1974, the favourite watch manufacturer of the schoolyard joined the fray. CASIO's CASIOTRON was actually quite an elegant looking timepiece, and what's more it could automatically work out the number of days in a month and whether or not it was a leap year. Later versions would bring with them the beloved chunky black plastic straps and, ergo, sweaty wrists, a nice musty smell and a collection of dead skin that would be uncovered when you finally took the thing off.

Sadly digital watches lost their appeal when home computers became more prevalent, and after a period in the Seventies during which watchmakers had genuinely believed that the days of the standard mechanical timepiece were numbered, the pendulum swung back towards traditional watch designs. Of late though, the inclusion of GPS and video recording functionality have re-energised the James Bond wannabe contingent, and one senses it is only a matter of time before CASIO hit the market with the first ever digital watch with built-in grappling hook, a book on sexual innuendos, or some other equally essential piece of spy kit.

Prestel
1974

The word Prestel sounded a bit like 'pastille,' and for many of us that was almost all we ever knew about this strange computer service. Although mentioned on the occasional *Tomorrow's World* feature in the Seventies and Eighties, it never really caught on in the way that its inventor, Sam Fedida, might have anticipated.

First demonstrated in 1974, Prestel received its UK launch in 1979. Backed by the British Post Office, it was a pioneering videotex service that gave users access to a wealth of local and national information via specially adapted television sets – in truth it looked rather like Ceefax. However, unlike teletext services, to access Prestel you actually had to dial up to a remote database before you could view any content; and even then certain pages came with an additional charge. Thus, once you totalled up the cost of buying the correct kind of telly, the call charge, the monthly subscription, plus any additional page charges, the total amount spent on trying to find out the average price of crops in East Anglia (not to mention that time taken to navigate to the correct page) was such that you might as well have jumped on a train to go there and have a look yourself.

What's more, you would often search fruitlessly for an important bit of information only to be directed to a page that gave you, not the answer, but infuriatingly a postal address of the relevant agency that you could have easily found yourself in the *Yellow Pages*. It is little surprise then, that Prestel failed to establish a viable consumer market, and by 1994 it was sold off and wound down. However, in some small sense the service still lives on and has some genuinely useful applications within business. Travel agents, for example, still use a videotex system modelled very closely on Prestel. Why they don't just use the Internet to book holidays like the rest of us is a bit of a mystery, particularly as you can get such good deals online.

Rubik's Cube
1980

At around the same time that **Pac-Man** was sending half the world bananas, a Hungarian chap called Erno Rubik was in the process of making a fortune off the back of an idea for a 'magic cube' that he had been working on since 1974. Released just in time for Christmas 1980, the Rubik's Cube was one of those maddeningly simple ideas that for a period of time seemed completely addictive, before fast becoming consigned to the litter bin of history as just another fad.

Its inclusion here is merited for two reasons: first of all the game itself is very similar to the steady string of hugely addictive computer **puzzle games** that have blossomed over the past decade or so (indeed in some respects playing with a Rubik's Cube is a bit like taking on a tactile version of **Tetris**); and secondly, Rubik's fan base seemed to consist of much the same people who would avidly spend their non-Rubik's cubing free time poking around with a **BBC Micro** or **VIC-20**. However, Erno's invention seals its place in our inventory thanks to the simple reason that it led to one of the most unlikely games releases of all time.

Yes, unbelievably in 1983, **Atari** released a computerized version of the Rubik's Cube for their 2600 console. Not only did this seem a bad idea in principle (why would anyone shell out the best part of £60 for a computer facsimile of something they could buy for real for just a fiver?), but it proved to be even worse in practice. Lacking the graphical ability to render the cube in three dimensions, the game allowed you to view only one side of the cube at any given time, meaning that whilst you tried to match up all the red squares on the bit you were working on, you had no idea how your various manoeuvres were affecting the other five sides. Incredibly, Atari had been working on a proper **3-D** version a year earlier but had abandoned it for reasons now unknown.

The game failed to sell in any great numbers, and today stands as testament to just how badly Atari seemed to lose their business nous in the early Eighties.

Simon
1978

Along with *Connect 4*, MB Games' *Simon* is surely the archetypal 'last day of term' game. In its day it was the biggest draw in the classroom, with loads of kids gathering round desperate for a go quite simply because it was an electronic toy with silicon chips and everything. *Simon* was one of the first mass-produced electronic games, and although the kids of today would doubtless give it short shrift, for an older generation the challenge of trying to remember and replicate a sequence of flash patterns and beeping noises was enough to keep them out of mischief for most of a drizzly morning. It also helped that *Simon* vaguely resembled the kind of portable talking computers that you could see in science fiction programmes and films contemporaneous to that time, meaning it wasn't inconceivable to imagine that *Simon* was a surrogate Orac (the grumpy portable computer in the television series *Blake's Seven*), or maybe Doctor Theopolis from *Buck Rogers in the 25th Century*.

Software Bundles
1982

There is nothing more frustrating than buying the latest state-of-the-art home computer or games machine, getting it home, setting it up and then finding you've got naff all to play on it. As the prices of computer systems continually fell throughout the Eighties and Nineties, they increasingly became impulse buys, meaning that if you weren't assured that within a hour of buying your new **Mega Drive** you would be immersed in *Sonic The Hedgehog* or some other top title, then you would leave it and simply rent a video for the evening instead.

As such, bundled software became an important weapon in the computer manufacturer's arsenal. Generally speaking, once a new system had been available in the shops for more than a few months it would be supplemented with free games and accessories as a way to maintain consumer interest. For **ZX Spectrum** users this initially meant the Psion 'Horizons' series (released in 1982). This was a collection of programs such as *Bubble Sort*, a utility that sorted cards into the correct numerical order; *Evolution,* which determined the population of a group of rabbits and foxes over time; and *Monte Carlo*, a deceptively exotically named program that simply generated random dice throws and mapped out the results against the expected results based on the laws of probability.

Thankfully, within just six years, prospective Spectrum owners were being offered something far more enticing in the shape of the *James Bond Action Pack*. This ace collection came in a Timothy Dalton as Bond box and contained not only a *James Bond* game but also mock secret agent documents (including a passport) and best of all, a nifty Sinclair Light Gun.

Over the years, software bundles became increasingly generous with the **Amiga** particularly renowned for its attractive deals including the much heralded 'Screen Gems' bundle of 1990, featuring free copies of *Back To the Future II, Days of Thunder, Shadow of the Beast 2* and *Night Breed*. Sadly, though (as was often the case with bundled games) with the exception of *Shadow of the Beast 2,* all of the other games were rubbish. This was the curious attraction of software bundles: you wouldn't countenance buying a machine that didn't come with them, but you always made sure you had enough money left over to buy a really decent game to go along with the ten or so crap ones you'd just acquired.

Tamagotchi
1996

In 1996 the company that had previously brought you the
*Power Rangers* unleashed another worldwide craze. This time it
was for key-ring sized LCD animals, that purported to be the
world's first 'virtual pets' (creators Bandai claiming they had
invented a whole new type of toy). Loosely translated, the word
'tamagotchi' means 'cute, loveable, egg', and basically the way
it worked was as follows: you purchased your *Tamagotchi* toy
and then activated it. This caused an egg to appear on the little
screen. After a few minutes, it would hatch and reveal a small
electronic creature, which from that point on would continue
to pester you for food, love and attention.

The purpose of the game (although the word 'game' isn't
wholly appropriate here) was to nurture your little electronic pet
through its brief time on Earth by providing it with the requisite
food, love and discipline (all determined by pressing the appropriate buttons). However, unlike more traditional toys the whole
point of *Tamagotchi* was that, like a pet, it could make demands
on your attention at any time, meaning that halfway through an
edition of *TFI Friday* the damned thing would start beeping at
you. Given that most games started and ended as and when you
determined, this was quite novel, but it was also rather irritating.

If you nurtured your pet successfully, by the time it was fully
grown (a day in our world represented approximately a year of
growth for your pet) it would have turned into a well-rounded
adult, fully able to make a decent contribution to society. However,
mismanagement and abuse would cause it to grow up indolent
and hostile, but happily it would slope off back to its own world a
lot quicker and allow you to start again with a new egg.

*Tamagotchi* was a big hit, and Bandai shifted around about
40 million units worldwide. Competitors were quick to muscle
in, and the likes of Tiger Electronics and **Nintendo** soon

released their own handheld pet games. Yet for many, deserting
*Tamagotchi* for a competitor would have been a little like trading in your beloved old moggie for an exciting new kitten –
tempting, but somehow very wrong. As such, there are still people today who every month or so, have to go through a genuine
grieving process as their latest well-rounded electronic pet bids
its farewell and returns to the planet Tamagotchi.

## Virtual Boy
## 1995

By the mid-Nineties, **Nintendo** had developed a reputation for
coming up with killer games machines. The **NES** and **SNES** had
both been great, and the **Game Boy** had, against the odds,
knocked all competition into a cocked hat. However, even the
most devoted Nintendophile must have raised an eyebrow
when they first heard about the Virtual Boy. The concept
seemed an amalgamation of some truly great, and truly awful
ideas, but then the Game Boy had looked that way on paper.

Released in 1995, the Virtual Boy was a cross between the
aforementioned Game Boy and a ViewMaster. To use it you had
to attach a pair of goggle-like visors to your face that would
block out all extraneous light and allow you to focus directly on
the **3-D** images created by the system. As a concept it sounded
very exciting and seemed to tap into the then current buzz
regarding all things **virtual reality**. Indeed the original design of
the Virtual Boy had included a head-tracking system, so that the
'virtual' world would move in accordance with your gaze. This
was dropped when it was deemed to be nausea-inducing.

However, there were just too many drawbacks. Although the
system was touted as being portable, it wasn't really practical to
play it on the move, and even if you did decide to indulge in
some outdoor Virtual Boy action, the whole unit (which came
with a stand) was just too cumbersome to carry around. Its

graphical capabilities were severely limited, and in an age where games such as *Ridge Racer* on the **PlayStation** were setting the bar, the Virtual Boy's reliance on red LEDs and mirrors might have created an effective illusion of 3-D, but it was an extremely simplistic one for all that.

Culturally too, the Virtual Boy seemed out of step with the times. The success of the PlayStation had caused a shift in perception of video games, so that they were now considered a legitimate social activity. But the Virtual Boy was a solitary pursuit. However its most critical flaw was its USP. Given it was all about a 3-D gaming experience, the still or moving images used to promote it looked rubbish. The Virtual Boy was simply something that you had to see in action. Nintendo attempted to get video stores to stock them so that potential buyers could come in and try one out on a rental basis before committing to purchasing, but it was futile.

Unsurprisingly, third party support from other software companies was minimal and the Virtual Boy died an ignoble death at the hands of a bemused, but largely uninterested gaming community.

## Virtual Reality
### 1962

'Awooga!' yelled *Red Dwarf* actor and Scouse poet Craig Charles during the course of each edition of the little remembered 1993 BBC2 game show *Cyberzone*. Utilising nascent virtual reality technology, each week contestants were pitted against each other in a series of games that took place in cyberspace (via a top of the range 486 **PC**). You probably barely remember the series, but at the time the BBC had high hopes for it, expecting the technology to evolve, allowing ever more exciting challenges to appear. However, *Cyberzone* ran for just one year – the technology was awkward and the games slow and stilted. Much like virtual reality itself in fact.

'[Virtual reality] will represent the greatest event in human evolution,' proclaimed author JG Ballard some years ago. 'For the first time, mankind will be able to deny reality and substitute its own version.' Although this sounds suitably revolutionary and exciting, it has to be said that even though everybody got themselves into quite a lather over the prospect of virtual reality (VR) back in the early Nineties, the expected infiltration into every corner of our lives has conspicuously failed to happen. With the notable exception of **Nintendo's Virtual Boy**, computer games (which now routinely feature the most complex looking **3-D** environments) are resolutely a VR-free zone.

Although it might have taken until the Nineties to attract people's attention to the virtues of VR, the concept has been around for a while. In 1962, one Morton Heilig patented an arcade game called the *Sensorama* that used 3-D stereoscopic images, smells and even artificially produced breezes to recreate the sensation of riding a motorcycle through southern California. It was an interesting premise, and in many ways ahead of its times, given that it would take another couple of decades before computers were sufficiently powerful to create proper virtual reality environments.

Our mental image of VR probably derives from the Nineties, and in particular breathless news stories and items on *Tomorrow's World* depicting someone wearing a visor and a glove. The graphics always looked pretty rudimentary, consisting of basic polygon shapes and little else; but being able to interact with a virtual environment did look like fun. However, VR's applications weren't just limited to gaming. Complex VR programs were created for scientists conducting molecular research; and VR technology has been used to enable architects to fashion a VR model of proposed new buildings before committing bricks to mortar. As well as being a pretty cool extra to offer your client, a VR model has the added benefit of allowing you to walk through your design and identify issues that might previously have been missed until after construction.

Undeniably such applications are fantastically useful, so why is it that the hubbub surrounding VR has all but gone away? Well, according to experts, the technology of the Nineties wasn't mature enough to meet our expectations, and it is only in recent years that computers have become powerful enough to cope with creating complex VR environments that can move in time with the turn of head (if there is a delay of more than fifteen milliseconds between you and the computer, the illusion is shattered). In addition, early users of VR technology complained of motion sickness and fatigue and it is only comparatively recently that researchers have been able to combat these symptoms.

So it is probably likely that in the next five or ten years the hype surrounding VR will kick off once again; only this time Craig Charles will get a halfway decent game show to host out of it.

# Credit Note

Plate 1 - *Carrier Command* screenshot courtesy of *Edge* magazine and is used with the permission of Ian Oliver.

Plate 2 - *Daley Thompson's Decathlon* screenshot courtesy of *www.crashonline.org.uk.* © Atari.

Plate 3 - *Dragon's Lair* screenshot used with permission of Bluth Group LTD. © 1983, Bluth Group LTD, characters by Don Bluth.

Plate 4 - *Football Manager* screenshot courtesy of Prism Leisure Corporation plc.

Plate 5 - Mario is © Nintendo.

Plate 6 - *Populous* artwork is © Electronic Arts Inc.

Plate 7 - *STOS* cover image courtesy of François Lionet and Clickteam.com.

Plate 8 - *Zaxxon* cartridge: Photograph by Rose Ruane.

Plate 9 - *Donkey Kong* is © Nintendo.

Plate 10- *Pac-Man* screenshot courtesy of *www.vgmuseum.com.* Pac-Man is © Namco Ltd., all right reserved.

Plate 11- Atari logo is © Atari.
 - Binatone: Photograph by Jack Kibble-White.

Plate 12- ZX Spectrum: Photograph by Jack Kibble-White.
 - ZX80: Photograph by Rose Ruane.

Plate 13- BBC Master: Photograph by Jack Kibble-White.
 - Amstrad CPC-464: Photograph by Jack Kibble-White.

Plate 14- GameBoy and *Tetris* cartridge: Photograph by Jack Kibble-White. *Tetris* GameBoy game and GameBoy are © Nintendo.
 - Mattel IntelliVision: Photography by Jack Kibble-White.

Plate 15- Mindlink is © Atari.
 - *Prestel* photograph courtesy of the Interactive Media Lab., University of Florida.

Plate 16- Computer magazines: Photograph by Jack Kibble-White.

# Index